WARRIOR

I guess it's ironic that I haven't toppled Castro's government but was involved in bringing down the head of the government of my own country; and that Castro, who tried several times to assassinate me, never could get to me, but my country put me behind bars.

—*Frank Sturgis to his nephew, Jim Hunt,*
in 1974 after serving fourteen months
in prison for his Watergate crimes

WARRIOR

*Frank Sturgis—The CIA's #1 Assassin-Spy,
Who Nearly Killed Castro but Was
Ambushed by Watergate*

Jim Hunt AND Bob Risch

A TOM DOHERTY ASSOCIATES BOOK • NEW YORK

WARRIOR: FRANK STURGIS—THE CIA'S #1 ASSASSIN-SPY, WHO NEARLY
KILLED CASTRO BUT WAS AMBUSHED BY WATERGATE

All photographs courtesy of Jan Sturgis, Frank's widow, unless noted otherwise.

A Forge Book
Published by Tom Doherty Associates, LLC
175 Fifth Avenue
New York, NY 10010

www.tor-forge.com

Forge® is a registered trademark of Tom Doherty Associates, LLC.

ISBN 978-0-7653-2863-2

First Edition: May 2011

Printed in the United States of America

0 9 8 7 6 5 4 3 2 1

To Frank
Via con dios, paquito

Contents

Acknowledgments

We would like to thank the following people for their assistance in researching and preparing this book: Frank's widow, Jan Sturgis; Frank and Jan's daughter, Autumn; Watergate participants Macho Barker and Rolando Martinez, and their attorney, Dan Schultz; Major Armin Frank, U.S. Marine Corps (Ret.); Ron Thompson; Gaeton Fonzi; A. J. Weberman; Jeff and Tina Siereveld (Madmacs); Carol Suhre; Kim Crowthers and Connie Steele; Megan Murphy; Diana Frost; Heather Saunders; Eric C. Meyer; Pam Gulleman; Bob's son, Dane; Jim's daughter, Sarah Hunt; and our wives, Nancy Risch and Laura Hunt. Thank you all.

Preface

Fearless men are a rare breed. But Jim's uncle Frank was fearless. It defined who he was. Those who knew him whom we interviewed for this book all said the same thing: "Nothing scared him." Yes, he was flamboyant and self-confident, sometimes to the point of cocky, but whatever spawned these traits also kept him from fear.

Jim lived with Frank in Miami and got to know him well. He was questioned by the Rockefeller Commission as to where Frank was on the day President Kennedy was assassinated. In many ways Frank was an enigma, even to his family. But it always boiled down to his courage. He continuously rose to the tests put before him; there was always a readiness to meet danger.

He also gave a damn about other people. He gave money to his friends and to the widows of his friends when he really didn't have it to give; he gave away his burial plot to someone in need; and he put himself in harm's way for underdogs time and time again. As one of his fellow Watergate burglars described him, "He was a tough guy with a good heart."

Most people who have heard of Frank remember him as a Watergate burglar, yet Watergate may have been his least dangerous mission. Elements of his other, and sometimes difficult to believe, lives (he had thirty-three aliases) are detailed in this book. They include encounters with world leaders and underworld leaders, assassinations, spying and counterspying, and a boatload of plots and mysteries. No wonder the press tagged him "a real-life James Bond." But as Frank said in his testimony before the Rockefeller Commission investigating JFK's assassination, "It was about Cuba . . . it was always about Cuba."

This book started as a song Jim wrote about some of Frank's exploits. When Bob, a friend of Jim's since the 1960s, heard it some two years ago, it sparked a conversation that eventually led to this story. We hope you find it as interesting as we did.

JIM HUNT *and* BOB RISCH
Spring 2008

WARRIOR

Prologue

★ ★ ★ ★ ★ ★ ★ ★ ★ ★

JUNE 17, 1972, 2:15 A.M.

This was a first for Frank Sturgis. Being locked up in an American jail. During his twenty-five-year career conducting clandestine and black-ops missions he had done hard time in jails in South and Central America and on some isolated islands. He had also been held in Havana's infamous El Morro prison, where dictator Fulgencio Batista's henchmen tortured him, after he was caught running guns and ammo for a beardless revolutionary named Fidel Castro. But, except as a police officer in Norfolk, Virginia, he had never seen the inside of a jail in his own country. All that and much more was about to change as he rode in a paddy wagon from the Watergate complex to the DC Jail.

Twenty minutes earlier, he and three Cuban friends, Bernard "Macho" Barker, Eugenio Rolando Martinez, and Vio González, and ex–FBI/CIA operative James McCord had been caught inside the headquarters of the Democratic National Committee, where they were installing bugs and copying files. Frank had been recruited for the mission by Barker, former Caribbean field director for the CIA, and E. Howard Hunt, the legendary "Eduardo" who was the chief CIA political officer for the Bay of Pigs invasion. Frank knew the other two Cubans, Martinez and González, from their CIA and anti-Castro work. They and Frank were told by Hunt and Barker that they were working for a top secret group that had jurisdiction over the CIA. Hunt's office was located in the White House, which led them to believe that this was a legitimate operation of national security. It wasn't. Their mission was to look for documents and other evidence showing that Fidel Castro was funneling money to the Democratic Party in hopes that Cuba would be better off with a president more liberal than the Republican nominee, incumbent president Richard Nixon.

As he rode along, Frank thought about his wife, Jan, and his stepdaughter back in Miami. In order to protect them, Frank had never revealed any details about his missions over the years. How would Jan survive financially if Frank were locked up for any length of time? What would their neighbors and friends think if news of the burglary broke? Would it be broadcast only in the D.C. area? What crime had he and the others actually committed? Simple burglary?

Frank and his fellow burglars were transported together, so they had the opportunity to talk. McCord took charge of the discussion; he told them to maintain silence on the true nature of their mission and said they would be "taken care of." He told them, "I know people. Someone will come and everything will be fine." Frank was not surprised and took comfort in McCord's promise. An unwritten rule of black ops was that you would be taken care of if you got caught. That was how President Eisenhower had handled the U-2 spy plane incident with the Russians, eventually securing the release of downed pilot Francis Gary Powers.

While Frank was worried about what the future would hold, he was not afraid. He had fought at Guadalcanal and Okinawa as a teenager. He had faced death more times than he cared to remember. By comparison, this seemed mild. Frank had total faith in his ability to survive. However, he was angry with himself. If McCord and Hunt had listened to him earlier that night, none of this would have happened. Frank and González, a master locksmith, were the first two to enter the Watergate Hotel that night. Earlier that day Hunt and McCord had taped open the hasps on the doors that led from the parking garage to a stairway that would take them to the fourth-floor offices of the Democratic National Committee. With a master locksmith on the team, Frank could not understand why they needed to use tape. What Frank saw when they reached the door that night concerned him even more— there was no tape on the door. This meant that someone had found and removed it. Frank used his walkie-talkie to report this to Hunt, who was waiting with McCord and the Cubans at the Howard Johnson motel across the street from the Watergate. Frank told them he thought they should abort the mission. After discussing the issue with McCord, Hunt radioed back that they were going ahead as planned. Even though he disagreed, Frank, who had served in all branches of the U.S. military, sucked it up and followed orders. González picked open the tapeless stairway door, and he and Frank ascended to the DNC offices, where González picked open the main office door. They had placed a piece of tape over the garage door so that Barker, Martinez, and McCord could join them. Frank reminded Barker to remove the tape once they got through the door.

Approximately fifteen minutes into the mission, McCord told Martinez that he needed to return to Howard Johnson's to get a piece of equipment. Martinez told him to tape the stairway door open while he went across the street, and to be sure to remove the tape when he returned. When McCord got back, Martinez asked if he had removed the tape and McCord said that he had. In fact, McCord lied. The tape was still on the door when it was discovered by the Watergate security guard who had removed it earlier. He called the D.C. police, who responded and arrested the burglars. Frank was not aware of McCord's duplicity as he rode in the paddy wagon. Later on, as the complex events of what would be known simply as "Watergate" unfolded, Frank suspected that McCord was a mole, working for some group or agency opposed to the work they were doing. But as Frank was taken from the paddy wagon to be processed at the DC Jail, he reiterated a promise he had made time and again over the last twenty-five years: that under no circumstances would he disclose the true nature of their mission. He was booked under one of his CIA aliases, Frank Hamilton. Neither he nor anyone else had any idea where all this would lead. Frank hoped it wouldn't put an end to the private war he had been waging since 1959 with his old friend Fidel to bring true democracy to Cuba

1

From Priest to Patriot

Before the war I had strong leanings toward becoming a Catholic priest. And, if the war hadn't come about, I would have. But then the war came, and I felt very patriotic and very strong in wanting to defend this country: patriotism became a substitute for the priesthood.

—**Frank Sturgis**, High Times *magazine, April 1977*

FRANK STURGIS DIED IN MIAMI ON DECEMBER 4, 1993, FIVE DAYS before his sixty-ninth birthday. He had gone to the VA hospital a few days earlier with stomach and back pain. The death certificate said he died of cancer, though none had been previously diagnosed. An autopsy was never performed. Less than a month before his death, Frank spent a week at the secret headquarters of an anti-Castro group, PUND (Partido de Unidad Nacional Democrático), located in the Everglades, where he conducted guerrilla survival training exercises. Frank seemed to be in good health when he returned to Miami. His only complaint was that he had what he thought was a pretty nasty bug bite on his back. He suspected it had come from a spider or some type of mosquito out in the Everglades. At the time, he recalled that six months earlier he'd gotten a similar bite on his back while standing outside the PUND headquarters in Miami. Other than that, for a man his age, he was remarkably fit. But, rather than celebrate his birthday on December 9, 1993, Frank was laid to rest.

Frank was born to Frank Angelo and Mary Fiorini on December 9, 1924, in Norfolk, Virginia. The Fiorini family was in the produce business. Frank's mother and father were both first-generation Italian-Americans. They were divorced in 1926, shortly after Frank's older sister, Carmella, was killed in a fire. From the very beginning, Frank's life was not easy. Frank and his mother left Norfolk and moved in with his maternal grandparents, the Vonas, at their house located at 5006 Wayne Avenue in Philadelphia. Also living there were Frank's aunt Katherine and her son, Joey, who was a few years younger than Frank. He was very close to his cousin and considered him a brother. (Unfortunately, Joey was later killed during the Korean War. Frank was deeply affected by his death, which he blamed on the Communists in North Korea and their ally, Red China. This was one of the factors that led Frank to become a very vocal and ardent anti-communist throughout his life.)

Frank had good memories of his childhood and received much support and encouragement from his family. He especially admired his grandfather Vona, who was a very positive male role model. Frank loved the stories and tall tales about knights and adventures in exotic locations that Grandfather Vona would make up for him when Frank was a child. Who could have known then that Frank would go on to have his own real-life adventures in such exotic locations?

Italian was spoken quite a bit in the household, so Frank grew up bilingual. As might be expected for someone with Frank's all-Italian lineage, he was raised Catholic. He went to a parochial elementary school and had vivid memories of the proverbial strict nuns who used to rap his knuckles with a ruler. He served as an altar boy in his parish and participated in practical jokes like lacing the communion wine with vodka and kneeling on the robes of the other altar boys. Despite these juvenile pranks, Frank had a deep and profound belief in Catholicism. He attended mass regularly and received the sacraments.

When Frank entered high school he made serious plans to become a priest. As he said in an April 1977 *High Times* magazine interview,

> *Before the war I had strong leanings toward becoming a Catholic priest. And, if the war hadn't come about, I would have. But then the war came, and I felt very patriotic and very strong in wanting to defend this country: patriotism became a substitute for the priesthood.*

For most of us, the closest we have come to a Pearl Harbor is what happened on September 11, 2001. But the attack on Pearl Harbor launched a world war fought on a much larger scale than our current wars on terrorism. Many Americans living during the 1940s had a very real fear of an armed land invasion by German or Japanese soldiers. During the first year and a half of fighting, things did not go well for the United States and its allies. Strategic islands in the South Pacific were falling to the Japanese, and the Germans had succeeded in driving British forces from the European mainland.

World War II impacted Frank in two very important ways. Like many other young men of his generation, he had strong patriotic feelings. The intensity that he brought to his religion became focused on his sense of duty and obligation to defend his country. Therefore, on October 5, 1942, in his senior year of high school, Frank joined the Marines in Philadelphia. Because he was only seventeen years old, his mother had to give her written permission. His term of enlistment was for "the duration of the national emergency." Basic training would take place at Parris Island, South Carolina. Also training there with him was the movie star Tyrone Power.

The other development that greatly influenced Frank and his later life was the decision made by FDR during the war to form two Marine raider units, patterned somewhat after British commandos who specialized in reconnaissance and hit-and-run raids behind enemy lines. The successful exploits of the British commandos as reported in the newspapers of the day provided one of the few bright spots in the way the war was going for the Allies.

On December 22, 1941, Colonel William J. "Wild Bill" Donovan sent a memo to President Franklin D. Roosevelt in which he suggested that the United States form a guerrilla corps, noting that "the whole art of guerrilla warfare lies in striking the enemy where he least expects it and yet where he is most vulnerable." He offered the British commandos as a model. It should be noted that Donovan was not an ordinary colonel. He had gone to Columbia Law School with President Roosevelt and remained a close friend. At the time Donovan wrote the memo, the president had appointed him "Coordinator of Information," which was actually the Army's spy agency that preceded the Office of Strategic Services (OSS). Following World War II the OSS morphed into the Central Intelligence Agency (CIA). Roosevelt greatly valued Donovan's opinions and ideas.

At the same time, but separate from Donovan's efforts, a Marine Corps major and an Army captain were also discussing the formation of a raider, or commando, force. Like Donovan, the Army captain was not your ordinary officer. He was James Roosevelt, the president's son. As such, he had better access to the president than did most generals, or anyone else for that matter.

Major Evans F. Carlson was no ordinary soldier either. He had joined the Army in 1912. Like Frank he was under the age limit but got by the recruiter. Some say he may have been as young as fourteen when he joined. He served under General John "Black Jack" Pershing during the Mexican Campaign. During World War I he fought in France and was wounded. When he left the Army in 1919 he was a captain. Three years later he wanted to reenlist, but the Army offered a rank below captain. Carlson refused to accept this demotion and, instead, he joined the Marines in 1923 as a private.

From 1927 to 1929 Carlson was with the Fourth Marines in Shanghai. Following that he spent three years fighting and learning guerrilla tactics in the jungles and mountains of Nicaragua during the campaign to capture the revolutionary rebel Augusto Sandino. He went back to China as an "observer" and watched as the Japanese seized control of Shanghai. The Marines gave him permission to accompany the Chinese Communist Party's Eighth Route Army under the leadership of Mao Tse-tung as they fought against the Japanese. It was during this period that Carlson formulated many of his ideas about guerrilla warfare. He greatly admired the strategy and discipline of Mao's army. Carlson wrote several books praising the Red Army, Mao, and Chou En-lai. He predicted (accurately as it turns out) that the Communists would ultimately defeat the Nationalist forces under Chiang Kai-shek. In the years before Pearl Harbor, Carlson urged the Marines and the U.S. government to provide more support to the Chinese Communists in their efforts against Japan. This advice was ignored, so Carlson resigned his Marine Corps commission in 1939.

But, in keeping with his sense of patriotism, Carlson rejoined the Marines in April 1941 and eventually achieved the rank of lieutenant colonel. He developed a friendship with Captain James Roosevelt, who firmly believed that guerrilla warfare tactics could be crucial to winning the war, especially in the Pacific Islands. They met and discussed the value of forming raider units as a part of the Marine Corps. As a result of their efforts, on January 13, 1942, Captain Roosevelt sent a letter to Marine Commandant General Thomas Holcomb recommending the creation of "a unit for purposes similar to [those of] the British Commandos and the Chinese Guerillas."

The letter was only two pages long, but it contained two detailed appendices prepared by Carlson setting out the organization and training of these fighting units. In contrast to the usual Marine chain of command protocol, Carlson did away with traditional ranks, dividing the unit into "leaders" and "fighters." Whenever possible, decisions in the battlefield would be based on input from all involved. Carlson believed that a "closer relationship" between leaders and fighters was essential to waging a successful guerrilla war. The training would include survival tactics and amphibious assaults. Since the 1930s, the Marines had been conducting exercises on Caribbean islands using rubber boats holding up to ten men; this became the basic structure for deployment of the raider brigades.

Frank talked about the special raider training in the 1977 *High Times* interview.

> *Not ever having killed a person in my life, then being trained and brainwashed to kill people in all different aspects of warfare and in hand-to-hand combat. Killing people in so many different manners. Going behind lines. Killing people with stilettos. With a knife. Silent killing. I was trained at this and I was very good at it.*

In addition to these killing skills, the raiders were trained to be highly mobile and to strike quickly. They were generally the first to land during the island-hopping campaign that eventually succeeded in removing the Japanese from the Pacific Theater. They often worked behind enemy lines conducting surveillance and disrupting enemy communications. To be a raider meant that you were in top physical shape and possessed the intelligence, bravery, and cunning to carry out these dangerous missions.

Interestingly, the letter that President Roosevelt's son sent to Marine Commandant Holcomb was not well received by much of the Marine brass. They believed that any Marine should be able to fulfill the role of raider and that the creation of special brigades was just another layer of bureaucracy that would siphon qualified men from the limited pool the Marines had.

The other thing that caused controversy was the rumor (and belief by some) that Carlson was a communist. He certainly was a Sinophile, at least when it came to Mao and the Red Army, but Carlson was too much of a patriot to be labeled a communist. And it should be remembered that his admiration for the Red Chinese predated the Cold War, at a time when the communist Soviet Union was our ally in the fight against Germany and Japan.

Despite the resistance, the Marine Raiders officially came into existence in February 1942. Carlson was put in charge of the Second Battalion, which was stationed in San Diego. For leadership of the

First Battalion, Holcomb selected Merritt "Red Mike" Edson. Like Carlson, Edson was a veteran of the Mexican Campaign and World War I, and he also fought in the "Banana Wars" in Central America. During the 1920s Edson commanded a 160-man unit in the jungles of Nicaragua in an effort to rid that country of the so-called *bandito* Augusto Sandino, for which he received his first Navy Cross for valor. Edson's experiences in Central America gave him a great deal of expertise in guerrilla war tactics.

The other common thread between Carlson and Edson was that the latter had also spent time in China shortly before Pearl Harbor and saw with his own eyes Japanese combat techniques as the Japanese took over the city of Shanghai in 1937. He would later use this knowledge to America's advantage against the Japanese during the island-hopping campaign in the Pacific.

Edson organized the First Battalion into eight-man squads. They initially trained at Quantico, Virginia, using the Potomac River for rubber boat exercises. Training emphasized weapons, marksmanship, demolitions, hand-to-hand fighting, and rigorous physical training. Edson expected his Raiders to average a pace of seven miles per hour on hikes, which is two times faster than ordinary infantry. His chain of command was more traditional than that used by Carlson in the Second Battalion, but he still allowed subordinates to speak their mind. Both battalions used the battle cry "Gung ho!"—Chinese for "work together."

At one time Frank possessed a fairly detailed file of his entire military record. Unfortunately it was literally blown away by Hurricane Andrew. Most of the government file is also not available. This may be due to a fire in the 1970s at the VA records facility located in St. Louis; or, as has been the case in other instances, much of his record may still be classified. A VA records request did generate five pages of Frank's Marine Corps record. He enlisted as "Frank Angelo Fiorini" in Philadelphia on October 5, 1942. His rank is listed as "private." He was immediately sent to Parris Island for basic training. On November 2,

1942, Frank was qualified in bayonet fighting and use of automatic weapons. By the twenty-seventh of that month he was certified as a "sharpshooter" on the rifle range.

Following basic training Frank was selected for Edson's Raiders and joined the unit in Samoa. This is where he first learned and utilized guerrilla war tactics. He was wounded two times, and in each instance he "jumped the hospital ship" before he was supposed to be released so he could rejoin his unit. He downplayed the severity of his wounds because he was afraid he might be shipped home. As he said, "I guess I was a little crazy."

According to author A. J. Weberman, Frank's unit received a special commendation from Secretary of the Navy James Forrestal for valor during fighting on New Georgia Island during July, August, and September 1943.[1] Frank received a second commendation for combat during the invasion of Guam in July and August 1944.[2] At that time he was also awarded a Purple Heart for his battle wounds, a bullet to his right wrist and a bayonet through his left foot. Frank also fought the Japanese on Guadalcanal, Emirau Island, and Okinawa.

Frank's "U.S. Marine Corps Report of Separation" lists his "military specialties" as "machine gun crewman, message center man, rifleman (F.T. leader) and Photostat operator." The "F.T." stands for "Fire Team," a Marine combat configuration consisting of four enlisted men usually operating Browning automatic rifles. Frank was farsighted, which gave him a big advantage in qualifying as a sharpshooter and a sniper. In his testimony before the Rockefeller Commission in 1975 Frank said, "So I was considered, with my Marine training for those years, to be an expert in all types of weapons."[3]

In addition to his battle scars, Frank suffered from malaria during the war. Throughout his life, this disease would occasionally flare up and he would have to take large amounts of quinine and aspirin. At the end of the war Frank received an honorable discharge. He sailed home from Guam on May 30, 1945, and arrived in Seattle on June 17.[4] His initial discharge from the Marines was at the ski resort in Sun

Valley, Idaho, which was being used by the Navy as a processing center. Because he was suffering from battle fatigue, or what was then called "war neurosis," he spent thirty days in treatment at a psychiatric facility in Klamath Falls, Oregon, prior to discharge.

During the 1977 interview Frank talked about what caused this condition:

> *I didn't realize that volunteering to join the service would radically change my whole concept of life. I was wounded twice. I received several medals and commendations. My last major operation was in Okinawa. I was sent back from a hospital ship with shell shock. They called it "psychoneurosis hysteria." I jumped ship many times to get back to my unit.*

According to military psychiatrist Dr. Roy Grinker, the incidence of war neurosis increased 300 percent during World War II when compared to World War I.[5] However, he divided this number into four groups, ranging from those who had just been inducted and might be looking for a way out of the military and the true sufferers like Frank whose condition arose from actual extended combat experiences. Symptoms included insomnia, weight loss, nightmares, indecision, fatigue, anxiety, and an inability to stop thinking about the horrors of combat.

Under today's psychiatric diagnostic terminology Frank's condition would be called post-traumatic stress disorder, or PTSD.[6] Basically it arises from exposure to severely traumatic events, with or without physical injury, that causes the person to repress the memories of those events. It continues to be an unfortunate consequence of warfare, as seen by the number of Vietnam and Iraq War veterans who suffer from it.

Something about the type of combat that Frank and other Marine Raiders went through can be seen in the following words written by James Forrestal in the commendation Frank and his unit received for their fighting on Guam in July 1944:

Functioning as a combat unit . . . forced a landing against strong hostile defenses and well camouflaged positions, steadily advancing inland under the relentless fury of the enemy's heavy artillery, mortar and small arms fire to secure a firm beachhead . . . Executing a difficult turning movement to the north this daring and courageous unit fought its way yard by yard through the mangrove swamps, dense jungles and over cliffs and though terrifically reduced in strength under the enemies [sic] fanatical counter-attacks, hunted the Japanese in caves, pill boxes and fox holes and exterminated them. By their individual acts of gallantry and their indomitable fighting teamwork throughout the bitter and costly struggle . . . [they] aided immeasurably in the restoration of Guam to our sovereignty.[7]

The treatment regimen used by Dr. Grinker and other psychiatrists caring for patients like Frank during World War II was called "narcosynthesis." The primary technique was to "uncover" the trauma that the soldier had been through and then engage in psychotherapy to directly confront the painful memories. Hypnosis had been used to aid in the "uncovering" but generally required an extended period of treatment. As a shortcut, Dr. Grinker recommended intravenous injections of Sodium Amytal or Sodium Pentothal, so-called "truth serum." The idea was to put the patient in a semiconscious state so that the traumatic memories could be talked out.[8] This type of treatment actually worked in most cases and must have worked for Frank as he was eventually able to make the transition from soldier to civilian.

Frank continued to have occasional bouts of insomnia and nightmares. One time the City of Miami was using low-flying small planes to spray for mosquitoes. A plane buzzed his neighborhood early one morning and Frank woke up and ran through the house completely disoriented, thinking that Japanese warplanes were attacking. Throughout his life, Frank had no love for the Japanese. Based upon his experiences in the Pacific Theater, he thought they were barbaric. At no time during his life did Frank own or drive a Japanese car.

Frank's Marine Raider training and battle experiences allowed him to maximize and maintain his great physical strength and stamina. And the training in guerrilla warfare that Frank received started his career as an expert in, and teacher of, that type of fighting. He trained guerrilla armies throughout Central and South America and Africa. To be a guerrilla or a raider meant you were intelligent and ready to act boldly and swiftly, relying more on stealth than firepower. The guerrilla was taught to think outside the box and to understand the political situation in any armed conflict and the importance of getting the support of the local populace. Most important, the guerrilla had to have the courage to undertake difficult and dangerous missions.

During his life, Frank embodied the spirit of a guerrilla warrior. When he died he was still teaching guerrilla war tactics and was in charge of counterintelligence for PUND. Over the years, a number of Cuban exiles who knew firsthand about Frank's anti-Castro missions and exploits have attested to his courage and leadership skills and his devotion to their cause. An FBI agent once called Frank "an assassin's assassin," and a New York reporter dubbed him "a real-life James Bond." Fidel Castro said Frank was "the most dangerous CIA spy [he] ever knew."

Frank's devotion to a cause did not begin with Cuba, and he had a gung-ho approach to life even before learning that concept in Edson's Raiders. His entire military experience, especially his years in the Marine Corps, provides evidence of his unselfish service to his country and his deeply held sense of patriotism. In the following pages you will see what Frank himself has said about this and make up your own mind. For example, was he truly acting as a patriot at Watergate or was he just picking up a paycheck?

What cannot be questioned is that Frank faithfully served the United States during World War II and thereafter. He was in all branches of the military and was honorably discharged from each one.

2

A Spy Is Born

I was a spy. I was involved in assassination plots and conspiracies to overthrow several foreign governments including Cuba, Panama, Guatemala, the Dominican Republic, and Haiti. I smuggled arms and men into Cuba for Castro and against Castro. I broke into intelligence files. I stole and photographed secret documents. That's what spies do.

—Frank in an interview with New York Daily News reporter Paul Meskil, June 20, 1975

FOLLOWING HIS HONORABLE DISCHARGE FROM THE MARINE CORPS in 1945, Frank visited his mother, who was living in Miami, and then settled in Norfolk, his birthplace. The emotional and psychological scars caused by his war experiences had taken their toll. As Frank said in the *High Times* interview,

Naturally, during wartime you're brainwashed to a point psychologically, where you have to kill the enemy, but now that the war is over, you have a trained professional man who's been trained and cannot adjust mentally to civilian life. So when I was discharged from the Marine Corps I became a plainclothes police officer.

Frank joined the Norfolk police force on June 5, 1946. Within a few months, he found evidence of corruption in the form of a payoff system that existed within the force, which he brought to the attention of his superiors. Instead of doing something about it, they told him to overlook these illegal activities. On October 5, 1946, Frank had an open confrontation with a sergeant over this at roll call and resigned that same day. For the next eighteen months he managed a Norfolk tavern called Havana-Madrid, which catered to foreigners, particularly Cuban merchant seamen. On November 9, 1947, Frank joined the Naval Reserve and was stationed at the Norfolk air base. During this time Frank was able to continue to work at the bar while learning a skill in the Navy he would use throughout his life—flying airplanes.

Frank was honorably discharged from the Navy on August 30, 1948, and the next day he joined the Army, his third and final armed services branch. He was immediately deployed to Berlin, where he became a member of General Lucius Clay's honor guard. At the end of World War II, Germany had been divided into two separate countries, East Germany and West Germany. Russia, a former member of the Allied forces, was given control over East Germany and set up a communist government. West Germany was established with its capitol in Bonn as a democracy under the supervision of the other Allied forces—the United States, France, and Great Britain. Berlin, the capital of Germany under Hitler, was located entirely within East Germany. The city itself was divided into four sectors, each controlled by the United States, France, and Great Britain on one side and the Russians on the other. These former allies who had defeated Hitler were now engaged in what was being called a "cold war" with their former ally. The Russians initiated the first major confrontation on June 24, 1948, by cutting off all highway and railroad traffic into the Allied sectors of West Berlin. The idea was to stop food and other necessary supplies from reaching the West Berliners. In response, Frank's commanding officer, General Clay, organized and launched a massive airlift of food and essential supplies as a way of circumventing the blockade. It ran around the clock, a plane landing about every twenty minutes. The airlift eventually succeeded in convincing the Russians to back down. Overland supply routes were re-opened by the Russians on May 11, 1949. Two weeks later Frank was granted an honorable discharge so he could help support his mother, who was in financial need.

During his Army tenure in Berlin and Heidelberg, Frank worked in an intelligence unit and had a top secret clearance. As a Marine Raider, Frank had his first involvement in intelligence activities during the island-hopping campaign because sometimes he would sneak behind enemy lines and gather data and intelligence information. In the Army, the primary intelligence target was the Russian communist government, which had its own force of agents and secret police who spied on the United States and the other Allied forces. Frank's intelligence work consisted of collating and analyzing intelligence data. Frank saw with his own eyes the threat that Russia and its totalitarian government posed to the United States. Like the death of his cousin, Joey, this was another factor that led Frank to become an ardent anti-communist, a position he would hold for the rest of his life. Intelligence gathering and spying were also lifelong pursuits. Frank's indoctrination into the world of spies and the "field work" they did received a serendipitous boost when, while stationed in Berlin, he rescued a beautiful Hungarian actress. As Frank told *High Times*:

> Well, I was in Berlin with a soldier friend of mine and we heard some screaming and ruckus that was going on in an alley. We went to investigate because we heard a woman's voice. And we got mixed up with three young Germans and had a nice little battle with them. The girl was pretty well beaten. Later I found out that she was a Hungarian actress, Jewish, and the three Germans belonged to the Nazi youth party that was still operating underground in Germany. Having saved her life, I developed a very good relationship with this young lady who started visiting me in the barracks and all. I didn't realize until later that she was the girlfriend of one of the army colonels who was on General Clay's staff. The Colonel found out about us and shipped me out of Berlin. Through a fickle finger of fate I wound up with the Army Security Agency. When I returned to

the States, I was still going with her. I became suspicious of some of her activities. I found out she was working very hard for the liberation of Israel and I told her I would certainly help her in Israel if I could because I was very sympathetic to the underdog. I returned to Europe, met her again and helped her in her activities over a period of years. I assisted her as a courier in some of the work she did for Israel. As the years went by her work became more serious and there were some things I could not do for her. Eventually, I lost contact with her, and to this day, I don't know if she is dead or alive.

Frank never revealed the name of this Israeli spy out of concern for her safety. Before the creation of Israel in 1948, she had been a member of Haganah (Hebrew for "The Defense"), a secret underground group organized in 1929 to promote statehood and protect Jewish interests in the Middle East. When she met Frank she was working as an intelligence agent for Israel. Through his contact with her, Frank developed the field skills used by spies. He began as a courier, learning how to code and decode, and ways to secretly transmit intelligence and disinformation.

After Frank returned to Norfolk in 1952, one of the first things he did was change his name. On September 23, 1952, he petitioned the Norfolk Circuit Court to change it from "Frank Angelo Fiorini" to "Frank Anthony Sturgis." In the court document, Frank said he wanted the change because his mother had divorced his father, Angelo, and married Ralph Sturgis, whose last name Frank wanted to take. During his testimony before the Rockefeller Commission in 1975, Frank said, "Well, the reason for that was that I felt there were too many Fiorinis. Frank Fiorini especially. . . . My mother wanted me to change the name, really, she influenced me to change the name from Fiorini to Sturgis, because she had a bad situation with my father."[1] It is true that there was no love lost between Frank's mother and father. However, it is far more likely that Frank's primary reason for the name change was to establish a second, or alias, identity for himself to use in the future should he return to intelligence and spy activities. Why else would he change his middle name along with his last name? Even after legally adopting his stepfather's name, Frank continued to call himself Frank Fiorini. He did not use the Sturgis name as a matter of course until the early 1970s.

Frank's first civilian job upon returning to Norfolk in 1952 was managing a tavern called the Café Society. The owner was Milton Bass. In 1973 Bass was interviewed by U.S. Probation Officer Frank Saunders, who prepared a sentencing report for Judge John Sirica, who was presiding over Frank's Watergate trial. Bass told Saunders that he found Frank "to be a very trustworthy and ambitious individual."[2] Frank and Bass formed a partnership to purchase a Virginia Beach bar/nightclub, The Top Hat. With Bass's encouragement and the help of the GI Bill, Frank spent two and a half years at The College of William & Mary. Although he had not graduated from high school when he joined the Marines, Frank received his GED while in the Corps. He kept up his flying skills as a lieutenant in the Civil Air Patrol, where he was a flight instructor. He also became licensed in Virginia as a real estate agent.

The Top Hat was successful, but Frank found it to be boring. He did not drink alcohol and was not a fan of the bar/nightclub lifestyle. By the mid-1950s he possessed a unique set of skills that were going to waste in the bar business. Frank was an expert in guerrilla warfare and arms and ammunition. He was in excellent physical shape. He was experienced in all aspects of intelligence work both as a spy and as a gatherer and processor of information. All he needed was a cause and a place to practice his skills.

3

The Cuban Revolution

¡Eso si es un yanqui bárbaro! (This is one hell of a Yankee!)

—*Fidel Castro describing Frank after witnessing his near impossible airplane landing delivering contraband weapons in the Sierra Maestra mountains, Cuba, 1958*

CUBA FIRST ENTERED THE U.S. POLITICAL SPOTLIGHT IN 1848 WHEN President Polk offered to purchase the island from Spain, but the offer was refused. Some fifty years later, in January 1898, President McKinley sent the USS *Maine* to Havana harbor to protect the eight thousand U.S. residents in Cuba, where a revolt against Spanish rule was under way. On February 15 the battleship was blown up by a Spanish mine, killing 266 U.S. sailors, which triggered the Spanish-American War, waged from April to August 1898. Teddy Roosevelt, whose "Rough Riders" gained fame in the battle of San Juan Hill, became president in 1901 and formally recognized the Republic of Cuba's independence on May 20, 1902. The United States retained the right to intervene in Cuban affairs and to establish a naval base at Guantánamo. A series of presidents led to Carlos Prío Socarrás, who was elected in 1948.

Prío was known as the "cordial president" as his administration had a healthy respect for freedom of expression. Democracy was alive and well until Prío was overthrown by a military coup led by Fulgencia Batista. But as befalls most dictatorships, the repressive regime spawned a revolution. Soon young Cubans were organizing an army under the leadership of a lanky, excitable rebel named Fidel Castro.

Fidel Alejandro Castro Ruz was born out of wedlock on a sugar plantation in Birán, Cuba, on August 13, 1926. Birán is in the Oriente province in the eastern part of Cuba, which is where, eventually, his revolution began. His father, Ángel, was an emigrant from Spain, and his mother, Lina, was a household servant on Ángel's sugar plantation. At the time of Fidel's birth, Ángel was married to Maria Luisa Argota. Fidel was raised in foster homes, and had the stigma of being illegitimate. His two brothers, Raúl and Ramón, and four sisters were also born out of wedlock. Fidel was not baptized in the Catholic faith until he was eight, which in Cuba was unusual. He grew to be over six feet tall, which in Cuba was also unusual. When Fidel was fifteen, Ángel married Fidel's mother after dissolving his first marriage. Thus Fidel was finally recognized by his father and "Castro" added to his surname.

Fidel finished his college education at a Jesuit school in Havana in 1945 and then entered law school at the University of Havana. Politics was a full-contact sport at the university and often degenerated into violent confrontations, accompanied sometimes by gunfire. Fidel, not one to back down, became involved in a shoot-out and killed the leader of a rival political faction. Rolando Martinez, who went on to be one of the Watergate burglars with Frank, not only was a witness to the shooting but also later testified to the incident in court. Fidel fled and hid out with a doctor and his family. Fidel grew close to them— evidently a little too close to the wife, who became pregnant by Fidel. The good physician threw him out, and he returned to Havana. In 1950 he finally received a law degree and began practicing with a firm in Havana that did work for the underprivileged.

In the late 1940s he had joined the Orthodox Party, which had as one of its platforms freedom from the United States' economic and political influence. In 1952, when General Fulgencia Batista led a military coup that ousted then-president Carlos Prío, Fidel was a candidate for the Cuban parliament. The coup caused the election not to be held. Fidel, like all young lawyers fresh from school, filed a suit. This one was against Batista, claiming he'd violated Cuba's 1940 constitution. The Batista-controlled legal infrastructure threw out his case without a hearing. But the die was cast. It was Castro v. Batista, and as Fidel said later, it was at this point he became convinced that revolution was the only way to depose Batista. Fidel then formed an underground group of supporters who began to collect guns and ammunition and plotted to overthrow the dictator.

On July 26, 1953 (July 26 was Carnival, and they hoped the garrison guards would be drunk), Castro's 135 student rebels, in a bold but ill-conceived plan, attacked Batista's largest garrison at Moncada Barracks, Santiago, in Cuba's Oriente province. More than sixty of the rebels were killed, and Fidel, who escaped briefly to the Sierra Maestra mountains, was captured, tried, convicted, and imprisoned on the Isle of Pines. At his trial he delivered his famous prediction. He warned the audience that this was just the beginning, that he would not be silenced. He concluded, "Condemn me, it does not matter: history will absolve me." Although he was sentenced to fifteen years, he served but two, being released in 1955 as part of a general amnesty.

Once out of prison, Fidel traveled to Mexico, where he met Ernesto "Che" Guevara and formed the 26th of July Movement (the date of the ill-fated attack on the Moncada Barracks) and plotted his revolution. The Moncada defeat became Fidel's alamo and the rallying cry for his revolutionary army, whose members wore "26 Julio" armbands. (One can be seen on Frank's left arm in the picture of Frank and Che Guevara on this book's cover and in the illustration section.) From Mexico Fidel traveled to the United States to raise money for his cause. He then returned to Mexico and he and eighty-one of his followers took off from Tuxpan aboard the yacht *Granma* and landed near Manzanillo, Cuba, on December 2, 1956. Batista, knowing more than a little about coups, had his men hunt down Castro. Most of Fidel's followers were killed. At this point, the remaining July 26 rebels went to the Sierra Maestra mountains to organize another rebel army. During this time Fidel made clandestine trips to the States looking for funding and help with his fight against Batista. On one such trip in 1957, Fidel and Frank met at the Flagler theater in Miami. Fidel was there trying to raise money and support from the Cuban exiles for his revolution. Frank also met Fidel's mother, Lina, who had accompanied him. Frank would later use her to make contact with Fidel. Frank was mesmerized by Fidel, who promised to restore democracy to Cuba. Frank had finally found a cause in which he firmly believed and one for which his unique set of skills could be put to good use. He devoted himself to a free Cuba and pledged his support to Fidel.

In the mid-1950s, Frank periodically visited his uncle Angelo Vona, who was married to a Cuban woman who was an integral part of the anti-Batista Cuban community in Miami. In 1957 Frank sold his interest in The Top Hat to his partner, Milton Bass, and moved to Miami permanently. His aunt's family was friendly with former president Carlos Prío, and Frank was introduced to him and to other anti-Batista Cubans, who were busy plotting their return to a Batista-free Cuba. Frank began to run secret night flights into Cuba for Prío. The contraband took the form of underground soldiers, weapons, explosives, and other war matériel. All to be used against the dictator Batista, or "La Hyena" as he was not so affectionately known in Miami. At the time, some of the anti-Batista Cubans in Miami were sending money to Mexico to support a beardless rebel named Fidel. Carlos Prío himself had met with Castro in the United States and had given him $50,000 for arms. After Frank met Fidel in Miami in 1957, Prío inquired as to whether Frank would be willing to go to Cuba, join up with this Castro fellow, and report back to the exiled powers in Miami as to just what was going on. The request was right down Frank's alley. He flew to Havana, and through the good offices of a Cuban priest, he was able to find Castro in the Sierra Maestra mountains.

Fidel remembered the skilled guerrilla fighter who had so passionately embraced the goal of a free Cuba. Frank spoke little Spanish at the time, but he spoke Italian, and Castro spoke some English, and together they made it work. Fidel said he could use someone like Frank. It was a fork in the road. Frank knew and liked Carlos Prío, but he also liked this unusually tall and excitable rebel. Both men had ambitions to lead Cuba; you had to be with one or the other. Frank explained later that he chose to throw in with Castro rather than Prío because Fidel was a soldier, a man of action, whereas Carlos was a politician, more a man of words. Politicians, Frank observed, told the truth maybe 20 percent of the time.

In the 1977 *High Times* interview, in answer to questions about how many men Castro had when Frank first arrived in the mountains and met Fidel in a small town called Santo Domingo, next to Pico Turquino (Cuba's highest mountain), and how Frank altered Fidel's concepts of tactics and strategy, Frank responded:

> *Less than 400 men. Ragged . . . you know . . . many of them were barefooted. They had weapons from 1800 and something, and shotguns . . . pitiful men . . . I helped quite a bit in training some of the officers and men in that type of fighting. And I started to develop a reputation among the exiles or, rather, the guerrillas in the mountains. Because they looked at me and said, "This guy's crazy." You know, one time they called me el jefe de caballo loco—that means Chief Crazy Horse—because I acted like an Indian and all. I was doing the same type of warfare I did when I was in the South Pacific for three years.*

Frank offered to train Castro's troops in guerrilla warfare. Fidel said he could certainly use that, but he had a more immediate need for guns and ammunition. In addition to being old, the weapons he had didn't match the ammunition. He asked Frank to straighten out this *mierda*. So Frank became a gunrunner. With anti-Batista money from the wealthy Cubans in Miami, Frank purchased boatloads of weapons and ammo from the International Armament Corporation located in Alexandria, Virginia. At the time, the world's largest dealer in surplus arms wasn't all that far from Frank's hometown of Norfolk. Frank became a one-man gunrunning operation, making daredevil flights to nearly nonexistent mountain airstrips. Other times he loaded up his Cadillac and took the ferry from Key West to Havana, often disguised as a priest. Also facilitating these runs was Frank's legitimate import/export business located in Miami. He earned the respect of Castro and the rebel troops not only for his courage but for the honesty with which he conducted the arms transactions. The Cuban rebels called him "Crazy Horse," and Fidel called him his "favorite warrior" and "one hell of a Yankee." In August 1958 Frank was just outside of Havana in his Cadillac full of contraband weapons when he was surrounded by Batista's men. They captured him and put him in the El Morro prison at the entrance to Havana's harbor. As Frank remembered, "They beat the hell out of me with bullwhips." But Frank wouldn't talk and was finally ordered deported. He returned to Florida with scars on his back and immediately packed up the next shipment of arms to be smuggled back to Castro, who was hiding in the Sierra Maestra mountains.

Andrew St. George was on a reporting assignment covering the revolution in Cuba when he met Frank fighting for Fidel in 1957. Some seventeen years later, in 1974, he wrote an article for *True* magazine. In it he relates why Fidel felt the way he did about Frank.

Frank was just a flyspeck in the blazing Cuban sky the day I caught my first glimpse of him in June 1957. In a moment or two he sounded like a buzzing fly. The twin Piper Apache engines were a distant whine, coming nearer, swelling greater, roaring deeper as Fidel Castro and Che Guevara and the rest of us stood watching in the jungle clearing, watching in silence as the plane suddenly coughed, tilted, slipped wing tip down into an incredible drunken descent, dropping like a kite in an air shaft, dropping to earth in that tiny hillside patch, one wing slashing sea-grape leaves, one prop buckling as it churned mud. Frank Fiorini had done the impossible, he had landed a supply plane at the jungle hideout of Fidel Castro's rebel army, the passenger seats buried under piles of Garand rifles and Mendoza machine guns, belted ammo and cans of three-in-one oil, other goods the guerrillas needed more than gold and, as Frank clambered out onto the wing, khaki shirt sweat-stained but the Italian-American grin flashing white-on-white, Fidel suddenly shouted in exploding admiration: "¡Eso si es un yanqui bárbaro!" (This is one helluva Yankee).

St. George confirms that Frank was Fidel's favorite "yanqui" and by far his most efficient gunrunner. He was not only the best bush pilot, but an honest one. St. George spends a paragraph explaining how it was not unusual for gunrunners to take a little something off the top for themselves. He then details Frank's "hand-scrawled accounts . . . folded and kept in a plastic envelope" . . . and that "when they were finally checked out, proved to be absolutely correct."

Another escapade involving Frank became front-page news worldwide, just what Castro was looking for to promote the revolution. On February 23, 1958, Juan Manuel Fangio, the reigning Formula One racing champion from Argentina, was in Havana for the Cuban Grand Prix sponsored by Batista himself. Fangio had won some two dozen grand prix races and had been world champion five times. Frank remembered that someone had floated the idea of kidnapping the famous race car driver and holding him for ransom. They thought that even if they didn't collect the ransom, they could at least get their cause in the media.

Frank admitted being involved in the kidnapping on the evening of February 23, 1958, when Fangio left his room and went to the lobby in the Hotel Lincoln. Frank and two other July 26th rebels grabbed him and spirited him off. The kidnapping garnered more coverage than Fidel's revolution had in two years of struggle.

On February 25 the race was run without Juan, but that night he was released. At the press conference he announced that he had been treated with great care by the civilized rebels and that neither he nor anyone else should bear them any ill will. Frank said that during the three days Juan spent with them, he was indoctrinated into the ideology of Fidel's revolution. The rebels released a statement that the Argentinean racer was a man of great charm whom they found to be a natural ally in their cause. It was one of the friendliest kidnappings in history.

At this time Frank also befriended a passionate young revolutionary who had come from Mexico with Fidel aboard the *Granma*. His name was Ernesto Guevara de la Serna. He went by "Che."

Guevara was born June 14, 1928, in Rosario, Argentina. In 1951, with his friend Alberto Granado, Guevara took a year off from his medical studies at the University of Buenos Aires to travel around South America on a 1939 Norton 500 motorcycle. He later wrote an account of his experience titled *The Motorcycle Diaries,* which was translated into English in 1996 and made into a movie in 2004. In 1953 he went to Guatemala, where, in a letter he wrote, he said he intended to perfect himself and "accomplish whatever [might] be necessary in order to become a true revolutionary." It was also here that he picked up "Che" as a nickname because of his continuous use of the Argentine salutation, which translates to "hey you" or just "hey."

Che traveled to Mexico City in September 1954 and ran into some Cuban exiles he had known in Guatemala. In 1955 he met Raúl Castro, and in July 1955 Raúl introduced him to Fidel and he joined Fidel's July 26th Brigade aimed at overthrowing Batista by revolution. On November 25, 1956, Che was aboard the cabin cruiser *Granma* as it left Tuxpan, Mexico, for Cuba. Castro brought eighty-one soldiers with him to attack Batista's forces and restart the revolution. Seventy of Fidel's soldiers were killed in the first few days of fighting. The remaining eleven retreated to the Sierra Maestra mountains to regroup. This is where Fidel pledged, "I will not shave until the revolution is over." It was during this battle with Batista's militia that Che literally laid down his medical kit in order to pick up a box of ammunition dropped by a comrade. This, he said later, marked his transition from doctor to soldier.

Frank also became fast friends with Cuban brothers Pedro and

Marcos Diaz Lanz. Castro made Pedro Lanz the commander in chief of the air force and his brother Marcos inspector general of the air force. The Diaz Lanz brothers relied on Frank's almost twenty years of military expertise to organize Castro's air force. They and Castro appointed Frank as their security and intelligence chief. A rare job for a U.S. citizen.

In March 1958, Frank opened a training camp in the Sierra Maestra mountains, where he taught Che and other July 26th rebel soldiers guerrilla warfare. In November, Frank and fellow pilot Pedro Diaz Lanz traveled from Cuba to Tucson and San Francisco to purchase two planes for Fidel, a C-46 transport and a B-25 bomber filled with munitions. Fidel's secretary had given Frank the number of a Swiss bank account, from which he made a $10,000 withdrawal for the B-25 and paid $112,000 for the C-46, registering both in his name.[1] The return route took them through Mexico, where they were arrested and jailed when they stopped to refuel. Eventually, they bought their way out with "*la morda*" ("the bite"), a common bribe. They made it back to Cuba just in time for the pivotal battle of the revolution.

Shortly before the Battle of Santa Clara in December 1958, Frank met two Latin men at the ranch of a Castro supporter, Cresentio Perez, in Oriente province. It turned out that these two were communists from Venezuela. As Frank later told the Rockefeller Commission:

> *And I found out at a later date, once the patrol came to pick up these two men and myself to go back to the mountains, I found out that these were two Venezuelan communists that came to see Fidel, and they had secret documents with them in code. I did not know that at the time. I was with them when we did meet Fidel. I have pictures of that. Where they gave him these documents, which I was led to believe from the information that I got were from the communist party in Venezuela who were going to support him if he wanted that support.*[2]

Frank with his own eyes saw the burgeoning Communist threat to the democratic revolution Fidel had promised. This was soon after

Frank first met CIA agent Clark Woolan, whose cover job was as an attaché at the U.S. consulate in Santiago de Cuba. Woolan approached Frank in the casino of the Casa Grande hotel and began to relate various details about Frank's life up to that point, including his military record. "He knew an awful lot about me. I could tell right away he was with the Company." Woolan "worked on [Frank's] patriotism as an American" and offered him money for information about Castro.[3] Frank refused the money but agreed to provide certain information about Castro's rebel army—"the movement of troops, the strength of the troops, the commanders of the different units, the weapons, and so forth."[4] Frank did not think he was being disloyal to Fidel by helping Woolan. "I told him . . . I would gladly help him, being an American, even though I sympathized with the Cubans in their fight against the dictatorship of Batista."[5]

In December 1958 Fidel ordered two offensives. While he led attacks against towns in eastern Cuba, the second major offensive was aimed at Santa Clara, the heavily armed fourth-largest Cuban city, situated between the rebels and Havana, their ultimate goal. Che Guevara, Jaime Vega, and Camilo Cienfuegos (his last name means "100 fires," very appropriate for a revolutionary) were sent against Santa Clara. Vega's rebels were ambushed and defeated by reinforcements that Batista had sent to the area. Cienfuegos, a close friend of Frank's, successfully attacked a garrison at Yaguajay. Che, aided by Frank and the weapons he had flown in, moved toward the city. On the rebels' shortwave radio band, Che was heard telling Cienfuegos to stay away because the prize of Santa Clara belonged to Che.

On December 28, on their way to Santa Clara, Guevara's troops were met by cheering throngs. Che's column captured the town of Caribarién in a one-day battle. The popular uprising that the rebels had hoped for was becoming a reality. Batista's troops at the next town of Camajuaní deserted, and Che's troops marched on to Santa Clara, arriving at the university on the edge of the city. Che divided his forces into two groups with 150 soldiers in each. One group marched south and engaged Batista's men in a fierce battle. While this fighting raged, the second rebel force attacked two Batista army garrisons. In a desperate move, Batista decided to bomb his own people in Santa Clara to keep the rebels from advancing.

Batista had also sent a nineteen-car armored train filled with reinforcements of 373 soldiers, some $4 million worth of munitions, and food for two months. On December 30, 1958, Frank and the others requisitioned some heavy equipment from the university, removed thirty feet of track, and derailed the train. Batista's soldiers surrendered, setting off a series of surrenders by government troops. The rebels now had a clear shot at Havana, and complete victory was in sight. Twelve hours after his Santa Clara defeat, Batista fled Havana for the Dominican Republic and Fidel claimed victory.

The victory at Santa Clara is memorialized on the Cuban three peso note. Fidel asked Frank to return to Santiago to pick up the C-46 and the B-25 and fly them to the air base near Havana. The revolution ended on New Year's Day, 1959.

4

Anti-Communist

*At that time it was not said that it was a communist government,
but it was a pink-type government. You had power struggles within
the government.*

—*Sworn testimony of Frank Sturgis to the
Rockefeller Commission, April 3, 1975*

ON NEW YEAR'S DAY, 1959, FRANK WAS STILL IN SANTIAGO WHEN HE
got word of the successful march on Havana and Batista's flight from
the country. Like the other rebels he celebrated their victory and
looked forward to Fidel's promise of a truly democratic Cuba. On the
other hand, by that time, Frank had firsthand knowledge of the growing influence of communists within the army and the government.
Given his deep-seated hatred of communism, there was no way that
Frank would be a part of a communist Cuba.

What bothered Frank most about communism as it existed in the
1950s was totalitarianism, the control of the citizen's total existence
and lack of individual freedoms. Politically, Frank was a registered
Democrat when he fought alongside Fidel. He believed strongly in
democracy and in the value of the rights and freedoms that he en-

joyed in the United States. Frank always said that he would have continued to support Castro even with some degree of socialism and
government ownership of certain resources as long as Castro's government was truly democratic. Instead, Fidel eventually developed a
repressive government based in large part on fear and strict adher-
ence to the party line. According to Frank, dissidents in Cuba were
routinely imprisoned or shot for opposing Castro's government. Castro had succeeded in replacing Batista's oppressive dictatorship with
one of his own.

However, as of January 10, 1959, when Frank first arrived in
Havana from Camp Tiro in Santiago, the jury was still out as to the
ultimate form the new Cuban government would take. There was
an ongoing power struggle between the communists and the anti-
communists. Frank described the regime as a "pink type government," meaning not totally red, the official color of the Communist
Party. Frank saw the threat posed by communism in Cuba not only
as anathema to his own political beliefs but also as a very real threat
to his home country, the United States. In the 1950s and '60s, the
Russian premier, Nikita Khrushchev, proclaimed to the citizens of
the United States, "We will bury you." It may have been a cold war,
but it was still a war that was being fought on a worldwide stage.
Frank worried that the communists might establish a foothold just
ninety miles away from the United States. Cuba, of course, was
much smaller than the United States, but strategically, it was huge;
nuclear missiles could land on major American cities in a matter of
minutes.

While Frank was fighting for Castro, his mother was living in
Norfolk. After not having heard from him for a number of months,
in November 1958 she was contacted by someone from the anti-Batista
crowd in Miami, who said that Frank had been killed. However, on
January 15, 1959, two weeks after Fidel's triumphant march into Havana, a photo of Frank appeared in the *Philadelphia Inquirer,* along
with a story, "Picture in Inquirer Disproves Death of Philadelphia
Rebel Fighter."

> Publication of a photograph of Frank Fiorini, captain in the
> Cuban rebel army, yesterday dispelled reports that the former
> Philadelphian had been killed in action eight months ago. Ac-
> cording to Mrs. Kathleen Parsons, of 544 E. Tulpehocken St.,
> Fiorini's aunt, word has been received from Cuba that the
> 32-year-old Castro aide is alive and well.

The article explains that some time ago Frank had been reported killed in Oriente Province, stronghold of Fidel's rebels, but *The Inquirer* had been responsible for proving this not true.

> The picture, published in *The Inquirer* yesterday, showed
> Fiorini standing atop a mass grave of 75 followers of the Ba-
> tista regime at Santiago. Later, an Associated Press correspon-
> dent reported he had spoken to Fiorini at a rebel army camp.

While this was good news for Frank's family, later, in 1960, this photo and others were used as reasons to revoke Frank's U.S. citizenship.

Frank was officially stationed at the air base at San Antonio de los Baños, twenty-six kilometers southwest of Havana, and he arrived there on January 10, 1959. The base had been built by the U.S. Army during World War II to house planes used to patrol the Caribbean for German U-boats. After the war it was turned over to Cuba and had been used by President Prío, and later by Batista, as the official headquarters of the Cuban air force. Frank was already a captain in the Rebel Army, and now Fidel appointed him to the post of chief of security and intelligence for the Cuban air force. The air base was adjacent to Camp Columbia, renamed Camp Liberty, which was the headquarters of Castro's July 26th Brigade. It was at the air base that Frank was associated with Pedro Diaz Lanz, chief of the Cuban air force, and Pedro's brother, Marcos, also an air force officer. Both of them were decidedly anti-communist and, like Frank, became more and more concerned as Castro's government swung in the communist direction. Frank recalled his last meeting in Santiago with Clark Woolan, who had asked him to contact Colonel Nichols and Major Van Horn, CIA agents working out of the embassy in Havana, if he wanted to pass on any further information. To combat or prevent a communist takeover, Frank decided to cooperate fully with Woolan's request and become a spy for the CIA. Frank met with Nichols "quite a number of times" and gave him copies of the photographs of the two Venezuelan communists who had met with Fidel.[1] Frank was again offered money for his help, which he refused. By this time, Frank had a "bitter taste . . . about the revolution."[2] He decided to do what he could to remove the growing communist influence from leaders like Che Guevara and Fidel's brother Raúl on Castro's revolution. At Colonel Nichols's request, Frank recruited military officers known to be anti-communists, such as the Diaz Lanz brothers. He even approached the chief of the army, who worked directly under Raúl Castro, Commander Camilo Cienfuegos, one of the heroes of the revolution. Using information Cienfuegos gave him, Frank was able to break into the army headquarters offices and take photographs of documents, which he gave to Colonel Nichols.

Frank developed his own intelligence network and shared information he gathered with the CIA. While recruiting individuals for this purpose, he came into contact with three brothers, Joaquim, Louis, and Sergio, from the Sangenes family. They had been anti-fascist soldiers in the Abraham Lincoln Brigade, which fought in the Spanish Civil War during the 1930s. After that they became ardent anti-communists, and they, like Frank, were becoming disenchanted with Fidel Castro. All three were officers in the July 26th Brigade, and they provided information to Frank's CIA contacts in Havana. After leaving Cuba for Miami in 1959 the three brothers became employed by the CIA. Joaquim—code name Sam Jennis—was Frank's primary CIA contact during most of his anti-Castro missions throughout the 1960s, especially regarding the Bay of Pigs. (He has another connection to Frank among certain conspiracy theorists regarding, believe it or not, the killing of Beatle John Lennon. They maintain that Sam Jennis was the doorman at the Dakota the night that Lennon was shot to death and that he was the actual killer.[3] Frank was supposedly an accessory because he stated publicly his belief, which was apparently incorrect, that Sam Jennis died in 1974, six years before the shooting.)

In addition to the Diaz Lanz and Sangenes brothers, Frank met and recruited Geraldine Shamma and her husband, Arturo, during the first half of 1959. Mrs. Shamma was Lebanese, and Arturo was a very wealthy Cuban, having made a fortune in tobacco. Mrs. Shamma became the CIA's main contact with the underground network of anti-Castro, anti-communist Cubans still living in Cuba. The Shammas made frequent trips between Havana and Miami, where they owned a house on Brickell Avenue. After being arrested by Raúl Castro and spending time in jail, they fled Cuba for good in 1959. The CIA used the Brickell Avenue residence as a safe house.

In January 1959, Fidel was not aware of the spy role Frank was beginning to play for the CIA. He still saw Frank as a trusted member of the Rebel Army who had been instrumental in the victory over Batista. For his part, Frank did not think he was being disloyal to Fidel. He was just trying to prevent the communists from co-opting the revolution. At this point, Frank's fight was with the communists, not Fidel.

Conspiracy theorist and co-author of *Coup d'État in America* A. J. Weberman and the Communist Party of Cuba both think that Frank was an agent of the CIA from the time he first started running guns and ammunition to help Castro's revolution in 1957. However, this view is not supported by the evidence. There is no written documentation concerning Frank's contact with the CIA and/or the FBI until the first half of 1959, after Fidel's victory. Frank's level of cooperation and information-gathering for the CIA increased and evolved as Castro's regime turned toward communism. Before then, Frank, somewhat of an idealist himself, believed in and supported the revolution. His original goal was to help get rid of Batista, whose repressive regime had resulted in many Cubans (including Frank's aunt) having to leave their homeland and live in exile. The only record of any contact between Frank and an agency of the U.S. government before 1959 is the report of his arrest in Miami by Customs agents on July 30, 1958, for gun-running. These charges were never pursued and were eventually dismissed in March 1959, probably because by then Frank was actively helping the CIA.

In light of Frank's demonstrated loyalty to the revolution, on January 14, 1959, Fidel asked him to take over the important position of Cuba's gambling minister, Fidel's direct liaison with all the casino and gaming device interests, a multimillion dollar business controlled by the Cuban and American mobs. In his testimony to the Rockefeller Commission, Frank explained what happened.

> STURGIS: *At one time while I was at the Prime Minister's Office there was a meeting and discussion with one of the woman ministers who was up in the mountains with Fidel as a rebel soldier. Her name was Pastorita. Commander Pastorita Nuñez. She was a commander and a lesbian. And Fidel asked me, please help Pastorita, because she is so tied up in work that you have to help her. And I said okay. The job I was supposed to do. I was supposed to take over or help her take over, the gambling casinos in Cuba.*
>
> OLSEN: *In all of Cuba or just a part.*
>
> STURGIS: *All of Cuba.*
>
> OLSEN: *And what did you do in connection with helping Miss Nuñez?*
>
> STURGIS: *Well, I made contact with all the different men in charge of the casinos. I put them on notice that Fidel and the government were going to have the laws changed. For instance he wanted only a certain amount of equipment in operation, and that each piece of equipment had to have a tax stamp on it. And any other type of equipment that did not have the tax stamp could not be used. Naturally, everybody was mad about that. Fidel at some of the meetings that he had—or rather that I was present at—mentioned that he was eventually going to close down the casinos. At one time, personally, he told me, Frank, I am going to run all these American gangsters out of Cuba. I am going to close down all the gambling casinos. I don't want them here. They are going to get out. I did tell him, well, if you do that, you are going to put Cuban people out of*

work. Maybe there is another way you can do it, and that is by having strict control over these people. He said, no, I don't want no control. They are going to leave. I am going to put them all in jail if possible. I am going to run them out of Cuba.[4]

The first item of business for Frank as gambling czar was to have tax stickers made up and begin collecting taxes from the casino owners, who were largely U.S. and Cuban mob figures. Frank was no more popular than any other tax collector in history. Shortly after the new taxes were instituted, Fidel ordered Frank to close all the casinos for twenty days while Fidel booted all the American mob bosses out of Cuba. A bold move. Gambling became one of the first businesses to be nationalized by Castro. The organized crime bosses were not happy. In fact, Frank tells a story of two men who came to see him about this time. The first was Hymie Levine, who let it be known that it would be worth a lot of money to the mob to get rid of Castro. Frank summed up his connection to the casino mob bosses in a 1975 interview with Paul Meskil, a reporter for the New York *Daily News*:

> I was in touch with all the casino owners and operators in Havana," said Frank Sturgis, who was Castro's casino inspector during this period. "Fidel ordered me to close all the casinos for 20 days. The owners got the hint. They knew he was preparing to shut them down permanently, which he did.
>
> "They were very, very mad. Those casinos were worth $100 million a year to the American crime syndicate. Every important mob boss in the United States had points (percentages) in the Cuban casinos. Each point was worth $30,000 to $100,000."
>
> Lansky and Trafficante were the top men in Cuban gambling. Lansky had direct business dealings with Batista. Trafficante had several casinos, including the Sans Souci.
>
> His Sans Souci partners included Norman Rothman of Miami Beach and the notorious Mannarino brothers, Gabriel and Sammy, Mafia chiefs in Pittsburgh. Rothman and the

Mannarinos tried to stop the Castro steamroller in 1959 by smuggling a planeload of arms—stolen from a National Guard armory in Ohio—to anti-Castro forces in Cuba.[5]

According to police and federal sources, Rothman was high up in the Cuban crime syndicate and shared his rackets profits with Batista's brother-in-law, General Roberto Fernández Miranda. Rothman returned to Florida soon after the Castro coup and, with his Cuban partners, bought the Biltmore Hotel in Miami Beach.

Rothman was convicted in 1959 on charges of attempting to transport 121 stolen army rifles to Cuba. Also convicted was Victor Carlucci, the son-in-law of Sammy Mannarino. Rothman and Mannarino were also indicted by a federal grand jury in Chicago in 1961 for trying to pledge thirty-four Canadian bonds in excess of $500,000. The bonds were traced to the burglary of an Ontario bank on May 4, 1958. There was a similar robbery in Montreal about the same time. This was the mob's contribution to the Bay of Pigs funding.

Frank's introduction to Hymie Levine began a relationship that lasted until Hymie's death in Miami in 1976. Hymie worked for Rothman, who owned part of the Sans Souci casino in Havana. Later Hymie vertically integrated and moved into the slot-machine business. He told Frank that he had previously been Dutch Schultz's partner in a slot-machine business in Upstate New York. Later, Lucky Luciano put a successful hit on Schultz and Hymie wound up owning more slots than he had before. Hymie introduced Frank to Jake Lansky and his brother Meyer, Joe Rivers, Charlie "The Blade" Tourine, Santo Trafficante from Tampa, and Sammy Mannarino, who controlled things in Pittsburgh. Frank was never a "made man," but he was well connected to the underworld.

Frank's introduction to the Cuban casino owners was facilitated by a man whose life Frank saved. In his own words:

Well. I did not meet Mr. Rothman up until that time that I saved the man. I took Stretch Rubin away from some rebel soldiers who wanted to

*shoot him. He had a bag of money on him. What he was doing was go-
ing into the Casa Grande hotel which had a gambling casino there and
slot machines. His job was to—he was like the collector for this outfit.
And he would collect all the money. And he had a big bag full of money.
And I came upon him as some rebel soldiers were dragging him away
and he was screaming and hollering and so forth, and they were going to
shoot him. And I took him away from the rebel soldiers. And he told me
that the situation was really bad there, that he was going to go to Havana, and so forth. And he asked me if I was going to Havana. And he
said, when you get up there, see me. I will be at whatever hotel—he mentioned it, but I forgot. But later on I found out that he worked for Norman Rothman who was the partner of General Clio Chivano. Chivano
was the brother-in-law of General Batista. Now Norman Rothman and
General Chivano were partners in the slot machine business. Later,
when I was in charge of that, I did meet Stretch Rubin when I made an
inspection of all the casinos, not knowing anyone, because I did not know
any of the gamblers or owners of those gambling casinos. I met Stretch,
who introduced me to a friend of his. His name was—I can't think of it,
the man he introduced me to—I will remember his name because we got
to be very good friends. He used to be the partner of Dutch Schultz. Mr.
Fletchenheimer, [sic] of the old days in New York. And he was his partner
in the slot machine business. In other words, this Jewish man, I forget the
name right this minute, was the partner of Dutch Schultz in the slot machine business in upper New York State. Hymie Levine is the name. Now
Stretch Rubin. I don't believe that is his real name. Stretch, I believe is—
you know how they call them muscles and egghead or whatever . . . I
didn't tell them that at the time, at the beginning, that Fidel was going to
get rid of them. What I did was to make my inspection of all the casinos
that came under my jurisdiction at that time, and advise them of new
laws that were being put into law, advise them of the tax stamps that had
to go on each piece of equipment, and that is just about it. And during
this period of time there was one more person he introduced me to—
Hymie Levine introduced me to a number of movie actors and actresses.
I did meet, at the Tropicana Night Club and gambling casino one night,*

sitting with Fidel's younger sister, Anna Castro, she called me over to the
table, and she was sitting down with a movie actor. His name was Hugh
O'Brien [sic] and I did meet Hugh O'Brien [sic] and I did meet Errol
Flynn and Lon Chaney, Jr.⁶

Errol Flynn had been one of Frank's idols due to the swashbuckling roles he played. Frank was very disappointed to find that Flynn was "a drunken degenerate who watched the revolution from his bar stool at the Tropicana Hotel." Flynn was in Havana with the blessing of Batista to work on a movie about "women revolutionaries" with director Victor Pahlen. After Castro's takeover in January 1959, they decided to curry favor from him by making a short documentary titled *The Truth About Fidel Castro's Revolution*. Flynn, complete with an elongated cigarette holder and seated in front of a wall map of the world, is the narrator. He tells the story of Castro's revolution from the birth of the July 26th Brigade to the triumphant march on Havana. The movie is an obvious propaganda piece that contains actual footage of the Battle of Santa Clara, some of Batista's atrocities and executions, and pre-Castro Havana nightlife. Flynn compares Castro to Salvatore Giuliano, "the Robin Hood of Sicily." Salvatore was the leader of an anti-communist group in the 1940s and had the rather unique idea that Sicily should become what would then have been the forty-ninth U.S. state.

Frank's association with Meyer Lansky, Santo Trafficante, and Sam Giancana grew out of their mutual interest in Cuba. Batista had befriended Meyer Lansky, and during the 1930s Meyer introduced Cuba to the mob, which began investing heavily. In the late '30s Lansky moved from Miami to Cuba, where he owned the Hotel Nacional casino and various racetracks in Havana. It was all good, and everyone was making a lot of money. In 1940 he moved back to Miami and then to New York in 1941, just before America entered the war. When Lansky left for New York he put Santo Trafficante in charge of the Cuba and Miami operations.

Lansky was also associated with Sam Giancana, whom he

introduced to Frank. Sam had been a "wheel man," or driver, for Al Capone in Chicago. He worked his way up, and in 1960, when the CIA approached him to kill Castro, he was the boss in Chicago. Later he was also part of the Judith Exner/John Kennedy/Sam Giancana love triangle that made the FBI very nervous.

While Frank performed his duties as Fidel's gambling czar, he continued to keep tabs on the increasing communist influence and looked for signs that Cuba would be restored to a true democracy. What he saw, he did not like. There had been plans to bring deposed president Carlos Prío back to Cuba from exile in Miami, but Prío was never offered the presidency. As in any revolution, there was a period of purging pro-Batista Cubans, who were ferreted out and captured and given a summary trial, usually followed by execution. Fidel's brother Raúl was in charge of the purge, and he was ruthless, much more so than Fidel. Frank saw evidence of this firsthand but denied taking part in the executions.

> *The revolution did end on January 1, 1959. When I came out of the mountains, I was at a camp site that I had, that I was in command of, called Camp Tiro. That is Camp Bullet in English. It was on top of a hill. And I had under my command approximately a thousand guajiros, they were peasants that I was trying to organize for Fidel on his triumphant tour to Havana. At the same time below this small mountain site is where Raoul [sic] Castro had his execution squads executing the Batista followers.[7]*

Over the next three months, Frank saw Raúl's purging begin to target anti-communists such as himself. What a different atmosphere the revolution had taken on. A few months earlier in the mountains of Oriente province they had all been part of a cause they believed in and had developed a genuine camaraderie. That esprit de corps was being replaced by suspicion and distrust. For example, Frank learned that Raúl had raised concerns about all the contact Frank was having with Colonel Nichols from the U.S. embassy. In an effort to conceal the real purpose of his meetings with Nichols,

Frank had Commander Diaz Lanz send Raúl a letter explaining that Frank was the air force's official liaison with the embassy and the meetings were therefore proper and necessary. Despite this, Raúl issued an order forbidding any and all contact between Frank, the Diaz Lanz brothers, and the American embassy.

By the end of March 1959 had Frank decided to take his concerns about the growing communist threat, which he had relayed to Nichols and Van Horn, directly to the FBI in Washington. As a cover story, Frank said that he was leaving Cuba to visit family members in Miami and Norfolk, Virginia. On March 31, 1959, Frank secretly went to Washington, D.C., and was interviewed by two FBI special agents, Krant and Nasca.[8] According to the FBI memo, Frank was "concerned with the growing menace of communism in the Cuban government," and offered his services in fighting against this infiltration. The agents listened to what Frank had to say, but because of the "highly unstable Cuban situation" and fear that Castro would claim American interference, no commitment was made to Frank. On the other hand, the FBI realized that Frank had "excellent potential to furnish valuable data and the door was left open for future contact." During the interview Frank expressed concern about the status of his American citizenship. He had been arrested on July 30, 1958, after the United States Customs Service found a large cache of guns and ammunition at a house he maintained in Miami. That case was still pending. Frank said that he "cherished his American citizenship and intended to protect it at all costs." The agents suggested he see legal attaché James Haverty in Havana after he got back. They did not tell Frank that Haverty was an FBI representative who would be keeping an eye on him.

Before beginning the interview, Frank showed the agents documents establishing proof of the three positions he then held in Cuba—gambling czar, director of security for the air force, and captain in Castro's July 26th Brigade. He told them there were known communists in the Cuban army like Che Guevara who were plotting to overthrow governments in the Dominican Republic, Panama, and Nicaragua. The communists hoped to capitalize on the political unrest and seize the opportunity to take over. He also provided the names and identities of eight "officials and leaders of the Cuban Government" who were "commonly referred to as communists in Cuba," including Che, whom Frank described as "a 'teacher' of military officers of the Cuban Armed Forces." Frank told the FBI that he was present at a recent indoctrination speech Che had given to air force officers that included attacks on Yankee imperialism. Frank said that because of his communist beliefs, Che was "intentionally keeping out of the public eye and awaiting developments which might present a better opportunity for him to press his beliefs upon the Cuban government." Frank also discussed the question of whether Fidel had been a communist all along:

> [Frank] stated that it is his belief that Castro is not a communist; however, he and the Diaz Lanz brothers and other anti-communists in the Cuban government are alarmed and concerned over the fact that known communists are being appointed to positions of power . . . there is a possibility because of the growing unemployment and accompanying unrest that the political situation might get out of control of Castro and that the communists might then take over the government. [Frank] stated that Castro is, in his opinion, a socialist and that he has the best interests of the Cuban people at heart; however, Castro is somewhat of an idealist, and it is his fear that Castro might be swayed by the communists to the belief that communism might be necessary to fulfill the purposes and ideals of the revolution.[9]

As it turned out, Frank's assessment of the future course of the Cuban Revolution was totally accurate. On October 22, 1959, Castro severed relations with the United States, while maintaining close ties with the Soviet Union, citing Frank's violation of Cuban air space as "Cuba's Pearl Harbor."

Frank's firsthand knowledge of the Castro regime supports the historical view that the U.S. government, and specifically President Eisenhower, is partially to blame for the loss of Cuba to the Soviet bloc. Shortly after arriving in Havana, Fidel began to seek aid from the

U.S. government. Frank accompanied Castro on a trip he made to Washington, D.C., in April 1959 for that purpose. However, Eisenhower refused to meet with Castro, shuffling him off to Vice President Richard Nixon and Undersecretary of State Christian Herter. The State Department had no plan or contingency for dealing with a populist leader such as Castro who was not the typical banana republic dictator (like Batista had been) and who might be an idealistic socialist or, "worse," a communist. "Co-existence" with a communist government ninety miles from the United States was out of the question during the Cold War. Frank said his contacts in the CIA were split into pro- and anti-Castro factions. With no clear governmental consensus and no plan to compete with the communists on their level in Cuba, it is little wonder that Fidel's government went from pink to deep, dark red.

In addition to providing information about Cuba and Castro to the CIA and the FBI, Frank offered a surefire solution to the problem of Castro—assassination. When he was stationed at the air force base near Havana he had three opportunities to assassinate Fidel. "In fact," he said, "I probably could have wiped out Raúl and Che at the same time and solved all our problems." These plans were discussed with Frank's CIA contact Colonel Nichols, at the U.S. embassy in February 1959. He described the scheme as follows:

> I would arrange an important conference at Campo Libertad [Camp Liberty, the combined army–air force base and headquarters formerly known as Camp Columbia]. All the top commanders would come to the base in their jeeps and cars. I was going to station gunners on the roofs [sic] to set up crossfire. I would have wiped out Fidel, his brother Raoul [sic] and all the top pro-communist military commanders in 30 seconds.[10]

He actually had the gunmen in place and ready to fire on two separate occasions, and they would have eliminated Fidel, Raúl, and Che. However, Frank never got the "green light" from Nichols and the

CIA. "They couldn't make up their minds. . . . They couldn't decide what to do."[11]

There were two other plans to kill Castro that were never carried out. One involved assassinating Castro on the second floor of the air force headquarters, where he would be meeting with his top military advisors. Frank acknowledged that this plan might result in the shooting of anti-communist officers but felt that the loss was worth it if Castro, his brother, and Che could be eliminated. The third plot involved planting in Castro's private office a briefcase full of plastic explosives that could be detonated from a distance with a radio signal. Frank had been able to enlist the cooperation and assistance of Castro's private secretary, Juan Orta, who was an anti-communist. In July 2007 Castro released an essay concerning yet another plot to have Orta assassinate him. Castro claims that by the time the plot was hatched, Orta no longer had the access to Castro needed to carry out the poisoning plan. Again, Frank never got the go-ahead from the CIA.

The other group that took an interest in eliminating Fidel was the American and Cuban mobsters had who lost a fortune due to his policies. In April 1959, while Frank was in charge of Cuba's casinos, he went with Fidel and company on a tour of United States trying to raise support for their new government. While they were in New York, the subject of the mob's desire to see Fidel out of the way was revisited. Fidel's entourage was booked into the Statler Hilton. Frank had registered under his real name and Cuban military rank. One night Frank was called by one of the security guards on duty in the lobby. No visitors were allowed up without permission. Frank told the guard to send up the visitor who was claiming to be Frank's uncle. It turned out to be one of the gambling mobsters, who said there were certain people who would pay $1 million for someone to kill Castro. Frank told him he wasn't for hire, but when he returned to Havana, Frank was approached by a CIA agent at the American embassy who was looking for information about Castro and Cuba, and Frank related the mob offer to him. This contact by Frank was the genesis of what would be an unholy alliance between the CIA and the mob that would surface in the future regarding further attempts to eliminate Castro and the assassination of President Kennedy.

Frank's tenure as gambling czar and tax collector brought him into contact with a lot of money, mostly in cash. Prior to that time Frank had been entrusted with money by Fidel to purchase guns and ammunition for the revolution. He usually received the money directly from one of Fidel's secretaries, often in the form of U.S. dollars. For larger purchases Frank was given the number of an account with a Swiss bank. Whenever Frank had purchased armaments to be smuggled into Cuba, he had been totally honest with Fidel, accounting for each dollar spent and keeping nothing for himself. However, as he saw the government turning to communism and the inevitable totalitarianism, Frank knew that his days in Cuba were numbered. He realized that his fight would now be against the Castro regime. What better way to finance his cause than with some of the money he was collecting for Fidel and the communists?

When Frank testified before the Rockefeller Commission, he told them that he left Cuba with "$3,000 or $4,000."[12] However, Frank confided privately that the actual amount was more like $750,000, which was a huge sum in 1959. He also helped finance his anti-Castro activities through his import/export business, which had offices in both Havana and Miami. It was somewhat ironic that Fidel was responsible for generating most of the cash that would be used against him, but Frank got no personal gain from this windfall. During the three years after he broke with Fidel he spent every bit of the money financing anti-Castro missions. This included purchasing a Coast Guard cutter, two forty-five-foot motor yachts, two racing hulls built by the Bertram shipbuilders in Fort Lauderdale that were capable of doing fifty miles per hour on the open ocean, and various weapons. He also financed and supported a cadre of anti-Castro Cubans from his house in Coral Gables.

By the beginning of June 1959 Frank had begun to lay plans for his eventual departure from Cuba. During the first week he flew the

B-25 by himself to Miami, ostensibly for "maintenance and repairs" to be done at the small Opa-locka Airport in the northwest part of the city. He took with him most of the cash he had been accumulating as gambling czar, to be placed in a Miami bank. Since he was an official representative of the Cuban government, Customs would not be a problem. Nor did he worry about being followed or spied on by agents working for Fidel and Raúl. At this early stage of the Castro takeover, there had not been sufficient time for the development of much of a spy network in Miami. While there, Frank signed a lease on a house in Coral Gables and looked in on his import/export business located on LeJeune Road. From his office he telephoned Carlos Prío and reported that the communists were poised to take over. He said that moderates in the cabinet were being replaced by radical communists and that Che had been made president of the Bank of Cuba and director of the Ministry of Industries, where he would direct economic policies. He also noted the increasing suppression of personal freedoms. The prospect of a truly democratic Cuba looked as dim as it had during the Batista regime. Frank returned to Havana knowing that he would ultimately have to split from Fidel.

Frank's decision to finally leave Cuba for good was not just based on his political differences with the communists; he feared for his life. On Monday, June 29, 1959, while in Havana, Frank received warnings from two separate sources—his friend and ally Sam Jennis and an anonymous "friend" working in Fidel's secret police, the G-2—that Raúl was about to arrest and try him for being a traitorous "anti-revolutionary." Frank therefore drove his jeep back to the air base at San Antonio de los Baños, went to his quarters, and packed two duffel bags with his uniforms and personal clothing. He also filled several large boxes with photos, his diary from the revolution, and copies of various documents he had obtained surreptitiously himself and through the cadre of spies in Cuba who had worked with him. With the help of a Cuban air force pilot Frank would later identify only as "Enrique," he fueled the B-25 and the C-46. They also loaded both planes with "as many guns and as much ammunition" as they could carry. Just before sunrise on June 30, 1959, with Frank at the controls of the B-25 and Enrique flying the C-46, they took off to the east from San Antonio de los Baños, then headed north directly over Havana toward Florida. A short while later they touched down at Opa-locka and Frank began what would be a lifelong struggle against his former comrade, Fidel.

While flying over Havana, Frank turned the plane a little to the east so he could better see the panorama of Havana and the harbor. Like one of his heroes, General Douglas MacArthur ("He wasn't a Marine, but he was a hell of a soldier"), he promised himself that someday he would return. Little did he know at the time that his return would occur the very next day. After arriving at Opa-locka, Frank received a frantic message from Marcos Diaz Lanz, asking that Frank return and exfiltrate him from Cuba too. Therefore, on July 1, 1959, Frank performed his first anti-Castro mission and flew back to San Antonio de los Baños, successfully bringing Marcos to Miami.

5

Anti-Castro

*Commander Cienfuegos, I believe because of his contact with me,
was executed by Raúl Castro.*

—**Sworn testimony of Frank Sturgis to the
Rockefeller Commission, April 3, 1975**

ONE OF THE FIRST THINGS FRANK DID AFTER LEAVING CASTRO AND
Cuba was to form an organization called the International Anti-
Communist Brigade. Incorporated under Florida law, its mission was
to fight communism, wherever it was being practiced, but Frank's
main target was Castro's Cuba. In addition to being anti-communist,
Frank was now anti-Castro. Frank did not just have political beliefs,
he lived them. He set up a military headquarters at his Coral Gables
house, where he stored a cache of armaments and kept a small commercial printing press. He first learned about printing machines during his training as a Marine Raider in World War II. He planned to
use the press to print anti-Castro literature and leaflets. There was
also a safe that held some of the cash that Frank had brought out of
Cuba. Living with him were three Cubans—his staff—two former

members of the July 26th Brigade and "Enrique," the pilot who had flown the C-46 from Cuba. Like Frank, they were anti-communists who believed Fidel had betrayed them and the democratic ideals of the revolution. Frank was their *jefe,* and he posted "Orders of the Day" on a large blackboard set up in the dining room. Various maps of Cuba and the Caribbean were mounted on two of the walls. On another was a large poster Frank had printed that proclaimed, *"Fidel fracaso"* ("Fidel failed").

On July 4, 1959, Frank launched his first true offensive against Castro by secretly landing twenty trained soldiers in the Escambray Mountains of Cuba to "compose the core of an anti-Castro guerilla group."[1] This was the first of many of Frank's missions into Cuba that would involve actions on behalf of the clandestine anti-Castro underground. Frank worked closely at this time with Marcos and Pedro Diaz Lanz. Pedro and his wife had left Cuba for Miami in a small boat several days before Frank's departure. Just prior to leaving, Pedro had taken over Radio Havana, an island-wide station, and delivered an hour-long scathing attack on Fidel, whom he accused of selling out to the communists, and the inevitable repressive regime that would be imposed. In keeping with their sense of patriotism and opposition to communism, on July 15, 1959, Frank and the Diaz Lanz brothers went to Washington, D.C., at their own expense and gave classified testimony about the situation in Cuba to a Senate committee investigating the threat of communism.

Shortly after Frank had set up his anti-Castro headquarters in Miami, he was told by an informant that his life was in danger. Fidel was sending two Mexican communists to kill him. Frank gave a description of the gunmen to the FBI and the CIA. The federal agents took Frank into protective custody with a twenty-four-hour guard at his house for two days. Then they flew him to Washington, D.C., and put him in a "safe house" for continued protection. After about a week, INS officers in Texas reported that they had apprehended the gunmen and prevented their entry into the United States.[2]

For Frank's third overt action against Castro, he and Pedro Diaz

Lanz dropped thousands of anti-Castro leaflets over several Cuban cities, including Havana, beginning on October 22, 1959. Fidel called this incursion "Cuba's Pearl Harbor" and used it as an excuse to formally sever diplomatic relations with the United States. The leaflets were printed on very thin, tissue-like paper. On each one was printed in bold black letters the same message on the poster in Frank's dining room, *"Fidel fracaso."* They also contained simple instructions for building gasoline bombs and encouraged the populace to burn down government buildings. Economic conditions in Cuba were not very good, and personal freedoms were being eradicated. Frank hoped to stir up resentment against Fidel on the part of the poor *guajiros* and the students and professionals.

Frank described the mission during which two hundred thousand leaflets were dropped on Havana in an interview with Paul Meskil of the New York *Daily News.*

> Pedro Diaz Lanz was the pilot and I was the co-pilot. Marcos Diaz Lanz and another Cuban were with us. Cuban Air Force fighters came after us but they missed us and almost shot their own planes down. The big guns at the Navy station and the Cabana fortress opened up and the angle of the guns was such that they were firing from the heights into the city. At least 36 people were killed or wounded.[3]

Frank said that although the B-25 was registered in his name, the CIA had provided the funds for maintenance and fuel for the mission.[4] Despite this CIA support and sanctioning, the B-25 was later impounded by U.S. Customs agents at the airstrip in Pompano Beach where Frank had landed it.[5] It was eventually released back to Frank to be used in the ill-fated Bay of Pigs invasion.

A week after the leaflet mission, Frank got the news that his friend and comrade Commander Camilo Cienfuegos had died in Cuba under mysterious circumstances. He was piloting his small Cessna from Camaguay to Havana and disappeared while over the ocean. An extensive search was conducted, but neither Cienfuegos nor his plane were ever found. Fidel praised Cienfuegos as a hero of the revolution, which indeed he was. He was the last person to board the *Granma* with Fidel on the voyage from Mexico that launched the revolution. Supposedly, Fidel allowed him on the crowded boat only because he was so thin. The official explanation for Cienfuegos's death was that it was an unfortunate "accident," but Frank disagreed. "Camilo was executed on orders from Raúl, in part because of his contact with me. My information is that he was shot down by a Cuban air force pilot." Frank explained that Cienfuegos was immensely popular with the Cuban people. He said, "Raúl was always very jealous of him, even when we were up in the mountains." That popularity was an impediment to the personality cult Raúl and Fidel were creating. Those who believe the official "accident" version point out that Cienfuegos was still supporting Fidel publicly in October 1959 when he endorsed the agrarian reform that nationalized and redistributed most of Cuba's farm land, including the farm owned by Fidel's family. They argue that Cienfuegos was, therefore, backing the Castro regime. Again, Frank disagreed. "Camilo may have been a socialist, or even a leftist, but he was no communist. We talked about this. He believed in democracy and personal freedom as deeply as I did. He stayed inside Cuba trying to stem the tide of totalitarianism being imposed by the Fidelistos."

In Frank's March 3, 1975, appearance before the Rockefeller Commission, during which he was questioned about his early CIA connections to Cuba, there were questions involving Guatemala and President Miguel Ydígoras Fuentes. After visiting Rafael Trujillo several times in the Dominican Republic seeking assistance for Pedro Diaz Lanz, in December 1959 Frank went to Guatemala and was successful in persuading President Ydígoras to not only give aid to Lanz but to allow invasion bases as well. Frank outlined the steps to set up such a base: establish trust with the government (Frank had an edge here because of his history in Cuba); get permission; come to a financial arrangement; and permit the host country to inspect the bases.

Frank's visit generated a lot of media publicity in Latin America, which forced him and Diaz Lanz to leave the country.[6] Nevertheless, bases were eventually established in Guatemala, where Frank trained soldiers for the Bay of Pigs invasion.

When Frank returned to Miami from Guatemala in January 1960, the Immigration and Naturalization Service revoked his citizenship by issuing a Certificate of Loss of Nationality.[7] This placed the burden on Frank to show why his citizenship should be restored. They also confiscated his passport. On January 7, 1960, Frank furnished the INS with a statement under oath denying any activities that would result in forfeiture of his American citizenship. However, the FBI reported to the INS that in March 1959 Frank had admitted to an agent that he was a captain in Fidel's army. There was also the January 1959 photo of Frank standing over a mass grave of Batista supporters and the caption, which identified him as a captain in the Cuban army. According to a January 14, 1960, FBI memo, Frank's case was "a hot potato" that was "being handled on the Washington level" and "the proceedings against [Frank] did not depend so much on the evidence as it did on the feelings of the State Department."[8] The INS held a formal hearing on February 23, 1960, and on April 26 the hearing officer issued a decision declaring that Frank had voluntarily expatriated himself due to his service in the Cuban armed forces. Frank was ordered to be deported from the United States as an illegal alien.

In response Frank filed an appeal, which allowed him to remain in the country. He then contacted Florida's senator George Smathers for assistance. Like Frank, Smathers was a former Marine and an ardent anti-communist. At the time, Smathers had been a senator for ten years. In his entire political career, which ended in 1969, Smathers never lost an election. As a southern Democrat, he was opposed to integration, but at the same time, he was close to President Kennedy. He was rumored to have ties with Santo Trafficante and the former Havana gambling crowd. For this reason, prior to the Castro takeover, Smathers had been a supporter of Batista's. By the time Frank contacted him in 1960, Smathers was anti-Castro and actively supported efforts to overthrow him. In light of this, it is not surprising that the senator agreed to help. The loss of his citizenship troubled Frank greatly. As much as he loved the Cuban people and wanted to help their cause for freedom, he said he never intended to surrender his American citizenship. He had heard about Americans who fought in such foreign skirmishes as the Spanish Civil War and never lost their citizenship. However, he acknowledged that his position in Castro's army and air force probably did violate the Neutrality Act.

Despite the evidence against him, Frank was supported by the CIA, which was preparing plans for an invasion of Cuba at the Bay of Pigs. Frank was an important part of those plans. He trained guerrillas, donated his airplane, and provided intelligence data to the planners. Further, he had demonstrated his loyalty to the United States by providing the CIA with information about Castro's government during the first six months of 1959. All in all, Frank was a valuable asset to the CIA. With the influence of the Agency and Senator Smathers, Frank's case was reopened in March 1961, just one month before the Bay of Pigs invasion. On March 14, 1961, the INS issued an order restoring Frank's citizenship. The reason given was that Undersecretary of State Christian Herter had "inadvertently" signed the Certificate of Loss of Nationality revoking Frank's citizenship. Frank offered no evidence himself at the hearing by exercising his fifth Amendment right to remain silent. He saw this whole episode as an example of an unwritten rule among spies that the government will take care of those involved in clandestine activities who keep their mouths shut.

Frank also credited the support of Senator Smathers for the restoration of his citizenship. During Frank's life, he maintained contact with the senator. For example, in 1968, when Frank and his crew ran aground near British Honduras on a mission to seize a Soviet or Cuban ship and exchange it for the USS *Pueblo*, which was being held by the North Koreans, they were arrested by Honduran police. The first person he called was Senator Smathers, who offered to intervene on Frank's behalf. He also asked Frank, "Why didn't you take me along?"

In March 1960, Frank was involved in the planning and execution of a plot to blow up a French ship, *La Coubre,* docked in Havana harbor loaded with munitions from Belgium. Ordinarily, ships with such dangerous cargo were off-loaded in the bay by smaller ships. However, Raúl Castro was in a hurry to process the shipment and ordered the ship to go directly to the dock. At the time, Frank operated a marine salvage business called The Hampton Roads Salvage Company, which was a front for his anti-Castro activities. Among the people who worked with Frank was a deep-sea diver who was also an expert in underwater demolition and explosives. With his help, anti-Castro agents were able to secretly place and then detonate a bomb on the hull of *La Coubre.* At least seventy-five people were killed in the explosion. Che Guevara, who was attending a meeting nearby, went to the scene and, as a physician, rendered aid to the wounded. It was at the memorial service for victims of *La Coubre* that Alberto Korda took the famous photo of a bereted Che that became an iconic poster during the 1960s.

After he exited Cuba, Frank made many intelligence-gathering trips for the CIA. He supplied details on planned assassinations including those of Joaquin Balaguer and Rafael Trujillo, both presidents of the Dominican Republic. In the early 1960s, Frank not only sneaked back into Cuba on a regular basis but also traveled to an array of Caribbean islands and Central American countries meeting with the heads of state. He visited the leaders of some dozen countries seeking assistance in the hoped-for war against Castro's Cuba. His access to these heads of state was made possible by a combination of CIA contacts and Frank's reputation from his Cuban escapades. Castro's revolutionaries had nicknamed him "Chief Crazy Horse" ("El Jefe de Caballo Loco") because of his stealth fighting skills and his complete lack of fear. As we have seen, Fidel himself once shouted, witnessing one of Frank's impossible landings on a mountaintop in Cuba, *"¡Eso si es un yanqui bárbaro!"* ("This is one hell of a Yankee"). It was a product of the training he had received as an Edson Raider and practiced for three years in the South Pacific proving grounds of Guam, Okinawa, and Guadalcanal. Frank had been introduced to island-hopping at the age of seventeen in the Solomons, where he saw so much intensive combat that he started to fall apart. Twenty years later he found himself island-hopping once again; and even though the war was now "cold," Frank would soon find that in some places it was still kill or be killed.

When you line up the leaders Frank visited in the 1960s (and in the '70s, '80s, and even into the early '90s), a pattern emerges. A cadre of strong anti-communists rose to the top in the Caribbean and Central America. It was the Cold War, and the revolutionary leaders that had taken power (sometimes with Frank's assistance as a guerrilla trainer and spy) proclaimed themselves bulwarks against Communism, which made them attractive to America and American business interests. However, in their respective quests for absolute power, and due to the negative changes that followed, many of these leaders soon were viewed as liabilities, and thus the United States and others sought out, and sometimes inserted, more moderate regimes. Leaders like François Duvalier in Haiti, for example, who had come to power as a medical doctor fighting a war on a crippling childhood disease. But the power seduced him and he became an incredible tyrant. This template was repeated in many banana republics, and the West became wary of these power-hungry anti-communist leaders who might spark follow-on revolutions that could go awry, as Fidel's had in Cuba. (When Aron Kay, known as "the Pieman," who had made a reputation by throwing pies in the faces of celebrities, tried to pie Frank in New York in 1977, he said he used a banana cream pie because of all the banana republics in which Frank had played a role.)

One of the first trips Frank made was to the Dominican Republic. Rafael Leónidas Trujillo Molina ruled the Dominican Republic from 1930 until 1961, when he was assassinated. The United States supported Trujillo and his position as one of Latin America's leading anti-communists. However, when his regime turned repressive, he was seen as expendable, and the same people, including Frank, who had saved his life by foiling an assassination plot by Castro, plotted his demise.

During the American occupation of his country (1916 to 1924) Trujillo had joined the Dominican National Guard. The guard was trained by the U.S. Marines to stabilize the country after the occupation. Finding the military life to his liking, Trujillo rose quickly through the ranks. His ambition rose quickly as well, and in 1930 he overthrew President Horacio Vásquez. Trujillo filled the country with statues of himself and renamed landmarks "Trujillo" this and "Trujillo" that.

Like some of the other anti-communist Latin American and Caribbean leaders, Trujillo ruled with absolute authority. He attempted to legitimize this voracious power by changing the constitution and holding elections wherein only Trujillo and members of his party ran for office. He ordered that schoolchildren recite prayers for "God, country, and Trujillo." Plaques were posted professing allegiance to the official state party; travel by citizens was severely restricted. The paranoia of similar absolute rulers (Duvalier of Haiti, Somoza of Nicaragua, Ydígoras of Guatemala, and others) was also visited on "El Chiro," or "The Goat," as Trujillo was tagged, in an allusion to his almost continual extramarital relationships. Trujillo's secret police, the SIM (Military Intelligence Service), reminiscent of the Tonton Macoute's in Haiti, jailed, tortured, and killed those who opposed. So much for a healthy discourse.

Trujillo had another nickname. He was also called "Chapitas" or "Bottle Cap." This sobriquet was applied to the Dominican leader because of his rather excessive use of medals, to which his picture in the photo section seems to bear witness. The Dominican children would fix bottle caps to their clothes in an attempt to emulate the overly decorated chest of Chapitas. El Chiro or Chapitas, "The Goat" or "Bottle Cap," take your pick.

In his testimony before the Rockefeller Commission Frank related the following:

STURGIS: *I was at the Biltmore Terrace Hotel on Miami Beach—I can't remember the year. But the man who was running or at least one of the*

men who was running the Biltmore Terrace Hotel was Norman Roth-
man. That place was supposedly a hang out of all the top Batista people
who came into exile. The top of the Biltmore Hotel was being readied for
President Batista who was in the Dominican Republic. I went to the
Biltmore. And I was introduced to an intelligence agent who was a close
buddy of General Trujillo's son, who I believe at the time was chief of
the Air Force, the Dominican Air Force. The man asked me, or approached
me in conversation and told me General Trujillo would like to speak
with the ex-Chief of Fidel's Air Force, Pedro Diaz Lanz. And if I could
make arrangements for the contact between him and Pedro, he would
appreciate it. And I did make contact. And Pedro did not want to go to
the Dominican Republic. So I said, I will go to the Dominican for you.
And I did. And it was set up and arranged by this intelligence agent.
OLSEN: *The intelligence agent of—*
STURGIS: *Trujillo, and I was received—I had carte blanc [sic] in the*
Dominican Republic. I stayed at the top hotel there; I think it was called
the Ambassador Hotel there in Santo Domingo. I was received at the
palace. I went directly with this intelligence agent to the Presidential of-
fice. Trujillo was present in his white uniform. Jonny [sic] Abbes, his Chief
of Intelligence, was there, a known past Communist, who I believe is still
a Communist or at least playing his little games.[9]

Frank also told of one visit he and Pedro Diaz Lanz had with Trujillo and Abbes. On one occasion in 1960, Trujillo offered Frank and
Pedro $1 million to lead an invasion of Cuba from the Dominican
Republic. Diaz Lanz declined, later telling his CIA bosses that he
didn't want to work for another dictator.

After Trujillo's rather public involvement in the assassination attempt of Venezuelan president Rómulo Betancourt in June 1960, the
United States and the Organization of American States imposed
sanctions on the Dominican Republic. The United States broke diplomatic relations in August 1960. It was clear that President Kennedy
wanted Trujillo (and those like him) replaced with democratic leaders as protection against the emergence of another Castro.

Aside from Trujillo's repressive tendencies and his almost public involvement in the attempt on the life of Betancourt, the Dominican leader's policy of *blanquisimo* certainly paved the way for his demise. Trujillo's plan to "whiten" the Dominican population resulted in the massacre of some twenty thousand dark-skinned Haitian sugarcane workers in 1937. This is a story in itself—complete with a poem by U.S. poet laureate Rita Dove—but suffice it here to say that these Haitian workers were identified as immigrants (the ill-defined border between the Dominican Republic and Haiti led to a host of issues) and then slaughtered if they could not pronounce the letter "r" in *perejil* (Spanish for parsley), which gave its name to the Parsley Massacre.

When Frank was involved with the Israeli underground in 1948, he had been told by the Israeli spy with whom he was working about Trujillo's unusual international policy of inviting Jewish emigrants from Europe in the 1930s when they were being refused admittance to other countries. He also invited Spanish exiles after the civil war there in 1930s. In retrospect, this encouragement of Europeans was perhaps an early attempt to bleach the mixed-race country under the aforementioned *blanquisimo* policy.

Soon after Castro came to power in Cuba, he attempted to expand his revolution to other countries. The Dominican Republic was one of the first targets. Frank had gathered intelligence on this, and a Cuban invasion had been foiled. Frank was there seeking bases and other aid for the counterrevolution against Castro. He was also consulted on training and matters pertaining to the Cuban air force. Later, when the regime turned repressive, Frank was there in quite a different role. In secret testimony before the Rockefeller Commission, Frank described the assassination plot not only in the Dominican Republic but those in four other countries as well.

In his attempts to enlist anti-Castro assistance from these leaders, Frank, with CIA assets, initially assisted these regimes because of their very pronounced anti-communist postures. Eventually, however, as noted above, intervention would occur to create the formation of a less reactionary government. Probably rightfully so, they feared that the repressive tactics of Trujillo, Duvalier, and the like would lead to what had occurred in nearby Cuba, where communism gained a foothold as a reaction to a repressive regime. Although the Dominican economy had prospered under Trujillo with the influx of foreign investment, his repression led the CIA, with Frank's assistance, to supply the weapons used in his assassination.

The assassination of Trujillo has been covered in books and articles. Frank has been associated with the event in various roles. A Dominican dissident, Lorenzo Berry, ran a supermarket in the capital, Trujillo City, called Wimpy's. Frank and at least one other (probably Frank Nelson, a syndicate associate) shipped weapons to the supermarket disguised as food. These weapons found their way into the hands of those who had no use for the Dominican president. On May 30, 1961, Trujillo and his chauffeur drove to one of "El Chiro"'s mistresses sometime after dark. Later, two carloads of assassins fired enough lead into the president to significantly increase his body weight. Whether the smuggled weapons were used (certainly the gunmen had access to guns in the Dominican Republic) was maybe not as important to the assassins as having guns sent from the United States for that purpose. Ties to the states in this mission certainly enhanced the perpetrators' position. The newspapers reported that on Tuesday, May 30, 1961, seven men ambushed the dictator as he left a residence in San Cristóbal. The accounts noted that Trujillo had been notorious for his terrorist methods. Reputedly he ordered the deaths of more than a thousand Dominicans in his first year in power and those of twenty thousand Haitian squatters seven years later.

The irony in the demise of Trujillo is that earlier (in June 1959) Frank's intelligence to the CIA had foiled an attempt by Castro to invade the Dominican Republic and assassinate Trujillo. Now, not two years later, Frank assisted in Trujillo's liquidation. Nothing is more constant than change. Trujillo is buried in the Père-Lachaise cemetery in Paris, far enough away to prevent tinkering with the corpse.

If Frank had cobbled together a résumé, certainly "training revolutionaries and freedom fighters" would have been near the top of page one, and under "desired geographical locations" would have been listed a number of the islands in the Caribbean and other tropical climes. However, as in any business, the clients you serve do not always appear as they really are, nor do they always turn out the way you, or even they, planned. Such was surely the case with François Duvalier and the dreaded Tonton Macoutes.

"Papa Doc" came to power in Haiti in 1957 in a democratic election. He had been the minister of health in a prior regime. In this position he gained notoriety for his fight against an insidious disease that had ravaged Haiti's children. The disease, called Yaws, is an infection that affects the skin, joints, and, if left untreated, later the bones, of the victim. It is transmitted by personal contact as well as by a small army of eye gnats. As health minister, Duvalier gained popular support for his war on this child-crippling scourge and paved the way for his election in 1957. But any compassion he may have exhibited as minister of health rapidly disappeared once he was in power. Like his peers in other island nations, his desire for absolute power turned him repressive. One year after his election, there was a coup attempt. Seeing what handwriting there was on the wall, Papa Doc amended the Haitian constitution (that had originally been written by future president Franklin Roosevelt), making himself president for life.

To help with the enforcement of this change, in 1959 he created the Tonton Macoutes. The name has an interesting derivation. Haitian children who have been good throughout the year are promised a Christmas visit by Tonton Noël. *Tonton* means uncle, so the visitor is literally Uncle Christmas. On the other side of the holiday ledger, however, is a character called Tonton Macoute, who allegedly snatches those children who have been bad, a fate certainly much scarier than the lump of coal that threatened America's youth. The word *macoute* translates to "gunnysack"—the burlap bag made of coarse jute material. So Tonton Macoute is literally Uncle Gunnysack, which in Haiti is equivalent to the bogeyman. And the Tonton Macoutes acted the part. Modeled on the Italian fascist "black shirts" and the German "brownshirts," the Macoutes became notorious for their widespread and brutal oppression of anyone who didn't see things their way. Their goal was to wipe out political dissidents, a program at which they proved alarmingly proficient. The Macoutes were led by Duvalier's second in command, Luckner Cambronne, and were known for wearing sunglasses. Their weapon of choice was the machete, and their signature was leaving victims hanging in public places as a warning to others. As if that weren't enough, they did their best to spread the story that they were voodoo demons and zombies. This death squad actually persisted after the Duvalier family reign and operated into the twenty-first century. Frank once admitted that the Macoutes came as close as anyone to scaring him.

Frank, true to form, traveled far and wide to train rebels, especially those who wanted nothing to do with communism. He would help their cause, seek aid for the invasion of Cuba, and return on a liquidation mission if they turned repressive and became liabilities. On many of these visits, Frank also represented American casino interests. The textbook case here of course was his unfailing support of Castro until the rebel leader began embracing communism. Frank went from trusted aide and confidant to would-be assassin. So it was in Haiti. Papa Doc Duvalier was initially seen as a positive change, and Frank helped him. Frank's insertion into Haiti was early in Papa Doc's reign. The CIA was trying to bolster the regime against communism, and Frank was practiced in just such an art. To keep Trujillo and Duvalier from being co-opted by the communists was the mission; Frank was the man. Never mind that both leaders would turn out to be in many ways less than spectacular human beings. On May 20, 1968, Frank's B-25 flew over Duvalier's palace and dropped two gasoline drums, leaving a huge crater. Working with the military arm of Cuba's underground and some former military associates, Frank drew up plans for Papa Doc's assassination, but Duvalier lasted three more years, until his son took over.

Papa Doc's corrupt and repressive regime drew an extremely negative response from the Kennedy White House. As stated above, the United States was exploring more moderate alternatives to Duvalier to prevent another Cuban-style revolution. Papa Doc would later brag that JFK's assassination was a result of Duvalier's placing a curse on him.

In 1986, fifteen years after Papa Doc's death, a mob of Haitians raided his burial place, intent on doing harm to his corpse, to ensure that on "judgment day" he would not be able to rise. To their dismay, however, they found that the body had been removed (ostensibly by those with a vested interest in assuring he *did* rise when the occasion warranted). Not wishing to be denied, the throng disinterred a nearby Papa Doc supporter and carried out their vengeance on his remains.

Amid his times seeking aid from the Banana Republics, Frank also formulated his own plots to assassinate Fidel. Perhaps the best known plan involved a former mistress of Fidel's, Marita Lorenz, who became a spy for Frank. She smuggled a lot of valuable information out of Cuba. As she said,

> Castro's rooms were full of guns and papers strewn all over the place. There was one filing cabinet that was never locked. It was full of money, documents and maps. I took stuff and slipped it to Frank, Fidel never knew. Frank said, "Get all the data you can," and I did. I was a regular Mata Hari.[10]

And she was. In 1960, Frank devised a scheme to have Marita put poison in Fidel's coffee. He gave her the pills to use, and she claimed later that she secreted them in a jar of face cream as she entered Cuba. A short time earlier, Frank had helped Marita escape from Cuba, so Fidel asked her why she had returned. She lied and said she'd left because she missed her mother and went to visit her in New York City. Fidel accepted her story and ordered food and coffee for the two of them. Then he fell asleep. Marita went to the bathroom and opened the jar of face cream. She felt around, but could not find the capsules. She told Frank she presumed they had melted. However, Frank believed Marita probably lost her nerve and invented the melting explanation. She had been deeply in love with Fidel for a long time, which prevented her from bringing harm to him. Frank didn't involve her in any more missions, although Marita reentered Frank's life with a bang in 1977 when she accused him of assassinating President Kennedy and threatening to kill her.

In 1961, Frank came into contact again with the Cuban and American mob bosses who had approached him in 1959 about assassinating Fidel. At this point the CIA was beginning to think that joining the mob in removing Castro might not be a bad idea, and Frank was the go-between. Frank's liaison to the underworld was Norman Rothman, and his business associates were Santo Trafficante, Johnny Roselli, Sammy Mannarino, Salvatore Granello, and Charlie Tourine. The mob didn't think that joining the CIA was such a bad idea either. Evidently the plan most favored by this new partnership was to hire Gaspare Magaddino, a sort of world-class hit man who had ended it for some fifty targets before he himself was shotgunned to death in Brooklyn in 1970. Gaspare had lived in Cuba and knew Havana well (which had its plusses and minuses), but for whatever reason, Magaddino didn't do the job. Johnny Roselli from Las Vegas got the nod. Poison was the weapon of choice, supplied by the CIA. Frank's friend, columnist Jack Anderson, reported that in 1961, agents gave Roselli some nasty stuff to put in Fidel's daily milk shake at the Havana Hilton. The plot failed when the complicit waiter appeared too nervous when delivering the deadly drink. Castro was suspicious and had the milk shake tested, and the waiter was executed.

Like most associations, the Frank Sturgis–mob connection was intended to be mutually beneficial. As Fidel's casino czar, Frank gained experience and information useful to those in the gambling enterprise. His access to Castro also made him attractive to the mob. When Fidel nationalized the casinos and booted the syndicate out of Cuba, those who were willing to liquidate Castro were in demand. The CIA had their own reasons for wanting him dead. In an ironic twist, the mob asked CIA-affiliated Frank to kill him, and the CIA asked mob-affiliated Sam Giancana to do the job. Turnabout is often fair play, but Fidel's security and an ample supply of luck have kept him alive while some of those interested in his demise have been less fortunate.

The extent of Frank's connections to the crime syndicate will probably never be known. Suffice it to say that they were interested in using him to protect their interests in Cuba, and when that didn't work out, they were interested in his help with eliminating the reason it hadn't. They also used him to investigate the possibilities of casino gambling on other islands and in other South and Central American countries. It was an agenda item on many of his trips to those regions.

Frank's connections with the underworld enabled the CIA to join forces with mob figures in attempts to dispose of Castro. These same connections involving Frank, the CIA, and the mob later led to theories about the assassination of President Kennedy.

Frank remembered several other assassination plots on Fidel in the mid-sixties, including planting dynamite in the garage under an apartment building that housed a bunch of Castro and Russian aides. Evidently Fidel had a habit of visiting this building at the same time every week; but before the plan could be executed, Castro's Soviet intelligence apparatus foiled the attempt. Another plan involved a sniper ambush at a funeral. The snipers opened up and sprayed the target jeep and killed the driver and the Fidel look-alike. It was one of his bodyguards, Alfredo Gamonal, who went to his death as a decoy.

Throughout his anti-Castro career, Frank participated in more than 150 air operations and 60 boat incursions. As Frank put it, these missions were done both "with the green light and without the green light," that is, with and without official government approval. For most of the air operations he used small single- or twin-engine planes, supplied by the CIA if they had requested the mission directly or rented from legitimate companies in south Florida for missions financed by private anti-Castro interests. He usually flew no higher than 100 to 150 feet after penetrating Cuban air space. This prevented radar detection but also made him vulnerable to small-arms fire from the ground. His only protection was a .45 revolver and his Marine knife.

Sometimes he would land on a mountain airstrip and drop off CIA counterspies who would infiltrate the Castro government. Other times he brought people out of Cuba.

During this time, Frank was never an official employee of the CIA but worked as an independent contractor. One of his main CIA contacts was Bernard "Macho" Barker, whom Frank described as the CIA's field director for Cuba and the Caribbean. As a cover for his real job, Macho ran a real estate business in Coral Gables. In a locked back room, Macho maintained his CIA office, which included a scrambled radio that he could use to call headquarters in Langley, Virginia. Frank was a frequent visitor, especially beginning in the summer of 1960. The CIA had big plans for Cuba. No more single incursions and infiltrations. There was now talk of a full-blown invasion with the support of the U.S. military. Macho enlisted Frank to help plan this mission and train the brigade that was being put together. This work would take Frank to several secret bases both inside and outside the United States, and, eventually, nearly to a place in Cuba called La Bahía de Cochinos, the Bay of Pigs.

6

The Bay of Pigs

My son is still too young to realize what has happened here, but I will make it my business to tell him the story of your courage as he grows up. It is my hope that he'll grow into a man at least half as brave as the members of Brigade 2506.

—Jacqueline Kennedy, in Spanish, to the forty thousand people gathered at Miami's Orange Bowl to celebrate the release of Brigade 2506 prisoners ransomed by her husband from Fidel Castro, December 29, 1962

IN FRANK'S OPINION, THE SEEDS FOR THE BAY OF PIGS WERE SEWN when communists began to become a part of Castro's revolution. He remembered them being everywhere, indoctrinating the rebel troops in communist ideology and being appointed by Fidel to important positions. Frank and his friend and daredevil pilot Pedro Diaz Lanz had had enough, and they told the communist air force advisors to go to hell. Obviously, Fidel was reneging on his promise of a democratic Cuba. It was no place for Frank. On June 30, 1959, Frank washed his hands of Castro's communism and left Cuba for Miami. This, Frank said, led directly to the Bay of Pigs invasion in April 1961.

During the two years in between, Frank carried on a war of his own against Castro, having clandestine meetings, making forays into Cuba with his boats and his trusty B-25, dropping arms, agents, leaflets, and bombs. Frank would receive covert phone messages from a man whose voice he recognized but whom he could not identify who would outline the next night's mission. Frank would take off from any one of a number of secret locations, and by the time he reached his target, he would be night flying. Many of these flights were made to enable U.S. tracking ships to locate the Cuban defenses sensing Frank's flights. Castro's anti-aircraft batteries would track Frank with their radar-guided canon and rocket launchers. Frank was not a stranger to danger, and he wasn't in it for the money. He was paid $500 per flight, and there were no benefits, like insurance. If he failed to return, his wife, Janet, would get double the amount for that flight.

The Bahía de Cochinos, or Bay of Pigs, is in southern Cuba, southeast of Havana. Old Cuban fishermen will tell you that *cochino,* or pig, is the name of a potentially poisonous triggerfish with curved blue stripes running down from the snout, giving it a somewhat disagreeable look. These fish are also piggish in their diet in that they will eat almost anything, including the ostensibly inedible spiny sea urchin by rolling them over with a jet of water and then attacking the underbelly, where the spines are weaker and smaller. The beach in the Bay of Pigs, where the assault landing actually took place, is the Playa Girón, named for a pirate, Gilbert Girón, who landed there in the 1660s.

In the spring of 1960, President Eisenhower's administration agreed to a CIA recommendation to equip and train anti-Castro Cuban exiles for a military action against Castro. Thirteen million dollars was appropriated toward that end. After all, Castro was a walking advertisement for Communism and lived only ninety miles from the U.S. coastline. The CIA began to recruit and train anti-Castro Cubans for this new expeditionary force, which came to be known as Brigade 2506. The brigade took its name, or rather its number, from the first recruit to die in training (in all, five died in the dangerous training exercises). When the CIA began recruiting, they assigned the recruits numbers, and to dress the recruitment efforts in the colors of success, they began the numbering with 2,500 to make it look like they had more men than they did. The seventh recruit, then, had been assigned the serial number 2506. His name was Carlos Santana. To honor him, the brigade took on his number.

According to Macho Barker, a CIA operative for thirty years and one of Frank's fellow Watergate burglars, he and E. Howard Hunt and Frank had a role in the planning of the assault and the training of the brigade. Frank trained recruits in the Sierra Madre mountains of Guatemala, on a small island in the Caribbean, in the Florida Everglades, and at Lake Pontchartrain near New Orleans. Two locations where landing exercises were carried out were Norman's Cay, a small privately owned island in the Caribbean, and Useppa Island off the southwest coast of Florida, where today a small museum recounts the activity. The basic plan to use a relatively small invading force in the hope that they could establish a beachhead and receive support from the local population was one that had worked in Cuba before, beginning with José Marti and with Fidel himself and his *Granma* guerrillas.

Originally this anti-Castro initiative was called "Operation Zapata" after the nearby Zapata peninsula of Cuba. Richard Bissell, one of three aides to then CIA director Allen Dulles, was put in charge of the mission. The original beachhead was to be near the city of Trinidad, 250 miles southeast of Havana in the foothills of the Escambray Mountains. This choice was based on the fact that Trinidad's residents had no love for Fidel, and therefore would more readily join or create a popular uprising when the exiled Cubans came ashore. Equally important were the mountains hard by the city that lent themselves to a guerrilla campaign in the event the landing met overwhelming resistance and the invaders needed a place to regroup. Throughout 1960 Frank had trained brigade personnel both in coastal landings (he had made many of these both as a Marine in the Solomon Islands and when running guns for Castro only a few years earlier) and mountain guerrilla warfare, in which he was also considered an expert. The planning of the invasion was as secret as they could make it, and details of Frank's role are nowhere to be found in writing. Oral accounts have been sketchy at best.

Early in 1961 President Kennedy became involved in the planning of the Bay of Pigs invasion, focusing on "acceptable" reasons why the United States would be involved in this effort to take down Castro. Kennedy's plan was to link the Bay of Pigs invasion to military shipments from Russia to Cuba that threatened U.S. security. Unfortunately, his advisors made changes to the original invasion plans, changes that would ultimately yield disastrous consequences. The new plans changed the landing area for Brigade 2506 to the Girón and Larga beaches in the Bay of Pigs, which would effectively cut off contact with anti-Castro Cubans in Trinidad City and eliminate the option of a mountain retreat should the landing go badly. Castro had the benefit of KGB intelligence-gathering from his Soviet sponsors. They had warned him that a U.S.-backed attack was imminent, and the word had spread. Also, only two weeks earlier Dr. José Miró Cardona, an anti-Castro political leader living in exile, had issued a call to arms from Miami. Castro's military prepared for an attack. The politicians couldn't keep the secret. There were, in fact, posters around Cuba warning of an impending attack. There would be no surprise. Frank had invested a lot of time and personal resources buying war matériel and training soldiers in various locations. His trainees would be dropped, for example, in the Everglades with literally nothing (sometimes a knife) and taught to survive and take out the enemy. Many anti-Castro Cuban exiles who had fled to Florida in the wake of Castro's communist rule had trained hard and parted with hard-earned livelihoods just for a chance to reclaim their homeland.

On the morning of Saturday, April 15, 1961, three flights of B-26 light bombers took off from covert bases in Nicaragua and shelled three Cuban airfields. Frank sat not so patiently in the B-25 bomber he had purchased with Castro's money three years earlier, in 1958. He was loaded with ordnance and was scheduled for the second wave of the support force to inflict damage on the enemy before the invaders hit the beach. He had begun flying for Fidel some four years before, and now he couldn't wait to fly against him. This was part of Operation Puma, which had been planned to include two days of air strikes to take out Fidel's air force and soften up the ground troops prior to the invasion. Since only a few years earlier Frank had been in charge of security for this same air force, he had good intelligence on the subject. Operation Puma was to provide the brigade with critical air superiority and ensure the success of the land invasion scheduled for April 17. But Operation Puma was not given a chance to succeed because President Kennedy canceled all but the first bombing run. He and his White House advisors were still casting about for excuses for the invasion.

The CIA had invented at least one plan to justify American intervention. One of the B-26's engine cowlings was made to look as if it had taken ground fire from Cuba while on a routine flight. By the time this cover story had been disseminated, the bombers had made their first run on Cuba, inflicting heavy damage, and had returned to their base in Nicaragua to refuel and arm for their second wave. However, when they landed, to their surprise, they found that the president had ordered an indefinite stand-down. Without air support, there was little chance of success. As part of the second air attack, Frank was waiting in his plane at a secret airstrip well within striking distance of the Bay of Pigs. However, when President Kennedy issued the stand-down order, Frank knew right away that the operation was doomed. He would never take off in his favorite B-25. The bombs would never find their mark. He would never be able to give aid to the men he had trained. As he told Frank Saunders of the United States Probation Service years later when he was incarcerated for Watergate and Judge Sirica ordered a pre-sentence investigation report, he and his fellow Watergate burglar and pilot Macho Barker sat in their planes at a secret air base utterly helpless and incredibly angry. There were to be no more military flights over Cuba. No more Operation Puma. No air superiority for Brigade 2506. Not much hope for a successful land invasion.

On Wednesday, April 17, 1961, four transport ships carried 1,511 anti-Castro Cubans into the Bay of Pigs. The new landing site had been changed only two days before. The transports were joined by two supply-laden infantry landing craft. The invaders were counting on support from local Cubans disenchanted with Castro, hoping that their landing would ignite an anti-Castro conflagration. It didn't happen. The forewarned Fidel had made sure that his militia had contained the dissidents in that area, and it didn't help that the new landing site at the Bay of Pigs was too far away for the invaders to establish contact with the Escambray rebels in the mountains. The invasion was foundering when President Kennedy delivered the coup de grâce by withholding air support from the aircraft carrier USS *Essex*. This critical fighter/bomber air support had been promised for the day of the invasion. Kennedy was ultimately persuaded, by his brother Bobby and others, that direct U.S. intervention could spark a war with the Soviet Union. He chose to keep the USS *Essex* and its complement of aircraft out of the action to lessen the risk of U.S.-Soviet conflict. It was the death knell for the brigade. There were those in the CIA who thought the president would at least send in some U.S. ground troops to even the odds, but that also failed to materialize. The brave men of Brigade 2506, who knew they were greatly outnumbered (fifty to one) going in, were now left to twist in the wind blowing in off the Bahía de Cochinos.

By the time the invasion attempt was over, on Sunday, April 21, the brigade had lost 68 of its soldiers, and 1,209 had been captured. As in any battle, casualty numbers are suspect, given their propaganda value. The 1,209 number, however, was reported by many sources. The captives were put on trial almost immediately. Most were given thirty-year prison terms; a few were executed summarily by firing squad. Of the countries still using this method of execution, Fidel's Cuba is the only place where, instead of being blindfolded, the prisoner is gagged. Without the gag, Fidel's soldiers would have to listen to the prisoner yell epithets at Fidel and call for a free Cuba. If Frank had been captured, he surely would have been executed. "Fidel sent gunmen after me here in the United States but never succeeded in eliminating me. As a prisoner in Cuba, I wouldn't have been so lucky." It hadn't deterred him a bit.

Many of the prisoners were tortured by Castro, but to a man they refused to give up any secret information. Their release was "purchased" with $53 million worth of food and medicine donated by private, charitable groups under the direction of President Kennedy's brother Bobby. At the last minute, Castro demanded an additional $2.9 million in cash as "reparations" for Cuba's losses during the invasion. Bobby was able to secure the additional funds from two sources, Cardinal Richard Cushing (the Boston area cardinal, close friend of the Kennedys) and retired general Lucius Clay, Frank's old boss in the Berlin airlift days, who was working as a Wall Street banker. Among the ransomed prisoners was Manolo Artime, leader of the Cuban government in exile and the odds-on favorite to be named president if Castro was toppled.

Though the estimates vary widely (from 2,000 to 5,000), Castro's military losses were substantial. Significant in these estimates were the 1,800 or so Castro troops lost to the first (and only) wave of bombing. This illustrates how essential the planned bombing raids were and how the outcome might have been altered had Kennedy allowed them to continue, followed by additional fighter/bomber support from the USS *Essex*. When the foot soldiers realized there was no air cover, it was too late to do much of anything about it. Had the original landing site been used, they could have retreated to the Escambray Mountains, but that option had also been taken from them. The bottom fell out. Frank and the other pilots sat helpless as 1,300 of their compatriots were killed or captured. The battle, without air support from the U.S., was hopelessly one-sided. Castro's forces numbered 50,000 against 1,500 invaders. Air support would have leveled the battlefield, in more ways than one. As it was, the land action was condemned to perdition.

A force of sailors and marines who were stationed at the U.S. naval base at Guantánamo, Cuba, were assigned to an assault craft unit. For days preceding the invasion, their unit had been under condition alpha, or high alert. They were not told the details, but it was obvious to everyone that something big was imminent. On the morning of April 17, they were deployed in an LSD (landing ship dock) containing a complement of landing craft. The ships from Guantánamo were joined by other craft from secret bases in the area and were at various locations in the sixty-mile stretch of ocean from the base at "Gitmo" to the Bay of Pigs. Their orders were to stand by. These were part of the ground forces that some thought JFK would send in to assist the anti-Castro invaders. However, when the disaster on the beach began to unfold, the orders for this "second wave" went from "stand by" to a "stand down." The sailors and marines returned to base. Frank and the others flew home.

The failure of the Bay of Pigs embarrassed the Kennedy administration, and the hunt for scapegoats began almost immediately. CIA director Allen Dulles and two of his deputies, Charles Cabell and Richard Bissell, were forced to resign. A CIA report, issued at the time and then ordered destroyed, termed the operation "the perfect failure." There was plenty of blame to go around, and a lot of it fell on E. Howard Hunt, Frank's longtime CIA contact and fellow Bay of Pigs operative. In his testimony before the Select Committee on the Assassination of President Kennedy on November 3, 1978, Hunt related:

> Let me interject this, if I may say, that at the time I left the Bay of Pigs Operation, in the wake of the failure of the Bay of Pigs and joined Allen Dulles' staff, it was principally to help Allen explain some of the things that went on that he hadn't known before in his exalted position, and it was made abundantly clear to me in a very pleasant way that having been stained with the failure of the Bay of Pigs that I was to have nothing further to do with Cuban operations.[1]

Frank was about as invested in the Bay of Pigs as a person could be, in every sense of the word. He was invested emotionally. Ever since he noticed communists showing up in Havana to assist Castro, Frank had dedicated himself to toppling Fidel and delivering a communist-free, free Cuba. He was invested physically. He trained recruits and armed recruits. He made countless clandestine incursions, sometimes around the clock. He helped with military strategy and with intelligence he had gathered. He dropped leaflets, agents, guns, munitions, and even bombs. And he was invested financially. Frank spent most of his own money on matériel for the Bay of Pigs, including airplanes, boats, arms, and munitions. He collected a variety of firearms and ammunition in quantity. He manufactured bombs. He printed anti-Castro leaflets on a press at his house and dropped them on Havana out of his own B-25. Frank put his life on the line for the Bay of Pigs mission in many ways, including foiling the assassins Fidel sent to kill him.

To Frank, the Bay of Pigs disaster took on biblical proportions. He spoke of sacrifice. Baker, Gray, Ray, and Shamburger are the names of four streets in Miami today, but in 1963 they were four American CIA operatives who died on the beaches of the Bay of Pigs. The fact that the invading troops were betrayed was something Frank could not forgive. While Frank and those like him were arming for battle, the politicians in Washington, headed by President Kennedy and his brother Bobby, the attorney general, were weighing two options: go ahead as planned or cancel the operation because of the specter of a possible war with Russia. The White House eventually chose to invade but with little determination. Arthur Schlesinger, in his Pulitzer Prize–winning *A Thousand Days,* delineates President Kennedy's indecision regarding support of the invasion. The scales of success for the operation had on one side doing what it took to win and on the other disguising U.S. involvement. In spite of all the changes made that weakened the chances of success, those around the planning table in Washington fooled themselves into thinking the plan was still viable. In the end President Kennedy abandoned Brigade 2506 to make plausible his denial that the United States was involved. According to Mr. Schlesinger, who was on hand at the time, the White House decided to "dump" Brigade 2506 into Cuba with little or no support, knowing, or at least being advised, that a fiasco was in the making. But the most sinister part of this plan was that the brigade was told nothing about the rug being pulled from beneath them. This, in Frank's eyes, made it despicable. To pull the promised support was horrible enough, but not to communicate this life-or-death decision to those about to enter harm's way on the beaches was treasonous and eminently unforgivable.

Shortly after the Bay of Pigs invasion was thwarted, Soviet premier Nikita Khrushchev accused President Kennedy of backing the attack. It had been no secret that the United States had hoped that Castro would fail after he turned to communism. During the Kennedy-Nixon campaign debates, Kennedy had proposed that the United States support Cuban exiles in an invasion. Khrushchev now railed against U.S. aggression, and in October 1962, some eighteen months after the Bay of Pigs, the specter of conflict with Cuba and the Soviet Union reappeared. The "Cuban Missile Crisis" was front and center. As we all know, President Kennedy did not blink, Khrushchev did not call him on it, and the worst was averted. Thirteen months later the president was assassinated, and President Johnson's focus was turned from Cuba to Vietnam. Not only was the CIA's influence in Miami considerably reduced, but initiatives against Cuba were downsized to the "cold war" task of gathering intelligence.

The Bay of Pigs was a watershed event for many. Frank was no exception. His government, one that he had served for most of his life, had let him down. The betrayal had resulted in the death and/or imprisonment of his fellow soldiers, many of whom he had trained personally. It had resulted in the dismantling of his dream. In his view, his president had committed treason. His personal war against Castro did not end—it would continue for the rest of his life—but the best opportunity he and the other anti-Castro soldiers would ever have was snatched from them in the worst way possible. To Frank it was cruel and unusual punishment.

As Frank had observed, the seeds of the Bay of Pigs were sown when communists became a part of Castro's revolution. Frank remembered that as being sometime in the autumn of 1958. So for him the Bay of Pigs had been in the making for four years. As far as President Kennedy's decision to stand down, Frank said he still blamed him for "the terrific mess" that gave Castro one of his biggest victories. "If

Khrushchev blinked a year later when he agreed to remove the missiles from Cuba, Kennedy sure as hell blinked at the Bay of Pigs. If Kennedy had been more courageous, there probably wouldn't have been a Cuban Missile Crisis," he said. If the Bay of Pigs embarrassed the Kennedy Administration, it made Frank crazy. As his friends remember, "The technology hadn't been invented that could measure how pissed off Frank was at President Kennedy." Frank had met JFK in Miami in 1960, before the Bay of Pigs disaster, and had liked him "right off the bat," but April 1961 changed that opinion to the furthest point imaginable.

Frank and about forty thousand other people attended a ceremony held at the Orange Bowl on December 29, 1962, to honor the release of the prisoners. The Brigade 2506 leaders invited President Kennedy, who was vacationing at his family's residence in Palm Beach. Frank attended out of respect for the brigade and those who had been killed, not to see the president. Perhaps to blunt any anticipated negative demonstrations by the Cuban exiles, the president brought the First Lady, Jackie, and his young son, John Jr. He made a speech proclaiming that he would "never abandon Cuba to communism." To many in the brigade, including Frank, the words rang hollow coming from someone whose indecisiveness had cost them an opportunity to literally change the course of Latin American history by ousting Castro. But the words spoken that day by Jackie were more meaningful and genuine. Clad in a pink sheath dress (the same shade she wore the next year in Dallas), she addressed the crowd of forty thousand in fluent Spanish, saying,

> My son is still too young to realize what has happened here, but I will make it my business to tell him the story of your courage as he grows up. It is my hope that he'll grow into a man at least half as brave as the members of Brigade 2506.[2]

Frank disagreed with the decision of the Brigade 2506 leadership to present President Kennedy their battle flag that day. Frank's friend

Manuel Artime was the one who gave Kennedy the flag. The president promised to keep the flag until it could be returned to the brigade "in a free Havana." Frank said they should have listened to him and not the president, because in 1976 the brigade had to hire a lawyer to get the flag back from Kennedy's archives. It was located in the dusty basement of the presidential museum and had never been displayed. The Bay of Pigs was obviously not a high point of President Kennedy's legacy.

During the 1962 Orange Bowl ceremony, there was a different celebration going on in Havana, some hundred miles away. Castro had invited communist leaders from all over the world to commemorate the anniversary of his triumph over Batista. He used the occasion to proclaim his victory at the Bay of Pigs, not only over the Cuban exiles, but also over the United States. "For the first time in history, imperialism has paid war indemnification," he declared. This was the $2.9 million Castro had demanded at the last minute in cash as "reparations" for Cuba's losses during the invasion. These words from Castro rang a lot truer than those spoken by President Kennedy that day in December 1962.

Today in Miami there is a memorial dedicated to the 2506 Brigade and those who were killed or captured at the Bay of Pigs. It is a simple obelisk engraved with, "To the martyrs of the assault brigade, April 17, 1961." There is also a shield bearing the brigade's emblem, a cross superimposed on the Cuban flag. At the top of the obelisk is a perpetual flame.

7

Missiles, Missions, and the Sword

We were kept in jail in Honduras . . . The jail, incidentally, was 156 years old. I was by myself in a cell five and a half feet wide and eleven feet long. We had one meal a day of fish heads and rice.

—**Frank quoted in an article in the Norfolk, Virginia,
Ledger-Star, November 14, 1968**

EVEN AFTER THE BAY OF PIGS DISASTER IN APRIL 1961, U.S. POLICY still supported the Cuban exiles in their quest to get rid of Castro. The CIA continued to be very active in the Miami area, working with anti-Castroites like Frank. Two years after first dropping leaflets on Havana, in October 1961, Frank began a series of leaflet missions as part of what he called Cellula Fantasma, or Operation Phantom Cell. He issued a press release claiming, "Operation Phantom has continually harassed Fidel Castro with its air and sea missions to his island since the early days of his takeover. It was only ten months after the Cuban Revolution, as Castro was purging his rebel ranks of those not in step with his newly revealed Communist ideals, that the first phantom bomber buzzed Havana."[1] This time Frank decided to rent small twin-engine planes, which would be launched from Norman's Cay in the Bahamas. Besides Frank, there were two other pilots, Robert Swanner and William J. Johnson. They flew leafleting missions on the weekend of December 15–17, 1961. Hundreds of thousands of leaflets were dropped, primarily over the Camaguay region of Cuba, where many of the people were not sympathetic to Castro.

Unfortunately, Johnson and Swanner did not return from their mission. Frank conducted an air search for the missing pilots but found nothing. Shortly before Christmas Day 1961, Johnson's widow reported that she and Swanner's widow had each received an anonymous telegram saying "Merry Christmas" along with $500. She said, "I knew the money had been sent by Fiorini and the CIA because it was the exact amount my husband would have been paid for the trip if he had returned."[2] Frank never formally acknowledged being the source of this money, though he was. He told his wife, Janet, "I wish I could have sent more." Two years later, a Cuban farmer who escaped to the United States told a Philadelphia newspaper that during the time in question he had seen a small plane dropping leaflets over the city of Matanzas shot down. It crashed into a sugar mill, killing those on board.[3] These leaflet missions generated a lot of publicity and were cited by Castro as the reason he ended diplomatic relations with the United States. However, they never succeeded in rallying Cubans to revolt against Castro. This was due largely to the repressive nature of Castro's totalitarian government, which violently stifled any attempt at free speech, and, perhaps, to the low literacy rate of the peasants.

In August 1962 Frank flew a twin engine plane that

> dropped food, medicines and anti-Castro pamphlets into a remote area of western Cuba's Pinar Del Rio Province . . . early yesterday it was reported today. The food, apparently intended for the enemies of Fidel Castro, was dropped at an unspecified spot. The leaflets fell on the village of Córtes, Las Martinas and El Campo. A fighter plane from the San Julian Air Base tried to intercept the invader but was unable to do so. The flight was arranged by a Cuban refugee group headed by Sturgis.[4]

Just a month before this leaflet mission, Frank had succeeded in infiltrating twenty anti-Castro guerrillas that he had personally trained at a secret camp in the Everglades into Cuba in a boat.[5]

During the early 1960s, as Frank continued his anti-Castro activities, he attracted a number of mercenaries and various con artists, prompting his wife to ask, "Don't you know any legitimate people?" On several occasions Frank assisted Macho Barker and the CIA in stopping planned anti-Castro actions by some of these groups deemed to be too provocative or risky. One of the legitimate people who was involved in the fight against Castro was Alexander Rorke Jr. He was a freelance journalist and photographer who had covered the "crisis in Cuba" for *Argosy* magazine.

Alex had recently been working with Frank and had gone along on some of the leaflet and bombing missions. Like Frank, Alex was an ardent anti-communist. He came from a prominent family in New York, where his father was a former prosecutor and a judge and his father-in-law was Sherman Billingsley, proprietor of the world-renowned Stork Club, New York City's premier entertainment spot. Rorke "attended the School of Foreign Service at Georgetown University in Washington, D.C., and held a bachelor's degree from St. John's University."[6] As Frank had done, Alex joined the armed services (Army) at age seventeen, "winding up as a Military Intelligence Specialist responsible for the security of five German Provinces."[7] After World War II, Alex completed his college education, becaming "a track star ... and an undefeated inter-collegiate debating champion."[8] He was once a contestant on a TV game show, *To Tell the Truth,* where celebrity panelists tried to match one of three contestants with their occupation. His occupation was "the reporter who covered the crisis in Cuba." Alex and his fellow contestants fooled three of the panel members—Rita Gann, Betty White, and Don Ameche—and as a result, they won $750. The fourth panel member, Tom Poston, correctly selected Alex.

Like Frank, Alex had spent time in a Cuban prison, though for different reasons. While Frank was imprisoned and tortured by

Batista for running guns to Fidel, Alex was arrested on direct orders from Raúl Castro in August 1959. Alex had gone to Cuba to cover a counterrevolutionary plot of Cuban officers to assassinate Fidel. He was held for nine days and told the FBI after his release that he had been "subjected to round-the-clock interrogation; and 'brain washing.'"[9] A slightly different story was later related to the FBI on February 7, 1961, by a former captain in Castro's Rebel Army, Rafael Huguet Del Valle. He said that he was the one who actually ordered Rorke's arrest when the latter showed up at the house of William Morgan, a major in the army who had fought against Batista. Huguet explained that at the time he and Morgan "were in the midst of a conspiracy in connection with the invasion of Cuba from the [Dominican Republic]."[10] They were afraid that Rorke would break the story and blow their cover. Huguet denied that they tortured or abused Rorke while he was being held but acknowledged that Rorke was transferred to the prison camp under the control of Raúl Castro at Camp Libertad before being finally released.

There is no question that Alex Rorke did more than just observe and report about the Cuban Revolution and the anti-Castro movement. As mentioned, he participated with Frank on leaflet missions. The FBI reported that Rorke and Frank

> were closely associated in Cuban revolutionary activities in Nassau, Miami and NYC. Rorke formed an organization in NYC to raise funds for Sturgis and then went on a speaking tour in this regard. He also made a trip to Central America in an effort to obtain a base of operations for Sturgis to use in his activities against Fidel Castro.[11]

In September 1962, Alex Rorke bought a house at 5106 Polk Street in Hollywood, Florida. He also purchased a thirty-five-foot cabin cruiser, *Violin III,* and a "bearcat airplane," both of which would be used in the anti-Castro cause. However, on October 15, 1962, a Cold War showdown between the United States and the Soviet Union over the placement of nuclear missiles in Cuba capable of reaching the

United States in a matter of minutes ultimately caused a shift away from overt American support for the anti-Castro fighters.

In 1959, Frank, with the assistance of Fidel's former mistress Marita Lorenz, had smuggled out of cuba copies of maps and diagrams of future missile sites on the island. On October 15, 1962, a U-2 spy plane took photos documenting that some of these sites were occupied, locked and loaded with nuclear missiles. President Kennedy announced this finding to the nation and demanded that Soviet premier Nikita Khrushchev remove the missiles. The president also ordered a naval blockade of Cuba to intercept any new shipments of nuclear arms. A direct confrontation between the two superpowers seemed inevitable because there was a Soviet freighter with just such cargo on its way to Havana.

Fortunately, there were behind-the-scenes discussions among the United States, the Soviets, and the Cubans to try to resolve the crisis. Because the United States had no formal diplomatic relationship with Cuba, President Kennedy sent State Department officials to meet secretly in Uruguay with the Cuban delegation, headed by Frank's former comrade in arms Che Guevara. It was Guevara who had been instrumental in persuading Castro to allow the placement of the nuclear missiles in Cuba. In a later interview with a British reporter, Che boasted that he would have pushed the button and fired the missiles if they had been under Cuban instead of Soviet control. However, during the negotiations in Uruguay, Che offered to pay reparations to American businesses that had been nationalized and sever all ties with the Soviet Union if the United States would promise to leave Cuba alone. President Kennedy rejected this proposal and warned that he would use force if necessary to prevent the nuclear-laden freighter from reaching Cuba. Ultimately, a deal was worked out directly between the superpowers, without much Cuban input, with the Soviets agreeing to remove the existing missiles and ship no more while the United States agreed to stop actively supporting the efforts of the anti-Castro fighters. A U.S. trade embargo would, however, remain in place.

Prior to the Cuban Missile Crisis in October 1962, Frank carried out a number of covert missions against Castro that were financed by the CIA. As an independent contractor, he would usually agree on a price for the mission and then receive a partial advance with the balance paid on successful completion. As an example, a flight to Cuba to drop leaflets or supplies would cost approximately $5,000 to cover all expenses, with one half paid in advance. Following Frank's testimony before the Rockefeller Commission regarding CIA activities in 1975, the staff attorney, Robert Olsen, incorrectly concluded that Frank never did any work for the CIA. This is the same Robert Olsen who had not heard of the movie star Errol Flynn when his name was brought up by Frank. Olsen and the committee must not have had access to the same classified CIA files that attorney Dan Schultz saw during his Watergate representation of Frank. Schultz was allowed to see these files because he was looking for evidence of CIA ties to Frank and the burglars to show that they thought Watergate was a government-sanctioned mission. Schultz told the authors that based upon what he saw, there is no doubt that Frank did quite a number of jobs for the CIA.

After the Cuban Missile Crisis the U.S. government not only withdrew support from the exile groups, but also actively intervened to stop such activities. An article in the April 12, 1963, edition of *Time* magazine titled "Anti-Anti-Castro Policy" told the story of how Alex Rorke's boat, the *Violin III*, was seized by British authorities in the Bahamas acting on information supplied by the U.S. government. "The U.S. not only withholds help from the raiders, but actively discourages them. Washington thinks that the raids do Castro no real harm, and in fact, encourage the Russians to keep their troops in Cuba." Rorke told the *Time* reporter that he and a crew of seventeen men were planning to transport guns and ammunition into Cuba and then seek out a Russian tanker and attack it with 20mm incendiary shells. Rorke said that some of the crew consisted of "U.S. college boys" from schools like Princeton, Harvard, Boston College, and the University of Miami.

According to an FBI surveillance memo, on December 28, 1962,

Rorke, his five-year-old son, and a friend left from the Miami area on the boat, which was being captained by Carlos "Cuco" Arce. They were intercepted by a U.S. Navy destroyer near Bull Key but were waived on without being inspected. At Anguilla Cay they rendez-voused with the *Sigma II,* manned by a Cuban exile and a crew of five men. Rorke joined them on a run to "an unnamed point in Cuba," where they successfully delivered arms and supplies to be used by the anti-Castro underground. On January 2, 1962, Rorke and his party returned by boat to Miami, and later that day met Frank at Miami International Airport. Frank introduced them to "a CIA source," pre-sumably Macho Barker. In March 1963 the FBI documented another mission in which Rorke participated with Frank and others. During the last week of the month, Zacarias Acosta, leader of an anti-Castro exile group, loaded up Rorke's boat, *Violin III,* with arms and muni-tions and left Naples headed for Key West. The FBI described what happened next.

At a point off Key West, Florida, Jerry Buchanan [an American anti-Castro operative] was put aboard the "Violin III" from a small launch which was also occupied by Alexander Rorke and Frank Fiorini [a/k/a Sturgis]. Fiorini was the Chief of the anti-Castro organization at Miami known as the International Anti-Communist Brigade. Rorke is the owner of the "Violin III." . . .

The overall plan called for a diversionary attack on a Cuban ship in or en route to Cuba. This attack was to cover the actual purpose of the strike, which was to put ashore in Cuba two landing forces, one under Comandante Emilio Duque in the Escambray area and another in Oriente. After these forces were successfully infiltrated they would be supplied by sea in operations which would involve Frank Fiorini [a/k/a Sturgis], an American soldier of fortune who had been involved in Cuban revolutionary activities. Plans for the strike, however, were suspended and there was no indication that they would be put into effect.[12]

The last time Frank saw Alex Rorke alive was on September 23, 1963, at the Opa-locka airport close to Frank's home. The following day, Rorke left in a twin-engine Beechcraft airplane being piloted by his friend Geoffrey Sullivan. Some reports said the plane left from the Fort Lauderdale airport, but Frank recalled having seen the plane at the Opa-locka airport, where he kept his B-25 and C-46. Also on the plane was a Cuban, Enrique Molina Rivera. There were some in the anti-Castro movement who suspected that Molina was a double agent still loyal to Fidel. The exact nature of Rorke's mission is unclear. His original flight plan indicated Managua, Nicaragua, as the final destination. Rorke's wife said that she thought he was going there to see Luis Somoza, former president of the country, for help in setting up an export-import business. However, after stopping to refuel in Cozumel, Mexico, he and Sullivan changed the flight plan, making Tegucigalpa, Honduras, their destination. A trip to Honduras would be consistent with efforts on behalf of Frank to develop guerrilla training bases and launching points for an attack on Cuba. Several people recalled that there were three persons aboard the plane in Cozumel, meaning that the Cuban, Molina, was still with Rorke and Sullivan. After refueling and taking off at 8:00 P.M., the airplane and its passengers were never seen again, nor has their exact fate ever been determined. Frank first became aware of the disappearance when he received a phone call from Nicaragua informing him that the plane was overdue. Frank immediately called the commander of naval intelligence in Miami. An air-sea search was launched by the Navy and the Air Force, but nothing was found.[13]

Over the next several weeks, Frank and others searched for the plane to no avail. Rorke's family offered a $25,000 reward, but nobody ever came forward with any information. Frank believed the plane was shot down over or near Cuba and was most likely lost at sea. There were rumors that Rorke and Sullivan had been captured alive by Castro's troops and were then held in a prison. Frank doubted that this was the case because Fidel would have publicized the capture to embarrass the United States. Frank later came to suspect that the CIA may have sabotaged Rorke's plane because they wanted to prevent him from further provoking the Castro regime. Conspiracy theorist A. J. Weberman concludes that it was Frank and another anti-Castro American, Gerald Patrick Hemming, who were responsible for the sabotage of Rorke's plane. He claims that Frank and Rorke had some unspecified "disagreement" and that Hemming wanted to kill Molina, whom he considered to be a double agent.[14] However, there certainly was no evidence of any animosity or disagreement between Frank and Rorke. Frank considered Rorke to be a friend and a valuable ally in the fight against Castro. He had demonstrated his courage and conviction by participating in a number of anti-Castro missions with Frank and others, and also raised private funds to help finance them. Marita Lorenz, who was recruited by Frank to assassinate Castro and who claimed that she had been in Dallas with Frank to participate in the JFK assassination, has alleged that Frank killed Rorke because of Rorke's refusal to also take part in the assassination plot. As with other of her allegations, she has offered no independent proof or corroboration of this claim. Even Weberman, who would love to prove Frank's involvement in the JFK killing, thinks Lorenz is a "congenital liar."[15] Frank had no reason to want to kill Rorke. Nor did he have any suspicions about Molina's being a double agent. The disappearance and presumed deaths of Rorke, Sullivan, and Molina in 1963 and the deaths of Swanner and Johnson in 1961 are significant for showing just how dangerous and risky the anti-Castro fight was for those like Frank.

In July 2007, Sullivan's daughter, Sherry, filed a suit against Fidel Castro, his brother Raúl, the Cuban army, and the Republic of Cuba, alleging that they shot down Sullivan and Rorke's plane over Cuba and "intentionally, unlawfully and with complete disregard for human life" imprisoned them as political prisoners, thereby causing their death. The suit was filed in Waldo County, Maine, Superior Court. Unfortunately, like Marita Lorenz, Sullivan's daughter has no evidence for her claim. "I don't have any actual proof that my father was executed, but I believe he was," she told the media.[16] Given the fact that the plane disappeared sometime after refueling it is more likely that there may have been some contamination of the fuel in Cozumel, Mexico. Moreover, as Frank pointed out, if Castro had captured Rorke, Sullivan, and Molina he surely would not have kept this fact a secret in light of the propaganda value.

The shift in U.S. policy after the Cuban Missile Crisis did not stop Frank from continuing to actively fight against Castro. For instance, in June 1964 he flew over Cuba to drop supplies to members of the anti-Castro underground, a mission he publicized in a press release from his International Anti-Communist Brigade. He was immediately contacted by federal agents, who threatened to prosecute him for various FAA infractions and for violating the Neutrality Act if, in fact, he had flown such a mission. To avoid any problems, Frank signed a statement saying, "To the best of my knowledge, a so-called 'Operation Phantom' raid in Cuba on 25 May, 1964, did not take place. I declare that U.S. radar defenses were not violated while leaving or entering U.S. territory."[17] However, as Frank related later, in this statement he was only referring to flights directly from the United States to Cuba, which, he said, would not include flights originating in one of the Bahamas and heading for Cuba. He did not want to risk losing his American citizenship again.

During this time, Frank also took part in some low-intensity warfare conducted against Castro dubbed "Operation Mongoose," which consisted of bombing sugar mills and factories and burning other of Fidel's assets. Frank made bombing runs and sea raids in what came to be almost weekly forays into Cuba. There was also an all-out media blitz being planned by the Kennedy administration after they lost face at the Bay of Pigs. Castro was going to be blamed for almost anything that went wrong in the States. For example, if John Glenn's rocket blew up, they were going to blame it on Fidel.

Because of the change in U.S. policy from actively supporting the Cuban exiles, most of Frank's work was done on behalf of groups that were privately funded. Much of the money came from anti-communist business interests in Central and South America. One such mission occurred in April 1967. Frank; his stepson, Ron Thompson; and a third man going under the alias of "Schneider" (the spelling of the name becomes important) loaded an old Cadillac with bombs and weapons and took off for Mexico.

"Schneider," whose nickname was Red, was a deep-sea diver and an expert in underwater explosives. The bombs were loaded in the door panel on the driver's side and the detonators were inside the passenger-side door. The plan was to get the car placed on a ship that had been delivering "machinery" to Castro. If they couldn't get the car aboard, Schneider would use his unique talents to blow the ship up. Ron was the photographer and Frank was in charge. Ron recently set the year by remembering that Bobby Goldsboro's "It's Too Late" was playing on the Cadillac's radio and on the jukeboxes in the places where they stopped on the way down. They had fake business cards identifying them as salvage divers. They stopped in Louisiana somewhere outside of New Orleans and somewhere in Texas. Frank had the other two wait in the car while he went into residences and had extended conversations. Once in Mexico, they stayed a night in Manatee Cenote and then traveled on to Tampico Bay. When they got to the ship they were supposed to blow up, it was flying a British flag. Because Great Britain was an ally in the Cold War, Frank had second thoughts and decided to scrub the mission.

On the way back to Miami, while still in Mexico, Frank made several phone calls. After one of them he announced that they had a problem. They therefore stopped between Mantee and Victoria and buried the bombs and detonators in "fairly deep" separate graves on a hillside. When they arrived at the U.S. border in Brownsville, Texas, they were pulled aside and taken to three separate rooms, where they were interrogated at length. While they were being questioned, Ron remembers, the authorities dismantled the Cadillac, "like they did to that car in *The French Connection*." They finally let Frank and Ron go but they detained Schneider. It seems that when they took his ID and asked him to spell his last name he came out with "S-n-y-d-e-r" and earned himself some jail time. CIA agent Macho Barker told the authors that it's a good idea for fake identities to have the same initials as the person's real name in case the authorities search clothing for laundry markings. It's probably also a good idea to pick a name that can't be spelled a half dozen ways.

On October 9, 1967, Frank's former fellow guerrilla Che Guevara, age thirty-nine, was captured in Bolivia and executed by the CIA. He was in Bolivia trying to foment a communist revolution with the support of the local population, which was largely Incan. CIA operative Félix Rodríguez, with the help of the locals, had been able to track Che down to a schoolhouse in La Higuera, Bolivia. The actual execution was carried out by Mario Terán, a Bolivian army sergeant. Che had left Cuba in 1965 over a disagreement with Fidel about whether Cuba should follow China's more radical brand of communism or maintain the alliance with the Soviets. Che opted for the Chinese path and worked actively to export communist revolutions to Central and South America and Africa.

Upon learning of Che's death, Frank said, "Che was known as an expert in guerrilla warfare because of two books he wrote, but the truth is, I taught him most of what he knew about it." Frank and Che had first met in January 1958 at a rebel camp in the Sierra Maestra mountains of Oriente province. Unlike Fidel, who Frank believed evolved from a socialist to a communist, Che, Frank thought, was a communist all along. "Che kept his true beliefs under wraps until after the January 1959 march on Havana. I reported all of this to the CIA and the FBI." Frank was surprised at the revolutionary icon status Che took on after his death. *Time* magazine called him one of the hundred most influential people of the twentieth century. Frank said, "To me, Che was always somewhat of an opportunist," citing Che's attempt to take full credit for the victory at Santa Clara when Commander Camilo Cienfuegos was equally responsible for the successful outcome. Frank also said that Che was himself responsible for getting caught because he violated a basic, cardinal rule of guerrilla warfare: learn to speak the local native dialect to win the trust and support of the *guajiros*. Che had erroneously learned Quechua, instead of the

Tupi-Guarani dialect spoken by the native Incas in the eastern lowlands of Bolivia where he was operating. As a result, Che never won their trust, and CIA agent Rodríguez had no trouble bribing some locals to reveal Che's hiding place.

Frank's last major offensive against Castro before the 1972 Watergate break-in was an escapade that wound up involving Mexico, Guatemala, Venezuela, Honduras, and Cuba. Code-named "Operation Sword," it took place in 1968, and though it rated fairly high on the creativity scale, it did not do that well in the execution phase. It began with recruitment that included an ad in a Fort Lauderdale newspaper offering adventure and good pay to those who could qualify. The ad yielded sixty responses, and the applicants were screened by Max Gonzalez, a friend of Frank's, who offered them varying amounts of money to "fight against Castro's forces in Cuba." Eventually eleven were selected. As Gonzales said to Paul Meskil, a reporter for the New York *Daily News* who ran a series of articles on Frank in April 1975, "They all had been in military service. Three had been in World War II; the others served in Korea and Vietnam. Most were young, but one was in his late 40's and had a drinking problem. He said he had never accomplished much in his life and had always wanted to go on some kind of an adventure, so Frank said, 'Well, if you stay sober, we'll take you along.'" The men were offered $10,000 each for a completed assignment. They were told it was to be a commando raid into Cuba to free political prisoners from Castro's concentration camps. Such was not the case.

The mercenaries were to meet in Guadalajara, Mexico, but when they arrived, the hotel they were supposed to stay in had been torn down. A case study for advance reservations. After two weeks' training in combat and Spanish, they traveled to Progreso, Mexico. On or about October 23, 1968, Frank and his crew chartered a thirty-foot fishing boat, the *Amigo,* for $250 worth of pesos and headed out from Progreso toward Cuba. The plan was to rendezvous with a second craft, under the control of a Cuban captain and crew who were disenchanted with Castro. Because of the nature of the ultimate goal of the mission (known only to Frank), Frank was secretive about the rendezvous spot and the course to reach it. The *Amigo* was ahead of schedule and Frank was directing a zigzag course as a means of delaying its arrival at the assigned rendezvous area. Because of this atypical course, some inclement weather, some outdated sea charts, and the captain's lack of familiarity with the area, the *Amigo* ran aground on a reef near the Turneffe Islands off Belize, British Honduras.

The FBI reported: "On October 23, 1968, and October 24, 1968, Sturgis and 12 other individuals were arrested by British Honduran authorities on charges of illegal entry. Various weapons, ammunitions and supplies were confiscated from the group at the time of the arrest."[18] Frank's cover story for the operation was that the plan was to leave Florida for Guatemala, where they would train at a camp. Frank had set up a camp—actually he had set up two camps, but they were in Mexico. One was in the mountains about a mile from the Guatemala/Mexican border. It rained much of the time they were there, and they called the base "Camp Mud." After two weeks, they moved to a camp on the beach near the Yucatán fishing village of Progreso. They called this, logically enough, "Camp Sand." The plan to train in Guatemala was changed because of heightened communist guerrilla activity at that time. They would then proceed by boat to Cuba on November 1, 1968, and hide out in a prearranged location in the Sierra Maestre mountains that Frank had come to know so well during Fidel's revolution. On January 1, 1969, they would execute a raid to free anti-Castro prisoners.

The real purpose of the mission, however, was to hijack a Soviet spy ship masquerading as a fishing trawler that was docked in Cuba at the time and ransom it for the U.S. spy ship *Pueblo* and its crew. The *Pueblo* had been captured by the North Koreans on January 23, 1968, and was still being held hostage. Frank told the men it was to be a commando raid into Cuba to free political prisoners from Castro's concentration camps. To embellish the tale, Frank showed the men a map of the locations of Cuban prisons and prison camps. He also had a fabricated list of prisoners that were to be freed. No one but Frank knew otherwise. But the objective was not to raid Cuba; it was to rendezvous with another ship off the coast of Mexico and, using this other ship, seize the Russian vessel. Frank had planned to meet the Cuban vessel, which with its pro-Western captain and crew wearing Cuban naval uniforms, would not raise suspicion when intercepting and boarding the Soviet vessel. The Cuban captain had sailing schedules with the arrivals and departures of all Soviet vessels in the Caribbean and the Gulf of Mexico. The plan was to hijack the Russian ship and take it to the coast of Venezuela. The orders were to not go into any port, but to stay off the coast. Certain officials in the Venezuelan government, who were aware of the plan, would then help with the negotiations.

There were other reports from the FBI that Frank and his "army" would assist the Guatemalan government in ridding the region of communist guerrillas. If this were accomplished, the Guatemalan government would assist in an invasion of Cuba. This and other reports at the time seem to be camouflage to conceal the actual plan. One of the better ruses was the invention by Frank of Colonel Francisco Quesada. Colonel Quesada, who was a complete fabrication, was rumored to be in charge of this operation to ransom the *Pueblo* and its crew. The good colonel was also rumored to be traveling throughout Central and South America raising funds and a mercenary army to fight communists throughout the Americas. The existence of Colonel Quesada became suspicious when he was described by Frank as a Latino, born in Argentina, who had seen action in four wars and served in all branches of the services, and was a pilot and an expert in conventional, guerrilla, and counterguerrilla warfare. He was also described as the prime organizer of the underground in Latin America. He allegedly had a price of $100,000 on his head by the communists, who had sent agents to kill him. Except for being born in Argentina and the reward money, the rest was Frank.

A postscript to this mission appeared as an article in the November 14, 1968, issue of the Norfolk, Virginia, *Ledger-Star.*

The latest chapter in the running saga of Norfolkian FRANK FIORINI'S fight with Fidel Castro includes an 11-day stay in a

British Honduras jail where he lost 20 pounds while living on fish heads and rice . . . FIORINI stated: "We left one of our camps on the Yucatan Peninsula in a 30-foot cabin cruiser called *The Amigo* . . . which ended up on a reef off the coast of Honduras . . . and limped into Belize . . . There, they began unloading the rifles and over $1,000 in medical supplies. Then the ship was taken over by British Army Units. We were kept in jail for four days before we had a hearing before a British Magistrate . . . I served as a spokesman and asked that we not be deported to Mexico as had been suggested. I knew it was filled with Castro sympathizers then and my life would be in great danger.

One of the recruits for "Operation Sword," Robert Curtis, testified in a court action growing out of the mission, "When we got to Guadalajara, the hotel we were supposed to go to was torn down. We went across the street to the Los Americanos Hotel. We left our car parked out front where Frank would see it. We waited three weeks, and we were running out of money so we went to a gun shop and sold my Japanese Nambu—an automatic pistol—for about $30."

Frank had planned and carried out this mission pretty much on his own, advertising for soldiers of fortune, training and equipping them, and coordinating with the anti-Castro Cuban naval personnel. The concept was good, the planning okay; the execution ran aground. But once again Frank landed on his feet.

By 1969 Frank had been fighting his battle with Fidel for ten years. He wasn't ready to give up, but he did start to wonder if he shouldn't take on some regular nine-to-five job to better support his wife, Janet, and her daughter, Gale. He therefore began working for the Pan-American Aluminum Company installing windows, primarily in the condominiums being built in and around Miami. He was later promoted to salesperson and began to earn a comfortable and steady income. He talked with Janet about the decision to focus more on his regular job and spend less time and resources on his fight with Fidel.

They had just seen a French movie with English subtitles starring Yves Montand, called *La Guerre Est Finie* (*The War Is Over*). Montand starred as an aging Basque radical who had been fighting the Spanish government for a number of years with little success. Although Montand played a communist, Frank could identify with him. The central question posed by the movie was whether it was time to give it up; after so many years, maybe the war really was over. For Frank, as long as totalitarianism reigned in Cuba, he was not ready to stop. His continued struggle to free Cuba from Fidel Castro would bring him to a place in Washington, D.C., called the Watergate.

8

Watergate—The Burglary

Watergate. We went in. We got caught. Nixon lost his job.

—*Bernard "Macho" Barker, summing up Watergate*
for the authors, January 2007

THE WORD "WATERGATE" HAS BECOME AN ICONIC PART OF OUR language. Originally referring only to a complex of hotel, apartment, retail, and office space in Washington, D.C., the word and the suffix "gate" are now well understood as generic terms for government corruption and misdeeds of all kinds. Thus, we have had "Iran/Contragate" under President Reagan, and "Monicagate" with President Clinton. NBC created "Heidigate" when they interrupted the last few minutes of the 1968 Super Bowl to show the movie *Heidi*. The word entered our popular music in 1974 in Lynyrd Skynyrd's song "Sweet Home Alabama," which includes the line, "Now Watergate does not bother me / Does your conscience bother you?" It is true that before Watergate there had been other political scandals in this country. President Grant's alcoholism, and the Teapot Dome Scandal in the

1920s when President Harding's friend and interior secretary, Albert Fall, took bribes in exchange for lucrative oil and gas leases of federal land come to mind. Some of these were embarrassing for those in office. But Watergate is the only scandal that resulted in the resignation of a president. Historians have generally divided Watergate into three phases—the break-in and trial of the burglars, the cover-up, and the Nixon White House tapes. Frank's role was primarily in the first phase, and that will be the focus of this chapter. In addition to consulting existing research sources on Watergate, the authors interviewed two of the burglars, Rolando Martinez and Macho Barker, and their lawyer, Dan Schultz.

In 1971 Frank and Janet were living in Miami at a house on NW 122nd Street. Frank was working for the Pan-American Aluminum Company as a salesman and sometime installer of windows. Janet worked in the art department of a local TV station, Channel 23. It had been ten years since the Bay of Pigs debacle and three years since Frank had launched a mission against Castro. The official policy of the United States was to impose an embargo and let Cuba "wither on the vine." As a result, CIA activity in Miami had been severely curtailed.

Despite this, Frank remained committed to waging what he always called "my war with Fidel." His fight was with Castro, not the Cuban people. Most of his recent efforts had been on behalf of private conservative interests in Latin and South America because of the slowdown in CIA activities. The CIA still worked in Miami and in the Caribbean, primarily collecting information and monitoring the activities of Cuban spies, in particular, double agent counterspies. Frank maintained his own intelligence network and had found plenty of evidence of Cuban involvement in the drug trade in the Caribbean and in Central and South America. Most of the money was going directly to Castro and his regime.

The other war that was on the minds of most Americans in 1971 was the one in Vietnam. Richard Nixon was elected president in 1968 on a promise to resolve the national morass in Southeast Asia. Talks began in Paris in 1969, and two years later, in 1971, not much progress was being made toward peace. In the meantime, many young American men continued to be killed on a daily basis. Most of these were draftees. In fact, on April 1, 1971, Nixon extended the draft for two years. There was a growing belief among Americans of all ages that the government was not being truthful about the situation in Vietnam, especially as regarded how well we were doing or not doing in winning the war.

Antiwar protests were abundant, beginning with the rally on the Capitol Mall in Washington, D.C., in October 1969 that was so well portrayed in the movie *Forrest Gump*. It was estimated that more than 250,000 people, the most ever to that date, crowded the Mall that day. Another 2 million people gathered for rallies in cities across the country. Later that same month, Lieutenant William Calley was convicted by a military court of murder for what was known as the My Lai Massacre. Calley and others had been accused of killing more than five hundred innocent civilian Vietnamese villagers. Events such as these led to even more of a division between Americans in favor of the war and those opposed. The fabric of the United States was being torn apart by Vietnam.

Frank was a dyed-in-the-wool anti-communist who saw the Red threat on a global level as the inevitable spread of communism. He was a believer in the "domino theory," that the loss of Vietnam to communism would result in similar governments throughout Southeast Asia coming under the domination of the Chinese Communists. But he also believed that the politicians were responsible for our poor performance and that if the military leaders were given more leeway, the war could be won. Frank had seen for himself what politicians could do to screw up a military operation when the Kennedys pulled the plug on air support at the Bay of Pigs.

In 1971, the possibility of overthrowing Castro or causing some kind of general uprising against his totalitarian regime seemed somewhat remote. Further, there was not much unity among the various anti-Castro groups in Miami, and this splintering hampered their efforts. Frank had witnessed the same phenomenon in island nations and Central American countries where revolutionary splinter groups had difficulty banding together because of perceived ideological differences and personal jealousies. Also, many of the Cubans in Miami who had fled Castro were doing pretty well economically and had lost some of their incentive to return to their homeland. Miami in the early 1960s was unlike most of the large cities in the north in that it had very little in the way of a middle class. This changed after Castro's revolution because many of the people he drove out of Cuba were professionals and members of the middle class. Cuban exiles in the early 1960s who had been doctors, lawyers, or engineers fled Cuba for Miami and took jobs as waiters, janitors, or gas station attendants in order to support their families and live in freedom. These hardworking people were devoted to making a better life for their children and they generally succeeded in doing so. According to Macho Barker, "The Cubans who 'lost' are living in Miami like kings, while the 'winners' in Cuba are still serfs suffering under a totalitarian government." He said that there were thousands of Cubans in Miami who came with nothing and were now millionaires. Today, Cuban exiles occupy a significant portion of Miami's middle and professional class.

With Castro so entrenched by 1971, maybe it was time for Frank to focus on his day job with the Pan-American Aluminum Company and give up the adventurous life he had been living. However, something happened in June 1971 that would eventually put Frank back in the news—the publication of *The Pentagon Papers*. This was a seven-thousand-page, forty-five-volume top secret study that had been commissioned in 1967 by Robert McNamara, the then secretary of defense. It looked at our involvement in Vietnam from 1945 to 1971, focusing on policy and military decisions that had been made. Contributors included people both within and without various government departments. One of those was Daniel Ellsberg, who held a PhD in economics and a position in America's premier think tank, the Rand Corporation, but who was physically working at the Pentagon.

Ellsberg has been described as both a committed Cold Warrior and a traitor. He had been a company commander in the Marine Corps before working at the Pentagon. He spent two years in Vietnam, 1964–1966, as a civilian for the State Department. Based upon his own personal experience and what he saw that others had written in *The Pentagon Papers* study, Ellsberg became convinced that the war was not winnable. He came to believe that others in the Defense and State departments felt the same way, but that political considerations prevented them from being honest with the American public. Instead, the government kept telling them that victory was just around the corner and the war continued to escalate. Ellsberg wanted to make this information public but knew that if he did so he would be committing a crime. He claimed to have tried to get antiwar members of Congress to release *The Pentagon Papers* on the Senate floor since they would be immune from prosecution, but no one was willing. He therefore decided to leak *The Pentagon Papers* to *The New York Times*, which began publishing excerpts on June 13, 1971.

The Nixon administration reacted quickly to stop this leak of top secret information, obtaining an injunction from a federal court prohibiting further publication. *The Times* appealed this decision, ultimately to the U.S. Supreme Court, which reversed the lower courts and dismissed the injunction as a prior restraint of free speech that was prohibited by the First Amendment. In the interim, Ellsberg released the *Papers* to a number of other newspapers across the country, which began publishing portions for the reading public. Nixon's people soon realized that it would be impossible to stop the dissemination of *The Pentagon Papers* and gave up. They still charged Ellsberg with theft, conspiracy, and espionage, but the judge declared a mistrial based largely on the fact that there was proof that Ellsberg's civil rights had been violated by the administration. He was never re-indicted.

To those who opposed the Vietnam War, Ellsberg was a hero who advanced the cause of democracy by exposing the "credibility gap" that existed between the American public and its government. He was not the only one committing potentially criminal acts to protest the war. The radical Weather Underground group set off a bomb at the Capitol, and in Baltimore, two "radical priests," the Berrigan brothers, led a group that broke into a Selective Service Draft headquarters and dumped pig blood all over the records. Four students who were protesting the war had been shot and killed by Ohio National Guardsmen at Kent State University (inspiring the song "Ohio," by Crosby, Stills, Nash, and Young). In a court brief filed by the U.S. attorney general in 1972, it was reported that there had been 1,562 bombing incidents, mainly at government facilities, as a part of the ongoing war protest during the first half of 1971.[1]

On the other side, Nixon's supporters—and there were many—saw themselves as the only true patriots and the antiwar people as a ragtag group of hippies. They considered Ellsberg a traitor. They believed that he had hurt the war effort and severely damaged America's image. Above all, President Nixon wanted to stop the leaks of sensitive and classified information, so he instructed his chief domestic policy aide, John Ehrlichman, to form an action group to deal with it. Logically enough, the group became known as the White House Plumbers. E. Howard Hunt, an ex–CIA agent, and G. Gordon Liddy, an attorney who had previously worked as an assistant U.S. district attorney in New York, as an FBI agent, and as a Treasury Department employee, were hired as White House aides in charge of the group's activities. Liddy was instructed to report directly to Jeb Magruder, a former Nixon White House aide who became deputy director of CREEP (Committee to Re-elect the President) under former attorney general John Mitchell in March 1971. As far as *The Pentagon Papers* leak was concerned, there was not much to investigate. Ellsberg acknowledged that he was the "leaker," and by then there was no way to stop the public from reading the study.

However, the Plumbers' mission soon expanded to include searching for other potential leakage problems and assisting in discrediting Ellsberg in the public's mind by finding damaging information about him. After the leak of *The Pentagon Papers,* the FBI began investigating Ellsberg as a possible spy. At the direction of the Nixon White House, agents tried to develop a psychological profile on him by interviewing and questioning his psychiatrist, Lewis Fielding. However, Dr. Fielding refused to talk to them due to the confidential relationship existing between psychiatrist and patient. Hunt and Liddy therefore decided to do a "black bag operation" by breaking into Dr. Fielding's office to photograph or copy Ellsberg's file. According to Liddy, the FBI believed that Ellsberg had given a copy of *The Pentagon Papers* directly to the Soviet Union at its embassy in Washington, D.C., and may have passed other top secret documents to the Soviets. Liddy hoped to find some reference to these activities in Ellsberg's patient file.

When E. Howard Hunt worked for the CIA in 1960 he was the chief political officer in Miami, where he lived with his family in Coconut Grove. His code name was "Eduardo." Hunt also wrote spy novels and mysteries. In 1949 he wrote a book called *Bimini Run* with a main character named Hank Sturgis. Some claim that Hunt based the character on Frank. However, Frank maintained throughout his life that he never met Hunt until 1972, when he joined the Plumbers. Further, Frank did not change his last name to Sturgis until 1952, three years after Hunt's book was published. Hunt's name choice was just a coincidence. One of Frank's main CIA contacts was Bernard "Macho" Barker, who was a "director of field operations" for Cuba, the Caribbean, and Central America and who reported to Hunt. (Incidentally, the Hunt that co-authored this book is not related to E. Howard). It was Hunt and Barker's job to help plan and execute the Bay of Pigs invasion and see that a government in exile was set up and ready to take over. Unfortunately, the invasion was a disaster, resulting in Hunt's career taking a nosedive; he left the CIA in 1970, four years after Barker did.

When interviewed for this book, Macho was ninety years old and very sharp mentally. He lived in a quiet neighborhood of one-story homes with his fourth wife, Dora, an attractive Cuban woman not half his age. She spoke little English and was very attentive to her husband.

Macho passed away in 2009. He was born in Havana in 1917. His father had emigrated there from Tennessee and eventually married Alicia Terry, a Cuban of Irish extraction. She was a very beautiful woman who came from a prominent family. He got the nickname Macho when he was five years old. His sister was "*la bebita*" (the little girl baby) and he was "*el macho*," the boy. It had nothing to do with his physical prowess. As he said, "You don't have much machismo when you're five years old." Macho grew up in the coastal city of Mariel (later of "boat lift" fame, or infamy). When he was sixteen his parents sent him to Long Island to finish his last two years of high school because they were worried about his safety due to his involvement with a revolutionary student group. He returned two years later and began studying engineering at the University of Havana. At the time, he held both Cuban and U.S. citizenship.

On December 8, 1942, the day after Pearl Harbor, Macho went to the American embassy in Havana and became the first Cuban-American to volunteer for the war effort. Like Frank, Macho was a very patriotic man. Typical of many Cubans, Macho had a deep love for the United States, remembering that we helped Cuba get its political freedom from Spain in 1898. He trained in Texas as an air cadet and ultimately became a bombardier on a B-17 stationed in England. One of the photos on the wall at Macho's house is a picture of the whole crew of ten men. At the time of the interview, only Macho and one other crewman were still alive. Dressed in his leather flight jacket, Macho looked like he had stepped out of that old comic strip "Terry and the Pirates." During World War II he and his crew were actually called that because Macho's full name at the time was Bernard Barker Terry, following the Hispanic practice of adding one's mother's maiden name after one's father's name, so he was called Bernard Terry. In February 1944, Macho's plane was shot down over Germany. He was able to bail out but was soon captured and became a POW. He stayed in a concentration camp for sixteen months until finally being liberated by the Russians in August 1945.

Following the war, Macho worked for a while as an assistant to Fulgencio Batista's chief of police. In the late 1950s he was running a large farm, Finca Clara, named after his first wife, whose family owned it. He described his job as "corn farmer." He was approached by both the CIA and the FBI about doing covert work to keep an eye on Castro's burgeoning revolution. He eventually became an employee of the CIA and developed a cadre of Cubans loyal to U.S. interests. After Castro seized power in January 1959, Barker stayed in Cuba, but, like Frank, he began to fear for his safety. Questions were being asked about his contacts with people from the American embassy. The CIA therefore decided to secretly exfiltrate him to Miami, where he would head up the field office for covert activities in Cuba and the rest of Latin America.

Macho is extremely proud of his work for the CIA over the years. "There is nothing in this world greater than being a CIA agent. You're serving your country in ways you can't believe," he said. For him, the CIA was a way of life. Even though he has been retired from the CIA for many years, Macho remains absolutely loyal to it. For example, he refuses to publicly disclose how he was exfiltrated from Cuba because the CIA still uses the same method today.

Like E. Howard Hunt's, Barker's career with the CIA took a hit due to the failure of the Bay of Pigs invasion. They had not seen each other in years when Hunt contacted Macho in April 1971 in Miami. They met, and Hunt gave Barker his unlisted White House number and later wrote to him on White House stationery.[2] In August 1971 Hunt returned to Miami and again met with Barker. He told him he was working for a White House organization "with greater jurisdiction than the FBI and the CIA."[3] Hunt further told him they needed to develop potentially embarrassing and damaging evidence about a "spy" who was suspected of passing classified information to the Russians. Hunt asked Barker to recruit a team to carry out the black bag operation Hunt and Liddy were planning. Barker selected two Cubans for the mission, Felipe de Diego and Eugenio Rolando Martinez. De Diego worked with Barker in his real estate business and was a long time "Company" man (i.e., CIA).

At that time, Martinez was still working for the CIA and met with his case officer on a weekly basis. He was with Barker during the April 1971 meeting with Hunt in Miami. Currently in his mid-eighties, Rolando has a thick head of white hair and looks to be in excellent shape.

His nickname is Musculito, muscleman, owing to his being a weight lifter. Like many Cubans, he is under six feet tall. Rolando came to Miami from Cuba sometime prior to Fidel's takeover in 1959. In the early 1950s he was with Fidel at the University of Havana at a time when Fidel was head of a student political organization. The leader of a rival group was shot to death, and there were those who thought that Fidel was the shooter. Rolando knows for a fact that Fidel did the killing because he was an eyewitness.

As explained by Barker, the CIA is organized on a "compartmentalization" or "need to know" basis. Individual CIA agents generally were not told about the overall details of a mission and received only as much information as was necessary to carry out their particular duties. CIA agents were trained to not ask questions about a mission beyond their own involvement. For instance, Macho Barker might know that the CIA wanted him to arrange to infiltrate a spy into Cuba, but he would not need to know exactly what the aim or goal of the mission was. This underlying precept—"need to know"—was a basic part of the mind-set of Frank and the other Watergate burglars when they broke into the Democratic National Committee headquarters in May and June 1972.

Beginning in the early 1960s Martinez made forays by boat into Cuba on behalf of the CIA hundreds of times. For one of the first missions, the CIA gave him a canoe to use. "It was an actual Indian canoe," he said with bemusement. Another time he transported two agents to the Cuban coast in a small motorboat that had been launched from a Navy "mother ship" in international waters. He dropped them off and was supposed to wait for their return at an appointed time. This occurred in a fairly populated area of the Cuban coast and Martinez was concerned about getting caught. When the agents failed to return as scheduled he had to make a decision to either wait and risk getting caught or leave them in Cuba. He decided to wait, which was a testament to his courage. (The agents eventually showed up two hours late.) Rolando said, "No, I was a coward. If I left them I knew I would have to explain to their widows why and I wasn't brave enough to face their families on that basis." Like many Cuban exiles, Rolando had a deep sense of family. The fact that he would have felt an obligation to personally deliver the bad news to men's wives is a prime example of this. He has been married to his wife, Cecil, for more than thirty years. He remains steadfast in his opposition to Castro and holds the post of second vice general secretary of MRR (Movimiento de Recuperación Revolucionaria), one of the oldest of the exile anti-Castro groups in Miami.

The spy business is like any large business organization in that there are those employees who actually do the work (the missions), and those who administer and oversee the workers. Martinez was definitely a mission man, or as he called himself, "an operative." Frank falls into the same category. Hunt and Barker, on the other hand, functioned more as administrators. During the 1960s Barker coordinated and gathered intelligence information, which he forwarded to his superiors in the CIA, but he was not that involved in the field. The same can be said about Hunt. Both of them were certainly known by Castro and his secret police to be CIA agents, so neither was a good candidate for undercover work. Placing Hunt and Barker into the administrator category did not lessen their value as spies for the CIA. However, there are those who think Hunt was a second-rate spy, especially when compared to his wife, Dorothy. An acquaintance of Hunt's described him as "totally self-absorbed, totally amoral and a danger to himself and anybody around him."[4]

The initial meeting that Hunt had with Barker and Martinez on April 16, 1971, was on the tenth anniversary of the ill-fated Bay of Pigs invasion. They met at the Bay of Pigs monument in Miami. This was the first time he actually met Hunt, though like Frank, Martinez had heard of Eduardo during the Bay of Pigs preparations. He wondered whether Hunt's connection to the White House might signal a renewed interest on the part of the Nixon administration in ridding Cuba of Castro. In fact, Hunt told them, "The whole Cuban thing is not over."

Hunt returned to Miami in August 1971 and met with Barker.

Hunt asked him if he would be willing to become "operational" again to conduct an illegal break-in to obtain information about a traitor.[5] Barker agreed to do so, and he contacted Martinez and Felipe de Diego to be part of the team. At this time, the only thing Martinez and de Diego were told was that their mission was covert and involved matters of national security. Several weeks later, Barker telephoned and told them to pack clothes for two to three days and meet him at the Miami airport at 9:00 A.M. the following morning, September 1. When they met, Barker told them only that they were going to Los Angeles. Martinez and de Diego knew not to ask a lot of questions. "They were trained agents, accustomed to rely on the discretion of their superiors and to operate entirely on a 'need to know basis.' "[6]

In October 1984, Martinez posted on the Internet an article detailing his part in the Los Angeles break-in of Ellsberg's psychiatrist's office, later, in Watergate, called "Mission Impossible."[7] On arriving in LA, Martinez, Barker, and de Diego checked into the Beverly Hills Hotel. The following day they met at the hotel and Hunt introduced them to Liddy, or as he called him, "George." Like Hunt at that time, Liddy was employed directly by the Nixon White House as a "consultant." For the first time, Barker and his team were told that the mission was to covertly enter the office of Dr. Lewis Fielding, find and photograph Ellsberg's patient file, and put it back where they found it. Martinez recalls that the briefing they received was not too detailed. The next day, September 3, 1971, they met again, and Hunt supplied them with photo equipment, phony identification papers, and disguises that he said had been supplied by the CIA. Then they went to Sears and bought uniforms for Barker and de Diego to use while posing as deliverymen. The plan was for them to deliver the photo equipment to Dr. Fielding's office while it was open and gain access to the rear door, which they would leave unlatched for entry later on. The idea was to leave no trace of what they were about to do.

They had to wait several hours after the office closed for the cleaning lady to leave. When they finally got to the rear door, they found that for some reason it was locked again. Martinez tried to cut a hole in the glass of the front door but the tool he had been given was so dull it could not do the job. He therefore used a small crowbar to break a window on the door and reached inside to unlock it. During the entry, Martinez said he "almost shot Barker." After he and de Diego were inside, Barker became separated from them. Martinez suddenly heard someone making whistling and grunting sounds, and as a precaution he drew the pistol he was carrying. Barker appeared out of the shadows, and fortunately Martinez did not fire before recognizing him. "Macho wasn't that experienced as an operations man," Martinez said, smiling.

To carry out the mission, they set up the photographic equipment and searched for Ellsberg's file. However, all they could find were Ellsberg's billing records (which contained no clinical information) and his telephone number, written in the doctor's personal address book. They photographed these and took some Polaroid shots of the office interior. Since their plan to leave no trace had been foiled by their having had to pry open the locked back door, Martinez scattered some pills he found in Dr. Fielding's desk that appeared to be vitamin C tablets on the floor to make it look like the break-in was drug related.[8] They left the building and met Hunt, who was waiting in his car for them. As they drove away, a police car appeared and followed them for several blocks. Martinez remembers thinking, "The police car was protecting us. That is the feeling you have when you are doing operations for the government. You think that every step has been taken to protect you."[9]

From there, they went back to the Beverly Hills Hotel, where they saw Liddy. Martinez was somewhat surprised to find that Hunt and Liddy were happy with the results of the mission even though they had not found Ellsberg's patient file. Both Hunt and Liddy emphasized the importance of the fact that they were able to carry out the mission without getting caught. Barker and Martinez wondered if this might have been a training exercise for some more important similar type of mission in the future. According to a memorandum to Judge Sirica from U.S. Probation Officer Frank Saunders, "Both [Martinez] and Barker were led to believe that what they were doing was the pre-lude to another attempt to free Cuba."[10] None of the three Miamians—Barker, Martinez, and de Diego—was in it for the money. "The only funds they received from Hunt in connection with the entry of Dr. Fielding's office were reimbursement for their living expenses, the costs of travel, and $100 for lost income."[11]

In October 1971 Hunt and Liddy's Plumbers group took on an added assignment—political espionage. It should not surprise any of us that both Democrats and Republicans have practiced "dirty tricks" ranging from planting spies in the campaign organization of an op-ponent to circulating inflammatory literature attributed to the other side. The people directing Nixon's reelection campaign were worried about being spied on by the Democrats. The head of the Nixon Com-mittee to Re-elect the President (CREEP) at this time was Francis Dale, an attorney from Cincinnati. At one time he was also editor of the city's major newspaper, the *Enquirer*. Dale always scheduled im-portant CREEP policy meetings in the steam room of a health club to be sure that they were not being bugged.

Nixon himself believed that the Democrats were spying on him. As he told his chief of staff, H. R. "Bob" Haldeman, "Goldwater put it in context; he said, 'Well for Christ's sake, everybody bugs everybody else.' We know that. We were bugged in '68 on the plane, and bugged in '62, uh, even running for governor [of California]."[12] (One of the more remarkable things that developed during the Watergate prose-cutions was the public disclosure of a secret, hidden tape-recording system installed by Nixon in various rooms in the White House, in-cluding the Oval Office. Nixon bugged himself! He claimed "executive privilege" and refused to turn over the tapes that had been subpoenaed by a House of Representatives committee investigating Watergate. The issue eventually went to the U.S. Supreme Court, which ordered that the tapes be turned over providing history with a contemporary record of the president's White House discussions before, during, and after Watergate.)

On December 12, 1971, Liddy resigned from the White House

staff and was immediately hired by CREEP. His duties included investigating the espionage activities of the Democrats. There were concerns that the Democrats were going to stage a huge antiwar protest at the Republican National Convention in Miami to disrupt it, as had happened to the Democrats in Chicago in 1968.[13] Additionally, leaks to the press were still occurring. On December 14 columnist Jack Anderson, a longtime friend and supporter of Frank's, wrote a story about India and Pakistan that contained quotes from notes taken at classified meetings held by Secretary of State Henry Kissinger. By this time, Hunt and Liddy's efforts focused more on political intelligence. They flew to Miami in late December and met an ex-FBI agent, Jack Bowman. They tried to enlist him to do surveillance at the Miami Convention Center, where the Democratic National Convention was to be held, but he was not interested.

In response to a request from Nixon's attorney general, John Mitchell, Liddy developed a comprehensive espionage program, which he code-named Gemstone. He presented it to Mitchell and other administration officials including President Nixon's legal counsel, John Dean, at a meeting held in Mitchell's office on February 4, 1972. Liddy explained that there were four separate programs, Diamond (removal and detention of violent demonstration leaders); Crystal (electronic surveillance); Sapphire (the prostitute program); Opal (the covert entry operation); and Ruby (the agents-in-place program). The estimated cost was $1 million.[14] Shortly thereafter, Mitchell resigned as attorney general and began to run Nixon's presidential campaign as head of CREEP. Campaign financing laws imposing limits on contributions were to become effective on April 7, 1972, so the Republicans were making a big push to solicit donations before then. As a result, they were able to raise a huge sum for the CREEP coffers. On March 20, 1972, Liddy met Mitchell at the latter's vacation home in Key Biscayne, Florida. Also present was Jeb Magruder, who had just been hired as Mitchell's chief deputy at CREEP. Mitchell approved spending $250,000 from CREEP to fund a scaled-down version of Gemstone. He instructed Liddy to report his activities to Magruder. Mitchell and

Magruder also specifically authorized breaking into the DNC Watergate headquarters and Democratic presidential candidate George McGovern's D.C. office to plant bugs and copy documents. Liddy was transferred to CREEP's finance committee and thus had direct access to the money. Liddy and Hunt made several trips to Miami and enlisted Barker in an attempt to "case out" the Miami location of the Democratic National Convention that was scheduled for July that year. Barker was able to obtain copies of the locations of all the air duct systems in the convention center.

Barker was also the recipient of money that was later traced back to CREEP during the prosecution of the Watergate cases. On April 5, 1972, CREEP'S treasurer, Maurice Stans, was given four checks totaling $89,000. On April 11 he received another check for $25,000. It came from a prominent Democrat named Dwayne Andreas who was a personal friend of Senator Hubert Humphrey, who had been beaten by Nixon in the 1968 election. Andreas did not want it known that he was contributing to the Republicans. In order to protect his identity, the $25,000 check and the other $89,000 (totaling $114,000) were deposited into Macho Barker's bank account in Miami.[15] During this time Barker made several trips to Washington, D.C., to see Hunt, and on a couple of occasions they met at the White House executive building. Hunt told him that they were planning entries into the headquarters of George McGovern and the national headquarters of the Democratic Party. Hunt told Barker they had good reason to believe that Castro was funneling money into the Democratic Party in the hopes of influencing the election. Apparently, Castro wanted a more liberal person in the White House. Hunt said the money was coming in two different ways. First, jai alai games in Miami were being fixed so that Cuban agents could bet large amounts of money and direct the winnings to the McGovern campaign. The second source of money was from the sale of narcotics flowing into the United States from Cuba. Supposedly, the militant Black Panthers were the main U.S. contact for these sales. Barker recalls that there were rumors about both of these things circulating in the Cuban exile community at the time.

Frank told the probation officer who prepared his pre-sentence investigation report for Judge Sirica that he was first recruited for the Watergate job by Macho Barker sometime in April 1972 and thereafter first met Hunt.[16] Barker repeated to Frank what he had been told by Hunt about suspected Castro involvement in funding the Democratic Party and told him that Hunt said they would be acting on behalf of a governmental group that had jurisdiction over both the CIA and the FBI. Like Barker, Frank was familiar with the rumors circulating among the exiles in Miami about Castro and the Democrats.[17] Barker said that their mission had been approved at the highest levels and that Hunt was working directly out of the White House. It was at this point that Barker recruited the rest of the team—Rolando Martinez, Reinaldo Pico, and Virgilio González, who was a locksmith. Hunt traveled to Miami and personally met with González before deciding to hire him. Perhaps Hunt had learned a lesson from the Fielding break-in, where there was nobody who could pick the lock when the original plan to leave the back door unlocked failed. Early on, Barker says he dropped Pico from the team because "he didn't have the nerve."

Barker also spoke with Frank about Daniel Ellsberg, though he never mentioned the Dr. Fielding break-in. Like Barker, Frank thought Ellsberg was a traitor who should be prosecuted. Barker said that Hunt and Liddy told him that Ellsberg was planning a big antiwar protest to disrupt the funeral of J. Edgar Hoover, who had died on May 1, 1972, and they wanted to prevent that from happening. Hoover had been director of the FBI for forty-eight years. At his death, the scandal involving Hoover's homosexuality and his penchant for dressing in women's clothes had not become public. However, Nixon must have had his suspicions because he was caught on the White House taping system telling his aide Bob Haldeman, "That old cocksucker was a morally depraved son of a bitch."[18] On the other hand, Nixon understood that Hoover enjoyed a good reputation with most Americans (Frank included) and saw the opportunity to generate some positive publicity from the funeral. As he told Haldeman, "By

God, Bob, let's go out there and put a torch on the boy."[19] To honor
Hoover, President Nixon delivered the eulogy and ordered that
Hoover's casket lie in state in the Capitol Building, which was where
Ellsberg and his demonstrators were expected to stage their protest.
At Hunt and Liddy's behest, Barker asked Frank to join a "group of
ten Cubans" who would go with him to Washington to confront the
demonstrators. Frank said he would be happy to help. On May 2,
1972, Barker went to his bank in Miami and withdrew $33,000, which
was the last of the $114,000 he had previously been given by Hunt and
Liddy. He then purchased airline tickets for himself, Frank, and the
others to fly to Washington.[20]

Barker recalled what happened next with obvious delight. After
arriving at National (now Reagan) Airport in Washington, they went
directly to the Capitol steps. Barker picked a location where the demonstrators would have to pass and stood abreast to block the way.
Barker positioned himself in the middle and put Frank on one side
and "a huge Cuban" on the other side. "I'm not that big, and I wanted
some muscle around me," he said. The protestors were chanting antiwar slogans as they slowly approached. Barker said that one of them
("He might have been a priest") made the mistake of raising his fist as
he moved toward Frank, who responded with a one-two punch that
flipped the protestor backward over two people. With that, the demonstrators began to retreat as Frank and the others chased them from
the Capitol steps. The police were called, but nobody was arrested.
Barker said his group celebrated with a good dinner before returning
to Miami the next day. Newspapers later reported that the "priest"
who threw the punch and who was "pummeled by an unidentified
counter-protestor" was one of the antiwar radical Catholic priests, the
Berrigan brothers.

In May 1972 when Frank took part in the Hoover funeral mission
he was still working for the Pan-American Aluminum Company, selling windows, primarily to condominium developers. He was paid on
commission, so he was able to take off from work from time to time to
do some White House "plumbing." Janet and Frank had just started

an art class at Miami-Dade Jr. College that met on Tuesday evenings. Janet was an accomplished artist, while Frank was a novice.

When Frank undertook a mission, he usually did not discuss anything about it with Janet. She would know how long he was expected to be gone but not always where he was going. After he returned from Hoover's funeral they had dinner at their favorite Italian restaurant, Mary's, and Frank did tell her about the confrontation with the demonstrators. He was proud to have taken a stand against those who he thought were dishonoring Hoover and the United States. He also told her something that turned out to be very prophetic—"We've got some jobs coming up, and if we get caught, a lot of high government officials will fall."

In preparation for the anticipated entry into the Democratic National Party offices, Liddy, Hunt, and Magruder were able to plant a loyal young Republican, Thomas J. Gregory, in the office of Senator George McGovern, the leading Democratic candidate, who was an extreme "dove" when it came to the war in Vietnam. Gregory had originally been placed in Senator Ed Muskie's office until the latter's popularity in the polls fell and it looked like McGovern would be the nominee. From his position in McGovern's office, Gregory had unlimited access to the Democratic National Committee offices at the Watergate. This allowed him to "case the joint" and provide information "regarding the location of pictures, air ducts, and other physical characteristics of the office" to Hunt and the others on numerous occasions prior to the first break-in.[21]

On May 22, 1972, Frank, Barker, Martinez, and González the locksmith flew from Miami to Washington, D.C. They checked into the five-star Hay-Adams hotel, located across the street from the White House. For the first time they were introduced to another person who would be participating in the break-in, James McCord. Hunt introduced him simply as "Jimmy." Hunt told them that McCord had worked for both the FBI and the CIA in the past and was an expert in the use of electronic surveillance equipment. Unlike Frank and the others, McCord had no known connection to the anti-Castro Cuban exiles in Miami. He had recently retired from the CIA after working there for nineteen years and had a private security business that did work directly for the White House. Thus, he was on the White House payroll when he became a part of the Watergate team. On May 5, 1972, McCord had checked into the Howard Johnson motel directly across the street from the DNC offices at the Watergate. He then ordered "$3,500 of electronic equipment," which was delivered on May 10. (Incidentally, McCord charged the Committee to Re-elect the President $2,000 more than he paid for it.)[22]

Rolando Martinez had his doubts about McCord from the start. As a veteran CIA operative, Martinez was familiar with the use of electronic surveillance equipment. The stuff that McCord had purchased was secondhand and cheap. Martinez could not understand why they did not have better equipment for such an important job. As we will see, there were other things about McCord that led Frank, Martinez, and Barker to believe that McCord actually sabotaged their mission and is the main reason they were caught. As time went by, they pieced more together and became increasingly convinced that McCord was acting as a double agent.

Barker enlisted Frank to provide the muscle for the group. He was certainly tough enough to play that role, as witnessed by the pummeling on the Capitol steps. G. Gordon Liddy recalls that in addition to Watergate, at one point they were checking out the possibility of breaking into one of McGovern's offices in Washington. There were security lights that were illuminating the rear door. Liddy used his gun to shoot one of them out but could not get the others. Then, Liddy said, "Frank Sturgis . . . bent over, put his hands on his knees, and I climbed up on his back and shot them out."[23] Frank, himself, described his role at Watergate as assisting González, "the pick man," and operating one of the walkie-talkies.[24]

On May 26, 1972, Frank and the others checked into the Watergate Hotel under false names as employees of a phony corporation called the Ameritus Company. The hotel was just one part of what was a complex of six interconnected buildings containing offices, apartments (six hundred total units), and retail space in addition to the hotel. It had been built by an Italian company, Società Generale Immobiliare in 1968, on ten acres in the Foggy Bottom area of Washington, D.C., about eight blocks from the White House. In the early 1970s, the Watergate was called "the White House West" due to the large number of Nixon cabinet members and officials who lived there.

The two eight-story office buildings are located at 600 New Hampshire Avenue NW and 2600 Virginia Avenue NW respectively. The Democratic National Committee headquarters occupied the sixth floor of the Virginia Avenue building, on the same street as the hotel. Barker arranged a dinner for Frank and the other "Ameritus" employees in one of the hotel's private banquet rooms that had access to the office building and the elevators to the sixth floor. Once the meal was under way, the plan was for Hunt to run a movie projector as a cover while the others did the break-in. However, as the evening progressed, there were still people working late in the DNC offices. At two o'clock in the morning the office was finally empty, but the Watergate security guards told Hunt et al that they would have to leave the banquet room. Hunt decided that he and González would hide in a closet while the rest left and would let them back into that portion of the Watergate when "the coast was clear." The closet that Hunt chose was used for storing liquor. What happened next is best described by Liddy in sworn testimony in a libel suit that was filed against him after Watergate.

> And later he [Hunt] related to me that as the night wore on and as the call of nature grew more urgent and he grew more desperate, he looked around and saw a bottle of Johnny Walker Red Label, that only had about an inch or so of booze left in it, but it was a full bottle by the time he got out of there the next day. And I have always counseled people who visit the Watergate Hotel, under no circumstances order Johnny Walker Red Label.[25]

After hiding out for several hours, Hunt and González were able to leave, but they could not open the door connecting to the office building, so the mission was aborted.

Hunt and Liddy decided to try again the following evening. This time they would wait until all the lights were off on the sixth floor and then go through the front door of the office building, signing in under their aliases. McCord led the way, telling the guard they saw that they were going to the Federal Reserve office on the eighth floor. From there, they walked two flights down the stairs to the sixth floor and the DNC offices. González began trying to pick open the lock. Martinez recalled that this went on for about an hour and that McCord would periodically leave and go back to the eighth floor. Around 2:00 A.M. Martinez went to that floor and found McCord talking to two security guards. At first, he thought they had been caught, but then he realized that McCord appeared to know the guards, who left to continue their rounds. Martinez wondered if McCord had a mole or a helper on the Watergate security staff. He and McCord went back to the sixth floor and it was decided to once again to abort the mission due to the failure of González to open the door. González said that he did not have all the tools he needed to do the job. So they left as a group, going out the front door.

González told Hunt that the tools he needed to open the door were in Miami. Hunt was very upset with González and ordered him to fly there that same day. Barker told González he might have to pay for his own ticket. Martinez and Frank intervened and told Barker that it was not González's fault. They pointed out that the preparations for the mission had been pretty inadequate. They had never been given complete floor plans of the sixth floor or any information about when the security guards would be making their rounds or how many of them there were. In fact, González was never told in advance exactly what type of doors he was expected to open.

González took an early-morning flight to Miami to retrieve the equipment he needed. He then flew back to Washington, arriving that same evening, May 28, 1972, and once again Frank, Barker, González,

Martinez, and McCord tried to enter the DNC offices. González and Frank went first, picking the lock on a garage exit door. From there, they were able to open the other doors, and they called Barker, Martinez, and McCord on a walkie-talkie and said, "The horse is in the house." Hunt and Liddy waited in Room 723 at the Howard Johnson motel located directly across the street from the Watergate office building where the DNC was located. McCord had set up a "listening post" in the room to monitor bugging devices that he was going to install on the telephones of DNC chairman Larry O'Brien's secretary, Ida "Maxie" Wells, and O'Brien's chief deputy, R. Spencer Oliver.[26] He told Martinez that he was going to install a third bugging device in a location that would make it unlikely to be discovered.[27]

While McCord was installing the bugs, Martinez took thirty or forty photos of documents handed to him by Barker and Frank. Most of these were lists of party contributors. The documents were then placed back where they had been found so as to leave no clue that there had been a break-in. However, there was one document that Frank did take with him. It was a Xerox of the face of a young woman who was kissing the glass on the copier. She had used lipstick to color in her lips. Underneath it she wrote, "For the real thing, call me at . . . ," and then gave a phone number. When it comes to sex, Democrats really do have more fun.

The installation of the bugs may have been the primary aim of the first break-in, but it was certainly not the only goal. In a 1974 *True Magazine* article, Frank said they were looking for documentary evidence of Castro's financial ties to the Democratic Party but found none. They also had been told by Hunt that the FBI suspected there might be a memorandum or other documentation prepared by the Castro regime listing all of the covert actions that had been carried out by the CIA against Cuba over prior years. The memorandum purportedly contained a proposal by Castro to reestablish economic ties with the United States in exchange for a promise to stop the covert missions. However, no evidence of this memorandum was found. The other thing they looked for was any "dirt"—what Liddy called "a shit file"—or derogatory information about the Republican Party. Finally, Hunt told them to be on the lookout for anything pertaining to Howard Hughes, the reclusive billionaire with ties to the CIA. Once again, they found no such evidence.

Frank and the others left the DNC offices at approximately 5:00 A.M. and returned to the hotel. Martinez gave the camera film to Hunt. Later that same day, May 29, 1972, they all flew back to Miami while McCord and Hunt stayed in Washington. To assist with monitoring the listening equipment in Room 723 at the Howard Johnson motel, McCord had hired Alfred Baldwin III, another former FBI agent. Baldwin came from a very prominent family of Democrats, yet he was hired to spy on the DNC.[28] This seems a little curious, especially considering the fact that during the subsequent prosecution of the various Watergate cases, Baldwin was the government's chief witness and was given immunity. It certainly raises the question of whether Baldwin was a "double agent" actually working for the Democrats.

The listening post set up by the "electronics expert," McCord, was not capable of recording the telephone conversations that were intercepted, even though such recording devices were readily available in 1972. As a result, McCord and Baldwin had to keep a written log of the phone calls and a written summary of the content. Liddy gave Magruder copies of these logs on June 8, 1972. He also told Magruder that one of the three bugs was not working. The next day, Liddy met with Magruder, who told him the logs were not "adequate." He instructed Liddy to arrange another break-in to replace the defective bug and photograph documents.[29] Magruder reiterated to Liddy to have his team look for any "dirt" that the DNC had on the Republicans. Magruder also authorized a break-in at the offices of Senator George McGovern.

On June 10, 1972, Hunt flew to Miami and met with Barker. He gave Barker some film to be developed and enlarged, which Barker took to Rich's Camera Shop in Miami. After dropping it off, Barker found out that the film was what Martinez had shot during the break-in. Martinez said that Barker became concerned about the security of the photos and sought help from him and Frank to retrieve them. "Barker was really excited," he recalls. They accompanied Barker to Rich's and "covered each door to the shop in case the police came while he was inside."[30] Realizing that the man at the shop had just enlarged pictures of documents being held by a gloved hand, Barker tried to buy his silence by giving him a $30 tip, whereupon the man said, "It's real cloak-and-dagger stuff, isn't it?"[31] A few days later, the man went to the FBI office in Miami and told them about the film. However, Barker had used a phony name and address when he dropped off the film, and the FBI was never able to make the connection back to Barker before he, Frank, and the others were arrested at Watergate.

Martinez thought "that it was crazy to have those important pictures developed in a common place in Miami." He considered telling Barker how wrong it was, but he knew that Barker trusted Hunt "totally" and would not question anything Hunt asked him to do. Martinez talked to Frank about his concerns, and they both had reservations about doing any more missions for Hunt and Barker.[32] However, on June 12, 1972, Magruder told Liddy and Hunt to do another break-in to replace the defective bug and to photograph more documents. Barker contacted Frank, Martinez, and González and said that Hunt wanted them to get ready for another job in Washington. Consistent with the "need to know" philosophy of the spy business, at this point neither Martinez nor Frank knew whether their previous efforts had yielded anything of value for Hunt and his superiors. As experienced professional operatives, they both had a sense of pride in the performance of their duties. Somewhat reluctantly, they decided to do one more mission. On instructions from Barker, the next day, June 13, Frank and Martinez purchased a box of surgical gloves and forty rolls of Tri-Ex film. At thirty-six exposures per role, this meant that they had the capability to take 1,440 photographs. Martinez told Barker he thought it would be impossible to take this many shots in a single mission.[33]

Nonetheless, Frank, Martinez, and González left Miami on Friday, June 16, 1972. Barker told them to dress in business suits and bring enough clothes for three or four days. They arrived at Washington National Airport about noon. While they were collecting their luggage, Frank saw his friend, columnist Jack Anderson. He introduced Anderson to Martinez and González, making up a story about how they were working on behalf of the Ameritus Corporation. What a scoop Anderson could have had if he had known their true purpose for being in Washington. Barker rented a car to drive them to the Howard Johnson motel across the street from the Watergate. Hunt had reserved rooms for them under aliases. Maybe Hunt was trying to save money, since the rates at Howard Johnson's were much cheaper than those at the Hay-Adams or the Watergate. We do know that there was enough money available for McCord to have been given $10,000 in consecutively numbered $100 bills, which he had deposited in his bank in Washington on June 12, 1972.[34] As they drove to the motel, Martinez and the others made some jokes about the car Barker had rented. It reminded them of a hearse. Could this have been a premonition?

Frank's wife, Janet, went to work at Channel 23 that Friday, June 16. It was Father's Day week end, and even though she did not expect Frank to be home by that Sunday, she thought about a present for him. She decided she would look for a desk lamp because the one on Frank's desk at home was no longer working. After work she went straight home and fixed dinner for herself and her daughter, Gale. She spent the rest of the evening reading one of the Tarzan novels by Edgar Rice Burroughs that she collected. On Saturday, she and Gale went to Miami Glades Shopping Center and bought a desk lamp for Frank. They returned home, where Janet did laundry and cleaned the house. She and Gale ate dinner at home and watched TV that night. However, she did not see any local or national news shows, nor had she read a newspaper that Saturday. With Father's Day coming, she hoped that Frank would call, though it would be unusual for him to do so. She knew he had gone to Washington, D.C., but did not know why or where he would be staying. Frank had told her he expected to be back by the middle of the following week. On Sunday morning, June 18, 1972, Janet and Gale went to the Presbyterian church they attended. As Janet sat in

church and listened to the sermon by the Reverend Paul Force she had
no idea that a little over twenty-four hours earlier Frank, Barker, Martinez, González, and McCord had been arrested by the D.C. police at
the offices of the DNC.

The events of June 16 and 17 that led to the arrests have been well-
documented. The afternoon of the 16th, Frank, Barker, Martinez, and
González checked into the Howard Johnson motel using aliases. At
6:30 P.M. McCord was seen at Liddy's office in the White House old
Executive Office Building.[35] From there McCord went straight to Room
723 at Howard Johnson's. At 8:30 P.M. Frank and the Miamians went
to dinner at the Watergate. It was reported that they dined on lobster.[36]
Martinez recalls that Barker "ate a lot and when he came back he felt
really bad."[37] They then met with Liddy and Hunt at Howard Johnson's to get "the briefing." Their goal was to replace the defective bugs
and photograph documents. Following that, they planned to break
into the McGovern headquarters and photograph more documents.

At the time, Martinez thought the plan was overly ambitious. Barker
said much the same thing during our 2007 interview. As loyal as he
was to Hunt, he did say that the reason the mission was botched and
they were caught was largely due to Hunt and Liddy "always being in a
rush. Liddy was manic. Gung-ho. He rushed too much. This led to errors." Martinez thought that Liddy was "a little weird, too." He said
that Liddy refused to proceed with the briefing until Hunt changed
the pants he was wearing. They were black with a white stripe and for
some reason Liddy did not want Hunt to wear them during the mission. Like a good soldier, Hunt changed his pants. He also donned a
red wig that he said had come from the CIA. He then passed out false
IDs, which had also been provided by the CIA. Frank's alias was
Frank Hamilton, one that he had used before when doing contract
work for the CIA. McCord's alias was Edward Martin and Barker's
was Frank Carter, an alias he had used while working for the CIA.
Hunt made each of them give him their real identification documents,
which he put in a briefcase that he left in the room. He told them to
take their room keys with them and gave Frank and the Cubans each

$200 in consecutively marked bills. Hunt said the money could be used as a "bribe" if they were caught.[38] They were also each given a set of rubber surgical gloves that Frank and Martinez had purchased in Miami. Following the briefing, McCord left, saying he had to buy some wire, batteries, and a battery charger. He returned at 10:00 P.M.

Martinez said the MO for this break-in was different from that for the previous one. This time, Hunt and McCord had entered the Watergate office building earlier that day during regular business hours, signed in under aliases, and then taped the stairwell doors on each of the eight floors of the building, giving them access through the hotel's parking garage. For fire escape purposes the doors opened from the floor but from the stairwell, the doors were locked, preventing reentry. During the previous break-in they had not used tape, relying instead on González to pick the locks. Barker could not understand the need to tape the doors this time. "Why do I need tape when I have an excellent 'pick-man'?" The other thing that is somewhat curious is the type of tape Hunt purchased to use—masking tape, instead of some type of clear cellophane tape, which might have been less visible.[39] Liddy later defended the tape plan by claiming that he had "intelligence" that indicated that the cleaning crews frequently taped the doors open and the security guards were aware of this and likely to ignore it.[40] Nevertheless, why take the chance if you already have a good pick-man? Finally, there is the issue of the position of the tape. It had been applied horizontally across the door bolt to keep it from springing out and locking shut. In this position, a portion of the tape was visible on the inside of the door itself. If, on the other hand, the tape had been applied vertically, on the edge of the door, it would have been hidden in the door frame. As with many aspects of Watergate, we know what happened—that is, the position of the tape—but not exactly why it happened. Was Hunt just being sloppy and living up to his reputation as a second-rate spy? Did McCord, who helped Hunt with the taping, deliberately leave a clue for the Watergate security guards?

Frank, Liddy, Hunt, Barker, Martinez, González, and McCord

watched from Room 214 at the Howard Johnson motel for the lights to go out on the sixth floor of the Watergate and the offices to empty of workers so they could make their entry. Baldwin was above them in Room 723, where the "listening post" had been set up by McCord, who had booked the room under his own name. From that vantage point, Baldwin's job was to be a lookout for the others. They had to wait so long that Hunt made a trip back to the Watergate to be sure that the doors were still taped open. He came back and reported that everything was still in place. Incidentally, years after the break-in and arrests, Hunt was being less than honest when he complained to the press, "I will always be called a Watergate burglar, even though I was never in the damn place."[41] He may not have been there when they were caught, but he had spent plenty of time in the Watergate before-hand.

Sometime around 1:00 A.M. Frank and González left the motel and crossed the street to the Watergate. Frank was carrying a walkie-talkie and a briefcase that contained some of the photographic equipment. González's briefcase contained his locksmith tools and picks. The only weapon between them was a pen-sized canister of tear gas in Frank's sport coat pocket. As instructed by Hunt, they had their Howard Johnson room keys with them, along with the $200 in cash. When Frank and González got to the basement door connecting the parking garage to the office building, they put on their surgical gloves and then made a startling discovery. There was no tape on the door. And on the floor in front of the door was a sack of mail.

Frank called back to the rest of the group and reported what they had found. He suggested they abort the mission since it was obvious that someone had discovered the tape. Martinez agreed with Frank. He also pointed out that for these types of clandestine operations there is an unwritten rule that the people performing the mission can call it off if they do not feel comfortable. McCord said they should go ahead as planned. Liddy and Hunt asked them to wait while they went to another room to make a phone call.[42] They returned a few minutes later and said the decision was to go ahead. Hunt called Frank on the walkie-talkie and told him to have González pick the lock on the door and tape it open. Barker, Martinez, and McCord then used the door to enter the stairwell and removed the tape before proceeding to the sixth floor, where González had picked open the stairwell door that led directly to the DNC headquarters. The suite occupied the entire floor, with twenty-nine separate offices, where approximately seventy persons worked.[43] However, after entering the offices, McCord told Barker and Martinez that he needed to go back to Howard Johnson's to get some equipment he had forgotten. Martinez told him to tape the door open again and be sure to remove the tape when he came back. Frank gave the walkie-talkie to Barker, but McCord told him to turn it off because there was too much static. He also told him to turn off the shortwave police scanner he was carrying. Martinez did not like the fact that they were without communication. He set up the photographic equipment and then he and Barker began searching for files. González started to work on picking the lock to Larry O'Brien's office, while Frank removed two ceiling tiles from an office immediately adjacent to O'Brien's. McCord wanted to use this access to slide a bugging device onto the false ceiling of O'Brien's office.

Ten or fifteen minutes after he had left, McCord rejoined the others inside the DNC offices. Martinez specifically asked him if he had removed the tape from the door. McCord said, "Yes, I did."[44] As it turns out, McCord lied. He left the tape on the door, and it was spotted by Watergate security guard Frank Wills, who became concerned because he had been the one who had previously removed the tape that had been placed originally by Hunt and McCord. That was the reason the tape was missing when Frank and González first arrived at the stairwell door. Because the tape had reappeared, Wills made a 911 call to the Washington, D.C., police at 1:52 A.M. and reported a possible break-in at the Watergate. Three plainclothes officers from the tactical squad, Sergeant Paul Leper and Officers John Barret and Carl Shollfer, responded and entered through the basement stairwell door that had been taped. Upon ascending, they discovered that all of the stairwell doors had been taped. Inside the DNC offices, Martinez had just finished setting up the photographic equipment when he heard noise like the shuffling of feet. Frank came to warn them that people had entered the office suite through the rear door that González had jimmied open. McCord led them into a small secretarial office and reception area and told them to crouch down behind the desk and try to stay out of sight. With so many individual offices in the suite (some, like O'Brien's were locked; others were unlocked) maybe they could still avoid detection. Unfortunately for Frank and the others, the D.C. police were very thorough in their search, and as a result they soon found the "burglars" in their hiding place. McCord "immediately jumped up and raised his hands in surrender."[45]

What happened next was described by Judge Sirica in his "Bench Book," a bound handwritten journal that he kept during the Watergate trials. Many judges keep such notes as a diary of cases, motions, and other matters that are heard in the courtroom. Judge Sirica's notes were made in a flowing hand with a pen and are generally legible. On January 10, 1973, the first day of Frank's Watergate trial, Judge Sirica began his notes. He wrote that when the police, with their guns drawn, confronted the burglars, Frank told them in a loud voice, "Be cool. Stay cool." Then he, Barker, González, and Martinez slowly got to their feet with their arms raised.[46] As mentioned, Barker recruited Frank to be the "muscle" of the operation, with a responsibility to protect them. By defusing a potentially fatal situation Frank was certainly doing that job. Barker agreed that Frank may have saved their lives at that point: "Frank was a true professional. He was a rock." Because the police did not have enough sets of handcuffs to cuff each prisoner, Barker and Martinez shared a set, so each had one hand free. In his free hand, Barker still had the walkie-talkie which he was able to turn on. He pushed the Talk button and delivered what Liddy remembered as a short, whispered transmission, "They got us."[47] From Room 214 at the Howard Johnson motel, Hunt and Liddy had seen the activity across the street, so they were not surprised by Barker's message. Baldwin was able to see that three police officers had entered the Watergate and tried to warn Frank and the others by calling on the walkie-talkie, but it was still turned off per orders from McCord.[48] Liddy started to pack up the electronic gear in the room, and Hunt went to see Baldwin in Room 723. He told him to move all of the equipment out of the room and load it in McCord's van and then drive it to McCord's house. Hunt also had a brief telephone conversation with a Washington attorney, Douglas Caddy, who, like Hunt, had worked for the Mullen Company, which was a CIA front.[49] Hunt told him that he needed legal representation for the burglars. Caddy said that he did not practice criminal law but he would be able to locate someone experienced in that field. He told Hunt to call him back. Hunt then returned to Room 214 and helped Liddy pack up as much of the eavesdropping equipment as they could carry. Liddy recalled that he was worried that they looked suspicious as they left because Hunt was carrying three overloaded briefcases and had stuffed an antenna down his pants leg, making him walk like a peg-legged pirate.[50] Maybe if Liddy had not made Hunt change pants before the break-in he would have been less noticeable. The historical record is not clear as to what happened to the CIA-issued red wig Hunt was wearing during the getaway.

Hunt and Liddy drove from the motel in their respective cars. Liddy went to his house, and Hunt went to his office in the White House Executive Office Building.[51] At 3:00 A.M. Hunt called Caddy again and asked to meet him right away. Caddy told Hunt to come to his house.[52] Hunt called and spoke with Macho Barker's wife in Miami at 3:24 A.M., presumably to tell her about the arrests. Hunt opened the small safe he kept in his office and removed $10,000 in cash that he had previously received from Liddy for "emergencies." He put $1,500 in his wallet and the remaining $8,500 in his coat pocket.[53] He then signed out of the Executive Office Building at 3:30 A.M. and drove to Caddy's house, arriving shortly thereafter. At 4:00 A.M. Baldwin arrived at McCord's house and dropped off the eavesdropping equipment that he had removed from the motel. An hour later, Hunt telephoned Hugh Sloan Jr., treasurer of CREEP, who authorized spending $8,000 to retain Caddy and "some other criminal lawyer."[54]

Liddy went to his office in the Executive Office Building at 8:20 A.M.

on Saturday. The first thing he did was find a document shredder and begin destroying the logs of the wiretaps and other incriminating documents.[55] Liddy had still not reported the disaster to his superior, Jeb Magruder, due to the fact that Magruder was in California with the head of CREEP, John Mitchell, so Liddy was dealing with a three-hour time difference. At 11:15 A.M. (8:15 A.M. California time) Liddy left for the White House and used his pass to gain entrance to a "situation room" that he knew had a secure phone line. From there he reached Magruder and told him to go to a Nike Missile base that was near the hotel and call back on a secure line.[56] Magruder called back in about fifteen minutes, though Liddy suspected he was not using a secure phone. When Liddy told him what had happened he was obviously very upset, especially because McCord could be traced back to CREEP and the White House. A few minutes later, Magruder called back again and told Liddy that John Mitchell wanted Liddy to personally contact the current attorney general, Richard Kleindienst, and tell him to find someone to represent McCord and get to him right away and tell him not to talk. Liddy succeeded in tracking Kleindienst down at a golf course and relayed Mitchell's request. Kleindienst refused to cooperate and was mad that Mitchell would ask him to do such a thing, especially since it could reflect badly on his boss, Nixon. Liddy then went back to the Executive Office Building and located a much larger shredder to finish what he had started earlier. "I didn't want somebody coming in with a search warrant finding anything that was incriminating. That's why God invented shredders," he said.[57]

After apprehending Frank and the others at the Watergate, the D.C. police called for a paddy wagon to transport them as a group to booking, and then to jail. During the trip McCord "took charge" and told them not to say a thing. "Don't give your names. Nothing. I know people. Don't worry, someone will come and everything will be all right. This thing will be solved."[58] At booking, they signed in under their aliases. The police then read them their Miranda rights and attempted to interrogate them. McCord recalls that Frank pretended to be a lawyer and spoke for the rest of them.[59] McCord does not report what Frank actually told the police, but it probably had something to do with their Fifth Amendment right to not be questioned or made to give evidence against themselves. Frank had certainly had enough brushes with the law in a variety of countries to be aware of his rights (or lack of rights, depending on which country was doing the arresting). Also, although Frank had been hired for "muscle," the truth is that he was no dummy. As a part of the sentencing that he eventually received from Judge Sirica, Frank underwent a psychological evaluation that included a measurement of IQ It was found to be 126, which indicates that he had "superior intelligence."[60] He was never shy about speaking up and expressing his opinions, and he enjoyed a good debate. The other reason Frank and the Cubans remained silent at this point was because they believed they had been carrying out an intelligence operation authorized by the White House. They thought that if they maintained their silence, somehow the government would intervene and have them set free. In essence, this is what McCord had told them in the paddy wagon.

Unfortunately for them, mere silence was not going to impede the police investigation. They were placed under arrest for one count each of felonious burglary and possession of implements of crime.[61] They were thoroughly searched, and their clothes and briefcases were confiscated. Police found the $200 in consecutively numbered bills that Hunt had given each of them, though, surprisingly, McCord only had 36¢ in his pocket.[62] Martinez was carrying a key that was later determined to open the lock of the desk of Maxine Wells, secretary to the DNC head, Larry O'Brien. It had been given to him by Hunt prior to the break-in. Since the mission's "mastermind," Hunt, made them carry their Howard Johnson room keys, it did not take the police long to have a judge issue search warrants for the rooms. There the D.C. police found another $4,200 in $100 bills of the same serial number sequence as the burglars were carrying.[63] They discovered more electronic bugging equipment and burglary tools in six suitcases. Most significant, they found the briefcase that Hunt had left behind that contained all of their real IDs. They also found the phone and address books of Martinez and Barker. Each contained the White House phone number of E. Howard Hunt.

At 4:00 P.M. on Saturday, June 17, 1972 (about the same time Janet was purchasing Frank's Father's Day present), Frank and the others appeared before Washington, D.C. Superior Court judge James A. Belson for an arraignment on the charges of burglary and possession of criminal tools, which had been filed as a "criminal information or complaint" by the D.C. police. The charges were filed using their real names. In criminal law the arraignment is the initial appearance in court where the defendant is expected to enter a plea of guilty, not guilty, or no contest. If the plea is "not guilty," the court then decides whether or not to set a bond and, if so, the amount and conditions of the bond. Representing them at this hearing was attorney Douglas Caddy, who had been retained by Hunt. When they first met with Caddy in the holding cell at the DC Jail before the arraignments that morning, he told them, "Olympus is watching over you."[64] To Frank and the others this meant that they would be protected and helped by the people in charge of the missions they had carried out. Caddy told the news media that he was a corporate lawyer who had met Barker a year earlier at the Army and Navy Club in Washington.[65] What Caddy did not reveal was that his connection to Barker and Hunt was through the CIA. Because he did not practice criminal law, Caddy brought another attorney as co-counsel, Joseph A. Rafferty Jr., an experienced criminal lawyer who did all the talking. Presumably, Caddy and Rafferty split the $8,000 fee that Hunt had obtained approval for from Hugh Sloan Jr., CREEP's treasurer. The state was represented by Assistant U.S. Attorney Earl Silbert, who was described as "the No. 2 man in the chief prosecutor's office."[66]

Rafferty entered not guilty pleas on behalf of the five defendants. Judge Belson then asked them to state their occupations. McCord volunteered that he had retired from the CIA two years earlier. This early disclosure by McCord of a CIA connection—sure to pique the interest of the prosecutor and the press—is another reason, in retrospect, why Frank, Barker, and Martinez eventually came to believe McCord was a double agent or "plant" whose real job was to see that they were caught so as to embarrass the Nixon administration. Barker responded on behalf of Frank, Martinez, and González that they were "anti-communists." Other than that, the defendants did not speak.[67] Silbert asked the judge to remand them to custody without bond, citing their use of false names, lack of community ties, and possession of a large amount of cash. Rafferty pointed out that the defendants were un-armed and that nobody was hurt during the confrontation with po-lice. Judge Belson decided to set a $50,000 cash or professional bond for Frank and each of the three Cubans and a $30,000 bond for Mc-Cord. (Measured in 2007 dollars, $50,000 is the equivalent of $225,000.) To get out of jail, Frank would have to deposit $50,000 into court or pay a professional bondsman a nonrefundable 10 percent fee ($5,000) to post it. The judge also specified that it would be a "reporting bond," meaning the defendants would have to stay in the Washington, D.C., area and personally appear before a probation officer on a weekly ba-sis. Unfortunately, Frank did not have the money for his bond, nor could he afford to relocate to D.C. while the criminal charges were pending. Unless the people who had hired him were going to keep the promise made by McCord in the paddy wagon and the one that Caddy made at the jail, Frank was going to stay in the DC Jail, an old, out-dated, overcrowded facility where they were being held. Frank ranked it just a small step above some of the Mexican jails he had been in. At least he would not have to face being tortured as Batista's henchmen had done to him in the old El Morro prison.

For the type of crimes Frank was facing, his bond was extraordi-narily high. Undoubtedly, the reason for this is that even at this early juncture, the police and prosecutor realized that they were dealing with something bigger than a simple breaking and entering. In his book, A Piece of Tape, McCord said that Sergeant Paul Leper, who had apprehended them at gunpoint, knew within hours that he "had a political espionage team" under arrest. For this reason, the FBI was called in immediately to take over the investigation. Prosecutor Sil-bert told Judge Belson that the defendants were "professionals with a 'clandestine' purpose."[68] On Sunday, June 18, the day after the arraignment, the *Washington Post* ran a story about the break-in that had been put together by a team of reporters, including Bob Woodward and Carl Bernstein, who later won a Pulitzer Prize for their reporting about Watergate and who authored a bestselling book, *All the President's Men*, about their experiences. (They also claim credit for "breaking" what came to be the Watergate scandal, but there are those, including Frank, who believe this claim is unfounded.) Nonetheless, the June 18 article that was sent on the wire to newspapers across the country contained a good deal of accurate information about Frank and the others. They reported on Frank's military experiences during and after World War II and his involvement with Cuba and Castro. He was described as a "soldier of fortune" and "head of the International Anti-Communist Brigade, after the Bay of Pigs invasion, that trained 23 Cuban exiles who in 1962 landed by boat in Cuba's Matanzas Province and set up guerrilla operations." There was no mention of the connection to the CIA that Barker and Martinez had. Martinez was described as a real estate agent who "violated immigration laws in 1958 by flying a private plane to Cuba." González's wife told a *Washington Post* reporter that her husband worked as a locksmith at the Missing Link Key Shop in Miami. The owner of the shop confirmed that González had worked there since 1959 and described him as "pro-American and anti-Castro."[69]

The first Janet heard about what had happened was when the attorney, Caddy, called her midafternoon on Sunday, June 18, 1972. She was absolutely stunned to hear that Frank had been caught inside the DNC Watergate offices. The words that Frank had told her at Mary's a few weeks earlier—"If we get caught, a lot of high government officials will fall"—rang in her head. She asked if she could talk to Frank, and Caddy told her the only way that could happen was for her to come to Washington, D.C., and visit him in the jail. He also explained what would be required financially to post the bond that Judge Belson had set. She said she did not have $5,000. Caddy left his number and told her to call if the financial situation changed. After she hung up, she went to the local 7-11 store and bought the Sunday *Miami Herald*. There on the front page was the *Washington Post* wire story that ran in the morning edition. She then realized why some people had given her funny looks in church earlier that day. She called Rev. Paul Force and offered to resign from her position as an elder in the church in light of Frank's arrest. Rev. Force told her, "Absolutely not. You know we love you, and we really love Frank. We will help in any way we can."

Unfortunately, not everyone was so supportive or understanding. Within days of the arrest she was contacted by Frank's boss at the Pan-American Aluminum Company, who told her they were firing Frank because of Watergate. With the loss of Frank's income and the inability to get him out of jail, Janet faced the prospect of having to live on her modest salary from Channel 23 (she took home approximately $125 a week). In addition to her daughter, Gale, Frank's mother, Mary, who had some serious medical problems, was living with them. Janet could not afford to lose time from work to go to Washington to see Frank. It would be another six weeks before she would see or talk to her husband.

Barker and Martinez were able to make bail within a few days of the arrest. Judge Belson modified the bonds to allow them to return to their homes in Miami, where they would report weekly at the local federal probation department. Barker called Janet and told her that he was working on raising the money for Frank's bond. At that point, he made no offer to help her financially with household expenses. During the last week of July, Janet received a call from Barker, who asked her to meet him the next day at Manuel Artime's office in southwest Miami. Artime was the head of the anti-Castro group and government in exile that Hunt and Barker had worked with leading up to the Bay of Pigs. Artime personally led the first wave of the invasion and was captured by Castro's forces. He was tried and found guilty of terrorism and put in jail. He eventually was freed along with other anti-Castro prisoners in exchange for the United States shipping millions of dollars worth of medical supplies and other goods to Cuba. If that invasion had succeeded in ousting Castro, Artime would have been the new leader of Cuba. Janet went to his office as instructed. Barker and Artime gave her $5,000 in cash to be used to post Frank's bail with a Washington, D.C., bond company. They also said they would pay for airline tickets so that she could go to Washington and fly back with Frank after he got out. Janet had to sign a receipt for the cash, which was designated as "charity." She later talked to Rev. Force about her plan to go to Washington and he immediately volunteered to accompany her at his own expense so he could act as a character witness for Frank at the bond hearing.

On July 28, 1972, the judge held a hearing to modify Frank's bond so that he could return to Miami as Barker and Martinez had done. Janet recalls that even though it was the middle of the summer, the courtroom was extremely cold. She said Frank looked "out of it"—like he was in a daze, which was unusual since he generally exuded confidence no matter what the situation. After six weeks in the old DC Jail, the enormity of the consequences that could result from the crimes he was charged with had taken its toll. On the flight home Frank was very quiet and felt claustrophobic. After they had been home for a few days, Frank returned to his old self. However, for the first time in his life, Frank came down with allergies that caused him to itch. He blamed it on conditions at the DC Jail, but clearly he was under a lot of stress, which probably played a large part. With the uncertainty of the outcome of the criminal prosecution hanging over his head and his national notoriety, Frank was unable to find a job, even on a temporary basis. Frank's trial had already begun.

9

Watergate—Law and Disorder

They were duped by high government officials.

—*Trial judge Gerhard Gesell*, U.S. v. Barker,
U.S. District Court for D.C.

They pled guilty because they believed national security interests precluded them from disclosing the nature of their activities, and because they interpreted the guilty plea of their supervisor, Hunt, as a directive that they follow the same course of action.

—*Appellate judge George MacKinnon*, U.S. v. Barker,
U.S. Court of Appeals—D.C. Circuit

WHILE FRANK REMAINED UNEMPLOYED IN MIAMI, A FEDERAL grand jury in Washington began hearing evidence about what was now being called simply "Watergate." A grand jury is usually composed of fifteen to twenty-three people, unlike a petit jury of six or twelve that decides civil and criminal suits. Both types of juries are guaranteed by the constitution and the bill of rights. The role of the grand jury is to decide if there is probable cause to bring criminal charges against a person. The only attorney involved is the prosecutor, who unilaterally decides what evidence to present. Originally designed as a safeguard against frivolous charges being filed against someone, in practice the grand jury is a prosecutorial tool to investigate alleged criminal acts and to bring multiple-count indictments arising out of that conduct. By stacking the criminal counts, the prosecutor generally has a significant bargaining tool during plea negotiations because conviction on multiple counts can result in the perpetrator's having to serve the sentence of each count consecutive to the others. This puts pressure on a defendant to accept a deal that includes dismissal of some of the counts. It would be unusual for a defendant to plead guilty to all counts of a multi-count indictment.

On September 15, 1972, the original criminal complaint filed by the D.C. police against Frank of one count of burglary and one count of possession of criminal tools was voluntarily dismissed by the prosecutor. On that same day, Frank, along with Barker, Martinez, and González, was indicted by the grand jury on a total of seven counts:

1.   Conspiracy in violation of 18 U.S. Code section 371;
2. & 3.   Burglary in violation of 22 DC Code section 1801(b);
4. & 5.   Illegal Interception of Oral and Wire Communication, in violation of 18 U.S. Code section 2511;
6. & 7.   Possession of illegal communication interception device in violation of 23 DC Code section 5439(a).

If they were convicted on each of these counts they would be facing up to fifty years in prison with consecutive sentences. The indictments came as no surprise. The media had reported regularly that summer about the activities of the grand jury. The actual proceedings were secret, but there were plenty of "leaks" to the press, including the fact that the investigation was focusing on "several other un-named individuals" who were part of the alleged conspiracy along with Frank and the three Cubans. These individuals turned out, of course, to be Hunt and Liddy. The prosecutor did not subpoena Frank or any of the others before the grand jury for the obvious reason that they would exercise their Fifth Amendment right not to testify.

Even without their testimony, the evidence of the actual burglary was overwhelming. As prosecutor Silbert had said, they were caught "red-handed" at the scene. The search at Howard Johnson's had yielded significant physical evidence, including the true identity documents that Hunt had left in the motel room. Additionally, $4,200 in consecutively numbered $100 bills matching the numbers on the cash the burglars were carrying had been left behind by Hunt and Liddy. Telephone/address books belonging to Barker and Martinez were found and each contained the White House phone number of Hunt. Barker used initials, writing "HH—WH 202-456-2282," a code that was easily broken. More electronic eavesdropping equipment was found in the "lookout" room because Baldwin neglected to remove all of it. That room was tied to McCord because he had rented it in his own name. He and Baldwin also had made a number of personal telephone calls from the room. By tracing these calls the FBI had no problem identifying Baldwin as being involved. Agents contacted him within days of the break-in, and by June 25, 1972, Baldwin had struck a deal to turn state's evidence against Frank, Barker, Martinez, González, McCord, Hunt, and Liddy. In exchange, Baldwin was given immunity from prosecution for the Watergate crimes that Frank and the others faced. By avoiding a felony conviction and accepting this deal, Baldwin, who was an attorney, also managed to avoid losing his right to practice law. Immunity was also given to Thomas Gregory, who had been hired by Hunt and Liddy to spy on the Democrats while working for the McGovern campaign's national committee. Gregory was able to corroborate much of Baldwin's testimony. Significantly, Baldwin told the FBI and the grand jury, and later testified against McCord and Liddy, that he personally had delivered the telephone logs that he and McCord had maintained to an official of CREEP. Thus, the FBI and the prosecutor knew early in the investigation about the ties from Frank and the others back to CREEP. From there it was just a stone's throw to the White House and Nixon.

In anticipation of the indictments, Barker, Frank, Martinez, and González decided to hire a new attorney. For some reason they were dissatisfied with Rafferty, who, along with Caddy, had represented them at their initial appearance following their arrests. One reason may have been their belief that Rafferty, like Caddy, was also working for the CIA. Caddy tried to have them hire Frank H. Strickler, a

Washington, D.C., attorney who later represented Nixon aide John Ehrlichman, but they distrusted his possible CIA ties. Although they continued to believe that the CIA was behind their mission and should do something to get them out of trouble, they had not received a clear indication from Hunt or anyone that this would happen. Since Hunt was working directly out of the White House, they weren't even sure if it was the CIA or some other government entity that they were working for. Also, they wanted an experienced criminal attorney who could bring some clout to their defense. Therefore, they selected Henry Rothblatt, a well-known trial lawyer from New York City. Rothblatt had gained notoriety by successfully defending Colonel Oran Henderson, who along with Lieutenant William Calley had been charged with the murders at My Lai. Although Rothblatt initially claimed that he was representing Frank et al for no fee in exchange for the massive publicity the trial would receive, Barker has said that Rothblatt was actually given $18,000 in cash as a retainer.[1] Barker said this money was part of a $50,000 payment he had received in a plain envelope from Dorothy Hunt, Howard's wife, when Barker went to meet Frank at the Miami airport following Frank's release on bail. He explained that the day before, he had received a phone call from an unidentified person who said that someone he knew would see him at the airport. Barker was not really surprised that it turned out to be Dorothy, who was always considered "the brains in the family."[2] Prior to the trial in January 1973, Barker estimated he received a total of $50,000 in plain envelopes from Dorothy. McCord retained his own attorney, Gerald Alch from Boston. Alch was a partner of F. Lee Bailey, who, like Rothblatt, was a high-profile trial lawyer. Another $18,000 of the $50,000 Barker received paid for McCord's lawyer. Hunt and Liddy hired D.C. attorneys William Bittman and Peter Maroulis, respectively.

During one of the first meetings that *Washington Post* reporters Woodward and Bernstein had with their confidential source, "Deep Throat" (named for a pornographic movie of the same name that was popular at the time), in June 1972, he told them that the key to getting to the bottom of Watergate was to "follow the money." It was later revealed that Deep Throat was W. Mark Felt, deputy director of the FBI, which was investigating Watergate. The FBI was doing exactly what Felt said—trying to determine who had paid for the Watergate operation. In addition to the cash found at the time of the arrests, the FBI was able to trace the three Republican campaign checks totaling $114,000 that had been deposited in Barker's account by way of a Mexican bank prior to the break-ins.

At the September 15, 1972, arraignments on the grand jury indictments, the attorneys on behalf of each of the defendants entered not guilty pleas. The judge presiding over the arraignment hearing was John Sirica, district court judge for the District of Columbia. Judge Sirica was sixty-eight years old and held the status of chief judge based on seniority of service. Ordinarily, in both federal and state courts, cases are randomly assigned by the clerk of courts who accepts them for filing. This rule prevents "forum shopping," whereby lawyers maneuver to have a case assigned to a particular judge of their liking. However, as chief judge, under the court's local rules, Judge Sirica was allowed to decide who would hear the Watergate cases. Given the growing media attention and the possible involvement of highly placed government officials, it is not surprising that he appointed himself. He had done the same thing earlier that spring with a sensational murder case that was extensively covered in the local media. Most federal district court judges do not hear that many criminal cases because they are usually brought in state courts. However, there is no state court in the District of Columbia, so the D.C. district court also acts as a criminal court for misdemeanors and felonies. Judge Sirica's nickname at the time was "Maximum John," owing to his penchant to impose the maximum sentence allowed. He had lived up to that name in the aforementioned murder case when he imposed the maximum sentences on the defendants.

Judge Sirica had been appointed to the bench by President Eisenhower, a Republican, in 1957. He had some things in common with Frank. Both men's parents were first-generation Italian-Americans. Their socioeconomic circumstances were similar. Like Frank, Sirica had lived for a while in Florida. Both were amateur boxers of some repute. On the other hand, the judge had not served at all in the military. In his book, Judge Sirica recounts that before becoming judge, he was offered the position of chief legal counsel for "red baiter" senator Joe McCarthy and the House Committee on Un-American Activities. Judge Sirica said he "found the offer very attractive."[3] McCarthy conducted numerous witch hunts with trumped-up charges accusing many innocent Americans of being communists and traitors. He was eventually exposed as a fraud and a liar by noted news reporter Edward R. Murrow. As much of an anti-communist as Frank was, he thought McCarthy was "an idiot" and a "phony" who actually hurt the cause of anti-communism with his lies and unsubstantiated charges.

In legal circles there is some debate about the proper role of a judge, particularly in a criminal prosecution. Should the judge be an umpire or a referee, responding to whatever matters the attorneys raise? Or should the judge participate actively by questioning witnesses and suggesting areas of inquiry during the trial? There is nothing in the code of judicial conduct that prohibits a judge from following one practice or the other; however, federal judges more often use the activist approach, and that is what Judge Sirica did in the Watergate cases. During pretrial conferences he pushed prosecutor Silbert to not only prove the elements of the various crimes charged against Frank and the others, but also to answer the question of their motive—why did they break in? As Judge Sirica said in his book,

> Technically, they didn't have to prove motive, only that the seven men were guilty of the charges against them. But the public was growing more and more suspicious. There had to be some reason these men went into the Watergate. Why not develop it? Why not get all the truth out and settle the question once and for all.[4]

Given this mind-set going into the trial, Judge Sirica was playing the role of prosecutor instead of that of impartial judge.

At the September 15, 1972, arraignment, Judge Sirica set a trial

date of November 15, 1972. The presidential election with Nixon running against McGovern would be held on November 3. Sirica notes
that "there was heavy pressure building to have the Watergate case tried
before November, to get the facts out in the open before the American
people cast their ballots in the presidential election."[5] He goes on to
point out that the earliest he could have started the trial was the end of
October, with little chance of getting a verdict before Election Day in
any event. From the start, Judge Sirica was aware of the political rami-
fications of the upcoming burglary and conspiracy trials. He was interested not only in proving that Frank and the others were guilty of
crimes, but also in learning why they had committed them. Judge
Sirica made it his mission to "get to the bottom" of Watergate. To ac-
commodate the crowd of people and media representatives who would
attend, Judge Sirica decided to use the ceremonial courtroom, which
was the largest one.

In late October 1972, Judge Sirica hurt his back while attending a
seminar for judges in New Orleans. As a result the trial had to be post-
poned until January 10, 1973. Frank continued to stay out on bond
with Janet in Miami. Janet recalls that Frank did a lot of the cooking
that fall and took care of his ailing mother. He was an excellent cook.
Janet is a big football fan, and it was the season that the Miami Dol-
phins went undefeated on their way to the NFL championship; she
and Frank watched the Super Bowl at their hotel room in Washington
that year, on the eve of the trial, before she returned to Miami the next
day. Frank and Janet had been able to spend Christmas together in
Miami. Money was tight, but they were able to buy each other rings
and presents for Janet's daughter, Gale. From his release on bail in July
1972 through the end of the year, Frank received $2,500 from Barker.
This amounted to less than half of Frank's take-home pay before he
was fired by the Pan-American Aluminum Company. During the same
period, Barker spent $7,000 on personal expenses.[6]

Several days before the trial, Judge Sirica had a conversation in his
chambers with the chief prosecutor, Earl Silbert, regarding "an administrative problem unconnected with the Watergate case."[7] It is certainly

plausible that Silbert saw the judge about some other case, but Judge Sirica then proceeded to bring up the Watergate trial without any of the defense attorneys being present. This amounted to an ex parte communication, which is improper and prohibited by the cannons of ethics. Judge Sirica violated this ethical rule by "advising" Silbert that he had "a great opportunity in this case if [he went] right down the middle, let the chips fall where they may," adding, "Don't let anyone put any pressure on you."[8] (This apparently did not include pressure from the judge). He gave Silbert a bound copy of a Congressional hearing from 1944 when Judge Sirica had been the attorney for the committee. He wanted Silbert to know how "whitewashers" [sic] were engineered. "And I wanted him to know that I had direct experience with cover-ups while serving as chief counsel to that committee."[9] In his zeal to discover why Watergate had occurred, Judge Sirica again demonstrated his bias. Forget about the basic presumption that an accused is innocent until proven guilty. In the judge's mind Frank and the co-defendants were guilty before the trial started.

Jury selection was set to start on January 8, 1973. Frank and the three Cubans continued to believe that if they maintained their silence, the people who had hired them would take care of things, by either having the charges dropped or commuting any sentence if they were convicted. Martinez maintains that there is an unwritten rule and expectation that the government would take care of you if you were caught doing undercover work.[10] This is what happened with Francis Gary Powers, the pilot who was captured by the Russians who shot down his U-2 spy plane over Soviet territory. President Eisenhower initially denied any knowledge of Powers or spying but worked behind the scene to secure his release. Powers went on to a successful career as one of the first helicopter traffic reporters in Los Angeles. Manuel Artime and the other Bay of Pigs captives who were eventually set free by Castro in exchange for medical supplies and money even though the United States denied responsibility for the failed invasion is another example. Their strategy at trial would be to maintain silence and let the prosecution try to prove its case. As far as their motivation was concerned, they were just "foot soldiers" with no direct connection to anyone at CREEP. Besides themselves, the only people that Frank and the others knew were involved in Watergate were Hunt and Liddy, both of whom were also under indictment, and Alfred Baldwin, who had turned state's evidence. Frank and the Cubans knew nothing of the extent of the Watergate conspiracy, which was in keeping with the "need to know" approach to intelligence work.

It took two days to pick a jury, which is pretty expeditious since there were four defense attorneys participating in the process along with the prosecutor. Prior to starting the trial, Frank and the others met with Rothblatt at the Arlington Towers to discuss strategy. He wanted to use the CIA as an explanation for their activities but they refused because, at the time, the involvement of the Plumbers in the break-in at Ellsberg's psychiatrist's office was not known. They felt bound to not disclose what they thought was a case of national security. During this meeting Hunt told them that he had decided to plead guilty. He felt that they had no defense to the crimes they were charged with. On a personal level, Hunt said the recent death of his wife, Dorothy, and the ensuing problems for his children made it impossible to go through "the ordeal of a trial."[11] Dorothy had been killed in a commercial jetliner crash while on approach to Midway Field in Chicago on December 10, 1972. Found among her belongings in the wreckage was $10,000 in $100 bills. One of the bills contained a handwritten note—"Good luck. F.S." This has led some conspiracy theorists to conclude that "F.S." was actually Frank Sturgis. According to Frank, this is absolutely untrue and is merely one of a number of coincidences surrounding the events in his life. At no time did any money pass directly from Frank to Dorothy Hunt or to anyone involved in Watergate. For that matter, Barker was the only person who gave any "Watergate" money to Frank.

However, there continues to be controversy and speculation about the circumstances of Dorothy Hunt's death. Some believe she was carrying something closer to $300,000 in cash and bearer bonds. It is undisputed that she purchased a $250,000 flight policy on her life before she boarded in Washington, D.C. What is also undisputed is that there were FBI agents at the crash scene before the fire department or any other agency responded. Generally, the FBI does not become involved in a crash until invited by the National Transportation Safety Board. On the other hand, as part of their ongoing investigation into Watergate, the FBI may have been monitoring the activities of Dorothy Hunt and therefore knew she was on the plane that crashed. But, still, why such a quick response? As to what Dorothy was doing with the money that was found, Hunt said that it was to be used as an investment in two Holiday Inn motels owned by a friend. A more likely explanation is that Dorothy was on her way to Canada to stash the money. According to Anthony Ulasewicz, an ex-NYPD officer who was the "bag man" for Watergate, he delivered a total of $154,000 to Dorothy Hunt before her death. All of this money came from CREEP.[12]

President Nixon knew as early as June 21, 1972 (three days after the break-in), that the Watergate burglars were looking for financial assistance. Liddy made the request to Nixon's chief aide, Bob Haldeman, who told Nixon about it.[13] They discussed the issue of whether the burglars might be able to blackmail them if the money was not paid. This conversation and others over the next two years provided clear evidence that the president and his top staff were well aware of the Watergate connection to CREEP and the White House. Ultimately, it was the cover-up and the attempt to thwart the FBI's investigation that caused the prosecution of more than thirty members of Nixon's administration and led to his resignation on August 8, 1974. Although President Nixon maintained throughout his life that he had no prior knowledge of the plans to break into the DNC and McGovern headquarters, Haldeman has recently said that in fact Nixon knew from the start.

As far as the blackmail question is concerned, from Frank's perspective he had little or no information that could have implicated Nixon or anyone on his staff other than Hunt and Liddy (who were already under arrest). However, the same cannot be said about E. Howard

Hunt. One of the "dirty tricks" he performed as a Plumber included fabricating State Department cables to show that President Kennedy had been directly involved in the assassination of Vietnam's prime minister Ngó Dinh Diem in 1963. Hunt then leaked them to the press to discredit the president's brother Ted Kennedy, who was a possible opponent in the upcoming election. On June 19, 1972, Hunt's safe at the White House was cracked and numerous documents were taken. Hunt believed that Nixon aides Charles Colson and John Dean orchestrated the burglary to retrieve potentially damaging documents, including the phony Diem cables.[14] It is likely that the safe held other secrets, because on June 29, 1972, Hunt's wife, Dorothy, demanded a payment of $450,000 from Maurice Stans at CREEP. She initially received much less, $40,000, but other payments followed, totaling at least $154,000 prior to her death in December 1972. White House tapes from August that year demonstrate that President Nixon was aware of these payments. Liddy also received large cash payments from CREEP, totaling $199,000.[15] Hunt received another $75,000 from CREEP on March 23, 1973.

Regardless of exactly how much money was paid as a consequence of Watergate, the fact is that Frank received none of it. As previously noted, he did get $2,500 from Barker during the months leading to the trial. Another $5,000 had been provided for his bail. After that he received nothing, which caused a serious hardship for his wife and family. Unfortunately, Frank also discovered that Macho Barker, who had been a friend for many years, was not sharing very much of the money he had received with the rest of them. For this and other reasons, while Frank was in prison with Barker he chose to end his friendship with him.

So, if Frank was not getting paid for his silence, why did he and the others follow Hunt's lead and plead guilty at the start of the trial? Frank called Janet the evening of Thursday, January 11, 1973, and told her that was the plan. She was not surprised and attributed it to Frank's Marine Corps training, which taught him to not question his superiors. If Hunt was pleading guilty and maintaining his silence, then the

Frank at eleven years old. Taken in Philadelphia on October 12, 1936.

William "Wild Bill" Donovan headed up CIA predecessor (OSS) and helped organize Marine Raiders. *(U.S. government photograph)*

LAZY - MARINES.

Merritt "Red Mike" Edson—leader of Frank's famed Marine Raider brigade during World War II. *(U.S. government photograph)*

These marines were not "lazy" for long. After boot camp they went directly to the South Pacific and into some of the most vicious combat of the war.

WhaT·A· bELLy·

Laundry day at boot camp, Parris Island.

Looking down "Main Street" of a Raider camp. South Pacific 1943.

Frank graduates from boot camp.

At Parris Island on the first anniversary of Pearl Harbor.

Three of Edson's finest in front of the ever-present fifty-five gallon fuel drums.

Battling the Japanese in the South Pacific.

(New Georgia) Dragon Peninsula 1943

Frank (in foreground) leads his "fire team" on New Georgia Island in the South Pacific.

Frank flanked by a flame thrower and munitions expert. He said his toughest battle was Guadalcanal, and his best was Okinawa (the last real battle of the war).

Frank was a Golden
Gloves boxing champ
in Philadelphia.

Comic relief in the Pacific Theater.

Refereeing fellow raiders somewhere
between Guadalcanal and Okinawa.

Written by Frank on the back of this photo: "In this picture are 6 marines of
the 1st Raider Bn. We just returned from an engagement and we brought
some junk back. We have a Jap rifle and bayonet and also a Jap skull."

Frank (second from right) was a permanent member of Gen. Lucius Clay's personal honor guard in Berlin.

Frank (second from left) in bombed-out Berlin at the time of the airlift in 1949.

In the army in Berlin on a relic from a bygone war.

In Berlin in 1948, where his spy career began as a courier for Haganah, the secret arm of the newly formed Jewish State.

Processing out of the Marines in Sun Valley, Idaho. Frank served in all branches of the U.S. military.

El Moro—where Frank was held prisoner and tortured by Batista's men in 1958.

This picture shows Frank, on the outside of the sandbags, turned toward Fidel (foot on sandbag).

Frank and Che Guevara in 1958 at a rebel camp in the mountains of Oriente Province, Cuba, where Frank instructed Che in guerilla warfare. Note Frank's July 26 armband.

Cuban rebels walking through a "friendly" village. Local farmers supported Castro's revolution against Batista.

Tending the wounded in the Sierra Maestra Mountains.

Pastorita Nuñez (in beret) was a female officer in Castro's rebel army, who rose to the rank of commander. When the revolution was won, Fidel put her in charge of all the casinos. Shortly thereafter he asked Frank to take over the duties. Below, Frank (second from right) observes the same piece of a Batista plane.

Castro's rebels burying the fallen.

Some of the "guajiros" Frank trained for Fidel.

Frank, a captain in Castro's Rebel army, with what appears to be an M-1 carbine with a large clip. He purchased weapons in the United States and delivered them via secret flights, landing on almost nonexistent airstrips in the Cuban mountains. Photograph circa 1958.

Frank astride a mass grave of Batista's soldiers. Although this picture verified the fact that Frank was still alive (his mother had been told that he was killed in action), it was also used to strip him of his U.S. citizenship. *(Courtesy of the Associated Press)*

Juan Fangio was the world champion Formula One racer from Argentina kidnapped by Frank to publicize Castro's revolution.

Meyer Lansky—well-known to Frank when Frank was Castro's casino czar in Havana in 1958.

Castro and his mistress, Marita Lorenz. Frank recruited her as a spy for the CIA.

Santos Trafficante Jr.—owner of Sans Souci Casino in Havana—was a Tampa mob boss known to Frank.

Carlos Marcello—
New Orleans
boss—was known
to Frank as part of
the Havana mob
connection.

Sam Giancana—
underworld
associate of
Frank's—was
the mob boss
of Chicago.

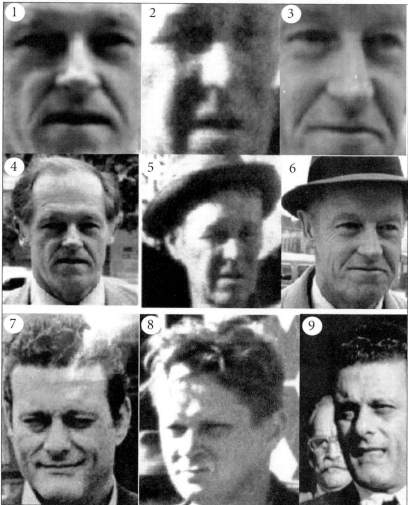

We think these pictures show that the "tramps" were in fact Gus Abrams and
Harold Doyle as the investigators said they were, rather than E. Howard Hunt
and Frank Sturgis. In the first row, E. Howard Hunt appears in photos 1 and 3,
Gus Abrams is in photo 2. In the second row, E. Howard Hunt appears in photos 4
and 6, Gus Abrams is in photo 5. In the third row, Frank Sturgis appears in
photos 7 and 9, Harold Doyle is in photo 8. *(Courtesy of A. J. Weberman)*

Pages where Frank's name allegedly appears in Oswald's address book. The enlarged images at the bottom are drawn from the text.
(Courtesy of A. J. Weberman)

The author's father, Jim Hunt, Frank's wife, Janet, and Frank, taken by the author shortly before Watergate. *(Courtesy of Jim Hunt)*

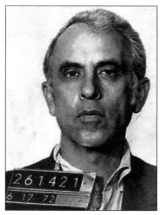

Rolando Martinez—
Watergate burglar and
close friend of Frank's.

Virgilio Gonzalez—
Watergate burglar and
locksmith.

Bernard "Macho" Barker—
arrested with Frank at
Watergate—longtime
CIA contact for Frank.

Frank's Watergate arrest
photo.

James McCord—arrested
with Frank at Watergate
break-in.

E. Howard Hunt—CIA spy, code
named "Eduardo"—planner of
Watergate and the Bay of Pigs
Invasion. *(Courtesy of St. John Hunt)*

John Sirica—
"Maximum"
John—was not
Frank's "Man of
the Year." *(Courtesy
of* Time *magazine)*

Romula Betancourt—Venezuelan president and associate of Frank.

"Bottlecap" Trujillo—Dominican dictator. Frank assisted in his demise.

Jonas Svimbi—an Angolan rebel leader who Frank aided in the fight against the communist government.

Miguel Ydigoras—president of Guatemala—was another national leader Frank assisted.

Memorandum

LE GRAND HOTEL

2. RUE SCRIBE
75442 PARIS Cedex 09
Tél. : 260-33-50
Télex : 220875

(uranium)

300 Bar's

ea. bar - 400 grams 235

stolen in London
ea. bar has (standard) Uranium London

100 gram of NR.
○ ○ ○ ○ — 4,000,000 ea. bar

" Carlos "

Frank's Paris notes regarding an offer to sell stolen uranium. The contact is a Mr. V. The seller is Carlos, the Venezuelan terrorist . . . who later became known as the "Jackal."

Frank with Angolan rebel leader Holden Roberto.

Frank next to his longtime fellow spy Marita Lorenz—Castro's former mistress—and Roberto and others.

Frank took these pictures at Holden Roberto's anticommunist rebel training camp in the Angolan bush.

Frank's secret camp in the Everglades where he trained anti-Castro guerillas. When he was investigated by the FBI and ATF, he characterized the group as "just some Boy Scouts learning ecology."

A somewhat indelicate message to Fidel from the Everglades.

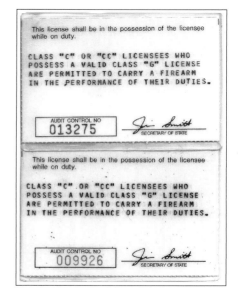

This license shall be in the possession of the licensee while on duty.

CLASS "C" OR "CC" LICENSEES WHO POSSESS A VALID CLASS "G" LICENSE ARE PERMITTED TO CARRY A FIREARM IN THE PERFORMANCE OF THEIR DUTIES.

AUDIT CONTROL NO
013275
SECRETARY OF STATE

This license shall be in the possession of the licensee while on duty.

CLASS "C" OR "CC" LICENSEES WHO POSSESS A VALID CLASS "G" LICENSE ARE PERMITTED TO CARRY A FIREARM IN THE PERFORMANCE OF THEIR DUTIES.

AUDIT CONTROL NO
009926
SECRETARY OF STATE

Frank had two private investigator licenses. Also pictured is his badge.

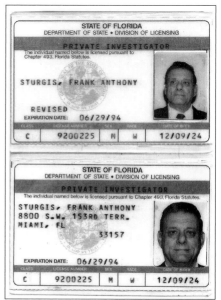

STATE OF FLORIDA
DEPARTMENT OF STATE • DIVISION OF LICENSING

PRIVATE INVESTIGATOR
The individual named below is licensed pursuant to Chapter 493, Florida Statutes.

STURGIS, FRANK ANTHONY

REVISED
EXPIRATION DATE: 06/29/94

CLASS	LICENSE NUMBER	SEX	RACE	DATE OF BIRTH
C	9200225	M	W	12/09/24

STATE OF FLORIDA
DEPARTMENT OF STATE • DIVISION OF LICENSING

PRIVATE INVESTIGATOR
The individual named below is licensed pursuant to Chapter 493, Florida Statutes.

STURGIS, FRANK ANTHONY
8800 S.W. 153RD TERR.
MIAMI, FL
33157

EXPIRATION DATE: 06/29/94

CLASS	LICENSE NUMBER	SEX	RACE	DATE OF BIRTH
C	9200225	M	W	12/09/24

Frank, Janet, and their daughter, Autumn.

Left to right: Wilfredo Navarro; Janet; Frank; Pedro Gomez; Janet's sister, Maxine Talley; and Autumn, age six months. Autumn's first of many trips to Disneyworld, Frank's favorite vacation spot.

Left to right: Frank; Janet; her mother, Elizabeth Hunt; Janet's daughter, Gale; the author, Jim Hunt; and his friend Dan Berger at Haulover Beach, Miami, July 1962.

rest should do so as well. At this point Frank and the Cubans still believed that the CIA or some other secret governmental group had been behind their mission and that some deus ex machina would be provided to commute any sentence or pardon any conviction. They also believed they were involved in a matter of top secret national security and were expected to not reveal it to anyone. It was later reported that their attorney, Henry Rothblatt, refused to continue representing them if they plead guilty. However, Dan Schultz, the Washington, D.C., attorney who later represented Frank, Barker, Martinez, and González after the guilty pleas, claims the real reason Rothblatt withdrew had to do with money, not trial strategy. Rothblatt wanted an additional $25,000 retainer paid into a trust account that he controlled and from which he could pay himself. Frank and the Cubans agreed to the retainer amount but wanted to approve any dispersal for fees. Whatever the reason, this attorney/client impasse was brought to Judge Sirica's attention through a letter delivered by Frank and his co-defendants on Friday morning, January 12, 1972. This was after he had accepted Hunt's guilty plea to all five counts against him.[16] The previous day, January 11, 1973, prosecutor Silbert had presented testimony from Baldwin and others establishing that Liddy and Hunt were the leaders and planners of this mission and that they had direct ties to CREEP. The evidence further confirmed the role of Frank and the others as mere foot soldiers in the burglary. Judge Sirica agreed to let Rothblatt withdraw and decided to appoint Alvin Newmyer, the judge's "long time friend" and "one of the leaders of the bar," to represent the Miami defendants at their guilty pleas. He adjourned over the weekend to allow Newmyer "to get on top of his case."[17] Accepting the fact that Mr. Newmyer was probably a skilled and experienced attorney, taking a weekend to get on top of a case as complex as Watergate is not nearly enough time. By appointing Newmyer, Judge Sirica was trying to deflect any argument on appeal that the guilty pleas were entered without the advice of an attorney.

On Monday, January 15, 1973, Frank and the others entered guilty pleas to all charges through their court-appointed attorney, Newmyer.

But Judge Sirica was not satisfied with just guilty pleas. As he said, "I was determined that despite their pleas, I would make an attempt to find out what else they knew about the case."[18] He grilled Martinez and Barker about the source of the money, the identities of others involved in the case, and any connection to the CIA. True to their code, they denied CIA involvement and shed no light on the funding issue. Judge Sirica therefore "gave up" and remanded Frank, Barker, Martinez, and González to the DC Jail on $100,000 bonds pending sentencing. Hunt was able to pay a bondsman, but Frank and the others could not afford to and waited in jail to be sentenced until after the case against Liddy and McCord was tried. The key witnesses against them were Baldwin and Gregory, who had been given immunity in exchange for their testimony. Baldwin provided a direct link to CREEP when he testified that he had personally delivered copies of the phone logs of intercepted conversations to its headquarters. Though neither Hunt nor Liddy testified at trial, other evidence established that at the time of the break-ins both were working directly out of the White House. Further, there was all the physical evidence that Hunt, Liddy, and Baldwin had left behind at the Howard Johnson motel.

McCord also did not take the stand. His attorney told Judge Sirica that he was going to argue that McCord acted under duress, because he had been hired originally to coordinate security for CREEP and he needed to break into the DNC to gather information on possible demonstrations and threats of violence at the Republican National Convention held in the summer of 1972. Sirica rejected this defense and instructed McCord's attorney not to use it. Liddy's lawyer argued that there was still reasonable doubt that Liddy was actually the ringleader of Watergate. Neither of these arguments worked. On January 30, 1973, after deliberating for one hour and forty minutes, the jury found Liddy and McCord guilty on all counts. As he had done with Frank, Judge Sirica set a $100,000 bond for each of them and scheduled sentencing for all the defendants on March 23, 1973.

Frank, Barker, Martinez, and González were without an attorney as they approached the sentencing date. As the days went by without any definite word from the CIA (or whichever governmental agency had hired them) they decided to find an attorney on their own. With financial support from CREEP now cut off, they looked to the anti-Castro community in Miami for grassroots financial help to retain one. Their old friend and Bay of Pigs survivor Manuel Artime agreed to organize and head up the Committee for the Defense of Watergate to raise the money. He contributed $6,000 of his own to get things started. To find a new lawyer Frank and the others took the somewhat unusual step of having Barker's daughter, Maria Elena, contact the federal prosecutor, Earl Silbert, for a recommendation. He suggested she contact Dan Schultz, who had spent several years as an assistant U.S. district attorney before leaving to enter private practice representing criminal defendants.

Schultz first met his clients in a holding cell at the DC Jail. In the beginning, he would meet with them as a group. They initially believed that he was connected to the CIA. For instance, when Schultz asked Martinez some questions about his work background, Martinez said, "Why are you asking? You already know all about me." It took several meetings before Martinez and the others came to believe that maybe Schultz was not a CIA plant. As Martinez opened up and talked about still being on the CIA payroll at the time of Watergate, and as Frank, Barker, and González talked about the CIA missions they had performed, Schultz began to see that they truly believed that they were performing a sanctioned, legitimate national security job at Watergate. In order to research this possible defense, Schultz requested and was granted CIA approval to review the agency's files on the defendants. He was given greater access to this information than the Watergate prosecutor had. The CIA even let him take notes, though they made and kept a copy of them at the end of each session. This prompted Schultz to start making fewer notes in a hand that was not very legible. He would then go back to his office after each session and dictate detailed notes. Some of the information that Schultz saw is still classified, and he cannot disclose details, but he confirms that even though Frank was not directly employed by the CIA, he did plenty of independent contract jobs for them over the years. The same was true for the locksmith, Virgilio González. His house had been routinely used as a store house and conduit for weapons and ammunition and enough explosives "to take out the whole neighborhood."

In preparation for deciding what sentences to impose, Judge Sirica ordered the D.C. probation department to prepare a "pre-sentence investigation report," or "PSI," on each of the defendants. This is common practice in both state and federal criminal courts where felonies are concerned. Ordinarily, these reports do not become a part of the official record in the case file kept in the clerk of courts office. However, copies of these PSIs were included in Judge Sirica's papers at the Library of Congress. The report on Frank consists of thirteen pages and is signed by Frank E. Saunders, U.S. probation officer, on behalf of his chief, George W. Howard. It was submitted to Judge Sirica on February 27, 1973, almost a month before sentencing. The report contains a detailed presentation of the origins of Watergate, beginning with the formation of the White House plumbers in 1971, as well as a thorough summary of Frank's life prior to Watergate. The probation department conducted a number of interviews with family members, including Janet, Frank's father (Angelo Fiorini), and several people who had known and worked with Frank in Norfolk and Virginia Beach in the 1940s and '50s. Judge Sirica was informed about Frank's childhood, including the tragic death of his sister in a house fire, the divorce of his parents, his Catholic education, and his growing up in his grandfather Vona's house in Philadelphia. Frank's exemplary war record was detailed, including his enrollment in all branches of the armed services.

There were positive comments about Frank's character from Milton Bass, who owned a tavern in Norfolk called the Café Society where Frank worked from 1952 to 1953. His decision to resign from the Norfolk police department over the corrupt payoff system was noted. Judge Sirica was also apprised of Frank's involvement with Cuba and Castro, including his capture and torture by Batista. The mission to drop anti-Castro leaflets over Havana on October 22, 1959, was documented, along with Frank's staunch anti-communist views and his patriotism. Frank was identified as one of the people at J. Edgar Hoover's funeral "who engaged the liberals on the Capitol steps" and got into a "scuffle" with them.[19] His prior criminal record was minimal—a fine of $15 for disorderly conduct in Portsmouth, Virginia, on October 2, 1942, a charge of illegal possession of "arms" in Miami on July 30, 1958 (when he was running guns and ammo to Castro), which was dismissed, and arrests in Mexico and the Bahamas for "revolutionary activities." Frank's marriage to Janet was described as "successful" and it was noted that they were "genuinely interested in each other" and that Frank had "completely accepted" his stepdaughter, Gale, as "his daughter."[20]

A major point in Frank's PSI is his "version" of the crimes to which he had pled guilty. Keep in mind that Frank disclosed this information in February 1973, before he and the others were given immunity to testify in the grand jury and Senate probes that were ongoing. Frank explained that he had been contacted by Macho Barker, who asked to meet him for lunch. At the meeting, Barker told him that "Castro money was coming into this country to support the McGovern campaign." Barker said he was working with a government group seeking evidence of this. Barker further told Frank that "what they were doing was perfectly legal." Frank also told the probation department investigator that there had been a prior attempt to break into the Watergate. He denied knowledge of the involvement of anyone beyond Hunt and Liddy. "Sturgis insists he knows nothing about this affair other than what was told him by Barker."[21] This statement is true and is indicative of Frank's role as a "foot soldier" in the Watergate affair.[22]

Despite this obvious circumstance and the fact that Frank had given information as to the motive for breaking into the DNC headquarters—that is, the Castro money connection—Judge Sirica states in his book, "None of the defendants had made any move toward telling the full truth about the crime. I began to wonder if, given a bit more time now that all seven had either pleaded guilty or been found guilty, they might reconsider their defiant stance."[23] What he says may have been true of Hunt, Liddy, and McCord, but not of Frank. The only important thing he had not disclosed as of February 1973 was his belief that they were performing a mission of national security for an agency with jurisdiction over both the CIA and the FBI. The reason for withholding this information was Frank's sincere belief that it was a secret operation that should not be disclosed.[24] As far as the legality of breaking in and conducting a warrantless search of the DNC, presidents in both political parties from Franklin Delano Roosevelt to Nixon claimed the right to authorize such searches and/or electronic surveillance in the interests of national security. Ironically, that rule of law was changed in an unrelated case by the U.S. Supreme Court on June 19, 1972, two days after the Watergate break-in.[25]

True to his nickname, "Maximum John," Judge Sirica "knew right away that [he] would give all seven men fairly stiff sentences."[26] In order to coerce them into giving testimony to the grand jury and the Senate committee, even though they had not yet been promised immunity, Judge Sirica hit on what he called a "tactic" to force their cooperation. It had actually been suggested to him by a reporter for the *Des Moines Register.* A federal statute on the books at that time, 18 United States Code section 4208(b), allowed a judge to order a provisional sentence if the court desired "more detailed information as a basis for determining the sentence to be imposed." The provisional sentence would be served over the next three to six months while the probation department conducted a study of each of the defendants. Following that, a final sentence would be imposed. Judge Sirica was delighted to find that this law gave him "a legal way to put off final sentencing until [he] could see just how well the defendants cooperated in the pending investigation."[27] He was also probably happy to see that this statute required him to impose the maximum sentences allowed for the crimes. On March 23, 1973, stacking up the seven counts of burglary and possession of wiretap tools consecutively, Judge Sirica sentenced Frank and each of his fellow burglars to fifty years in prison. This is more years than even a convicted murderer would get.

In his book, Judge Sirica says that he never really intended to have the defendants serve this maximum sentence. He also claims he needed "more information than had been furnished to [him] by the probation officer in his presentencing reports."[28] However, at no point did Judge Sirica specify exactly what additional information he needed from Frank or any of the defendants. He knew from Frank's PSI that he was essentially a first-time offender who had readily admitted his crimes. He had strong ties to a family that he helped to support. Probation Officer Saunders found him to be "a fearsome fighter of communism" and "an intensely loyal person" who took on "the charisma of a 'soldier of fortune.'"[29] He was obviously not a career burglar. There was no concern that Frank would repeat this type of behavior in the future. What other information did Judge Sirica need? There are four basic considerations that due process of law requires when a criminal defendant is sentenced. First, what form of punishment or retribution is just under the circumstances, depending on the heinousness of the crime. Second, is there a need to protect the public from the defendant? Third, will the sentence deter others from committing similar offenses in the future? Fourth, to what extent is the defendant capable of being rehabilitated to be allowed back into society? In imposing the maximum interim sentences, Judge Sirica served none of these purposes. Rather his purposes were twofold: to coerce the defendants into talking and to further his prosecutorial quest to "get to the bottom of Watergate." Frank's constitutional rights were ignored by Judge Sirica. Usually, the probation department preparing the PSI makes a recommendation as to whether the defendant should be imprisoned or placed on probation. Interestingly, the PSI prepared by Mr. Saunders on Frank in February 1973 made no mention of this one way or the other, though he does conclude, "The ordinary elements of 'rehabilitation' are not an issue with respect to this man."[30] This is an acknowledgement that the sentence Frank was going to receive had more to do with the ongoing Watergate probes than it did with matters ordinarily considered during sentencing.

Janet got the news about Frank's fifty-year sentence while working at Channel 23 in Miami. She was absolutely stunned by the severity of it. Maximum John was receiving maximum media exposure, a result that he obviously intended. He wanted to send a message to others who might have been involved in Watergate. That Judge Sirica was "media savvy" is also illustrated by another thing he did at the sentencing on March 23, 1973. On March 19, 1973, the defendant James McCord hand-delivered a letter to Judge Sirica's chambers. In the practice of criminal law it is not all that unusual for a defendant to write directly to the judge without informing his attorney, as McCord had done. This is especially true when the defendant is awaiting sentencing and is looking for some mercy from the court. Nonetheless, Judge Sirica was worried that the letter might contain a bribe and he wanted a "witness" to his opening it.[31] He therefore called federal prosecutors Earl Silbert and Harold Titus to his chambers along with a member of the probation department. Also present were the judge's two law clerks and his court reporter, who would transcribe what was said. Interestingly, the judge did not feel compelled to invite McCord's attorney to the meeting. To their credit, Silbert and Titus saw this as unethical ex parte contact and therefore asked to be excused from the meeting before anything happened, and Judge Sirica acquiesced. In the presence of the others, he opened the envelope and found two letters inside. One was a copy of a letter McCord had previously sent to the *New York Times* denying a story that claimed McCord had engaged in "strong-arm tactics." The judge was puzzled as to why McCord had sent this letter.

The second letter from McCord contained claims and information that Judge Sirica credited with "breaking the dam" on the Watergate investigation.[32] McCord began the letter by noting that he felt prevented from testifying or talking about the details of Watergate because of concerns about his Fifth Amendment right against self-incrimination and due to the fact that he was likely to be sued in a civil action because of the break-in and the interception of private telephone conversations. Despite these concerns, McCord went on to list six points about Watergate:

1. "Political pressure" had been applied to make the defendants plead guilty and remain silent.

2. Perjury, the giving of false sworn testimony, had occurred during the trial.

3. "Others" involved in Watergate had not been identified by witnesses who could have done so.

4. This was not a CIA operation, though the "Cubans" might have been misled into believing that. "I know for a fact that it was not."

5. Some witnesses made "honest errors" of fact.

6. His "motivations were different than those of the others involved."[33]

McCord ended the letter with a request to meet with Judge Sirica privately because he did not feel confident in talking to an FBI agent.

As Judge Sirica read this letter aloud to those in his chambers he began to think, "This is it; this is it, this is the break I've been waiting for." Because he got the letter on March 19, his birthday, he said, "This is the best damned birthday present I've ever gotten . . . I always told you I felt someone would talk. This is going to break this case wide open."[34] Even though this letter was potentially key evidence in the Justice Department's ongoing grand jury probe of Watergate, Judge Sirica decided to not turn it over to them. Instead, in order to guarantee the maximum media impact, he decided to wait until the sentencings on March 23, 1973, and then read the letter publicly into the record. He was later heavily criticized by Attorney General Richard Kleindienst for not promptly turning the letter over to be used as a tool in the grand jury investigation. Sometimes, this type of evidence is best kept confidential so as to not tip off those who may be impacted by it. In terms of the separation of powers among judicial, legislative, and executive that is the foundation of our form of government, clearly the prosecution of Watergate was the responsibility of the executive branch, not Judge Sirica. Despite this basic constitutional tenet, Judge Sirica was "infuriated" by the critical letter from Kleindienst.[35] He was expecting the Justice Department to "congratulate" him for making the letter public. This attitude is indicative of

Judge Sirica's wanting to take credit for cracking the Watergate investigation at the expense of his role as an unbiased judge. In this way he is much like the reporters Woodward and Bernstein, who take similar credit in *All the President's Men*. For an illuminating analysis of the fallacy of the Woodward/Bernstein claim, see the July 1974 *Commentary* magazine article by Edward Jay Epstein, "Did the Press Uncover Watergate?"[36] He correctly concludes "that it was not the press, which exposed Watergate; it was agencies of the government itself." Frank agreed. This is the reason for the question in the Trivial Pursuit game "Who did convicted Watergate burglar Frank Sturgis say were the two most overrated people in America?" Answer? "Woodward and Bernstein."

At the March 23, 1973, sentencing hearing Judge Sirica began by reading the McCord letter. It must have been an emotional moment for him because as he read it aloud he developed chest pains that caused him to take a twenty-minute recess. Following that, he returned and imposed the maximum provisional sentences of thirty-five years for Hunt, and fifty years for Frank, Barker, González, and Martinez. In his book, Judge Sirica mistakenly says that the sentence was actually forty years.[37] According to the February 27, 1973, PSI for Frank, the maximum prison terms for each of the seven counts to which Frank pled guilty—five years for conspiracy, thirty years for two counts of burglary, five years for wiretapping, and ten years for two counts of possessing wiretap equipment—total fifty years. At the hearing, Judge Sirica told the defendants that their cooperation in the investigation would be a major factor in the final sentences he would impose. Liddy received a prison term of from six years, eight months to twenty years and a fine of $40,000.

Frank was stunned by the length of the sentence. It was not until after the hearing that his attorney, Dan Schultz, was able to explain that the sentence was provisional and not final. Even with that explanation, Frank was worried. He expected some type of maximum final sentence from Maximum John, but not fifty years. The disclosure of McCord's letter, in retrospect, had a major impact on the future course of Frank's case. Even before the letter, he and the Miamians suspected that McCord was some kind of "plant" or double agent. Unlike them, he had no ties or allegiance to the anti-Castro cause. McCord was hired as an electronics expert but used shoddy equipment that did not always work properly, resulting in the need for the second entry into the DNC, when they were caught. On that evening he had left for over an hour, supposedly to buy batteries. During the burglary he left to get some equipment and did not remove the tape on the door even though he told Martinez he had. During their initial appearance the following day, McCord volunteered the information that he had worked for the CIA. Frank later learned that McCord was in contact with a CIA handler on a weekly basis during the Watergate events. All of this evidence points to the fact that McCord was some sort of double agent intent on sabotaging their efforts and unraveling the conspiracy to its highest levels to harm the Nixon administration.

As far as McCord's claim in the letter that Watergate was not a CIA operation although he and the "Cubans" may have been deliberately misled to believe that it was, as of March 1973, Frank and the Cubans were beginning to have their doubts about CIA sanctioning of their operation, even though the Agency had provided their false identities at Watergate and had supplied disguises used in the Ellsberg psychiatrist's office break-in. Even McCord's assertion that the CIA was not behind the operation could be interpreted as disinformation or a lack of such information on McCord's part consistent with compartmentalization. However, as the Senate committee and the grand jury did their work over the summer of 1973, the information that leaked out strongly suggested a simple political motive for the break-ins— one party wanted to gather political information on the other through illegal means. "In particular, the Committee and the public were informed in detail of the genesis of 'Operation Gemstone,' characterized in the Committee's report as 'a comprehensive political intelligence-gathering program for CRP.'"[38] It did not become "clear" until after "three months of testimony" that Nixon's attempt to limit the Watergate investigation "was not for sensitive national security reasons, but for purely political purposes." Frank faced the growing realization that their mission may have had nothing to do with national security or matters involving Cuba. As federal judge Gerhard Gesell later said in the Ellsberg psychiatrist break-in trial, "You were duped by high Government officials."[39]

They discussed this issue over the summer with Dan Schultz, and he concluded that Frank and his fellow burglars might have a legitimate defense to the charges against them. Their previous lawyer, Rothblatt, was going to argue that they lacked criminal intent, one of the essential elements of the crimes that the prosecution had the burden of proving beyond a reasonable doubt. Under the law, intent is a weak defense because it can be proven by merely showing that the defendants knew or should have known the consequences of their illegal activities (i.e., committing a burglary at the Watergate is an illegal act, which is what the defendant must have wanted and intended). Schultz came up with a different approach, the assertion of an affirmative defense, which he called "good faith reliance on apparent authority." The concept was not entirely new to the law. For example, if a person who is trying to subdue another person shows you a badge identifying himself as an officer of the law and enlists your assistance, if it later develops that the badge was phony and the arrest illegal, you have an affirmative defense to a charge of false arrest or kidnapping. In Frank's case there was ample evidence of a good faith belief that Watergate was a national security operation sanctioned by the CIA and the Nixon White House. The problem with raising the defense at this point, the end of the summer of 1973, was that they had entered guilty pleas some eight months earlier. If Schultz was going to be able to use this affirmative defense, he was going to have to persuade Judge Sirica to allow the defendants to withdraw their guilty pleas. Schultz filed a motion requesting this relief and Judge Sirica ordered Schultz to file detailed affidavits from each of the defendants to support their belief that they were on a legitimate mission at Watergate. He set a deadline of September 14, 1973, to file them.

Dan Schultz's effort to file these documents provides one of the more humorous moments of the trial. On the last day for filing, Schultz went to the DC Jail holding cell where the defendants had been brought from Danbury so they could appear before the Ervin Committee. Schultz had them sign the affidavits, which he notarized and packed in a briefcase he had borrowed from another attorney in the office and latched the double locks. It was 3:30 P.M. and he needed to get to the clerk's office to file before 4:00. After leaving the holding cell, Schultz realized that when he'd shut the briefcase it had locked and he did not have they key. There was not enough time to return to his office, get the key, and file before 4:00. This would have been a problem except for the fact that one of Schultz's clients, Virgilio González, was an expert locksmith. González said, "Don't worry, Dan. Put that briefcase up against the iron bars and I'll get it open." True to his word, González was able to open the locks in a matter of seconds, and the motions and affidavits were removed and filed. Talk about assisting in your defense.

After imposing maximum fifty-year sentences on Frank and his fellow burglars, on March 23, 1973, Judge Sirica ordered that they be held at the DC Jail so they could be called as witnesses before the grand jury that was continuing its probe of Watergate. To encourage their candor and avoid Fifth Amendment concerns about self-incrimination, Judge Sirica decided to grant them immunity. This is in contrast to their status at the time of their guilty pleas earlier in January when Judge Sirica did his Perry Mason best to get them to "talk" and help him "get to the bottom of Watergate." At that point, they had no immunity at all. True to his reputation as a hanging judge, Judge Sirica granted "use immunity," which offers the least amount of protection. Under use immunity the defendant cannot be prosecuted for crimes uncovered during his own testimony. This does not prevent the prosecutor from presenting evidence from other persons or sources to prove criminal misconduct against the defendant. The other type of protection, "full immunity," means just what it says. The person testifying cannot be prosecuted, period. This is the type of immunity that had been given to Alfred Baldwin and Thomas Gregory to secure their testimony in the trial of

Liddy and McCord. As it turns out, for Frank, use immunity offered plenty of protection because he had already been convicted of all potential criminal acts arising out of Watergate. Whatever he knew had been brought out through witnesses in the prosecution of McCord and Liddy. At this point Frank had nothing to hide. He still believed that Watergate was a government-sanctioned operation involving matters of national security and that is what he told the grand jury, though privately, he and Martinez began to wonder if Hunt had lied to them.

In March 1973, the break-in at Ellsberg's psychiatrist's office by Barker, Martinez, de Diego, Liddy, and Hunt was still not known about by anyone except the participants. Barker said in January 2007 that Hunt instructed him to not mention the Ellsberg matter to the grand jury because it was "a national security case." Therefore, Barker did not tell the grand jury about it, nor did Martinez. What happened next is described in a report by Probation Officer Saunders to Judge Sirica:

> Hunt went before the Grand Jury following Barker. When Hunt returned to the cell block, he advised those in the cell block that he told the grand jury about the Ellsberg matter. Supposedly, Liddy was in the cell at the time and hollered, "Get that s.o.b. out of this cell before I kill him." Apparently, Liddy has not said another word to Hunt since that time.[40]

Before disclosing the Ellsberg break-in, Hunt received full immunity on condition that he also testify against Barker and Martinez in their criminal cases. Hunt, of course, readily accepted immunity. Barker later recalled that it hurt him to watch Hunt testify against him and accuse him of doing things that Hunt had actually done. "Not only did he rat us out, even with immunity he lied about the extent of his own involvement." Despite that, until his death Barker still held Hunt in high esteem and would have "gladly laid down [his] life for him."

In April 1973, while Frank was still being held at the DC Jail, his mother, Mary, died at his home in Miami. She had been very ill due to

complications from diabetes and heart disease. Since his original incarceration, Janet had written a letter to him each and every day, but
she had no way to reach him on short notice by phone. She therefore
called Dan Schultz and asked for his help. He told her he would request a furlough from Judge Sirica to allow Frank to travel to Miami
for the funeral. The judge was kind enough to grant the request and
word was sent to the U.S. Marshals office to arrange for Frank's travel
to Miami. The first thing Frank knew anything about this was when a
marshal came to the jail and told him he was being taken to Miami for
"a family matter." Frank asked the marshal to elaborate, but for some
reason he refused to do so. Maybe he did not feel comfortable delivering such bad news. In any event, it wasn't until Frank met Janet at the
airport in Miami that he learned of his mother's death. He was allowed to spend the next two nights at home before returning to jail.
Frank's relationship with his mother was very close, certainly more so
than that with his father, and he was grief-stricken over her death. He
knew her health was not that good, but he blamed himself for not being
there more for her. Several months after her death, when Frank was being evaluated by a psychologist, George Steinfeld, as a part of the "study"
that Judge Sirica had ordered, he talked about his feelings. Dr. Steinfeld
reported, "As he started talking about this, he broke down and became
extremely emotionally upset. It was 10 to 15 minutes before Mr. Sturgis
could pull himself together to continue talking about what has been
happening to him of late."[41] Down deep Frank really was what Rolando
Martinez called him, "A tough guy with a good heart."

Frank and all the other defendants were transferred to the federal
medium security prison in Danbury, Connecticut, on May 25, 1973.
All told, Frank had spent a miserable five and a half months in the
overcrowded DC Jail. Danbury was a welcome change. Frank and the
others slept on bunk beds in locked dormitories holding up to forty
prisoners. Toilets and showers were shared. They were allowed to exercise and performed menial jobs. It was no country club (that would
come later), but it was better than where they had been. Frank never
felt threatened at any of the jails where he had been held, including

the old DC Jail. The inmates did not mess with Frank or Rolando Martinez, the weight lifter. Frank generally got along with all segments of the prison and jail populations. However, the same cannot be said for Macho Barker. Martinez and Frank had to rescue Macho on several occasions. Frank came to Macho's aid despite the growing estrangement between them.

The ostensible reason for their being sent to Danbury was so that the "study" that Judge Sirica had ordered before imposing a final sentence could be conducted. The unspoken reason was to continue to confine the defendants even though they had given grand jury testimony until they could appear before Senator Ervin's committee investigating Watergate. To this end, Judge Sirica again granted them use immunity. Frank thought he would be at Danbury pending the "outcome of the Watergate investigation."[42]

One of the psychological tests that Dr. Steinfeld gave to Frank was the Minnesota Multiphasic Personality Inventory, or MMPI. This test, consisting of some five hundred true-or-false statements, continues to be widely accepted in mental health and legal circles for its accuracy. One of its unique features is a scale that assesses whether the person being tested is being truthful. It is extremely adept at identifying true major psychiatric illnesses and most personality disorders. Frank passed his MMPI with flying colors. In the words of Dr. Steinfeld, "Results of the MMPI corroborate the clinical impression during the interview. The pattern of scores in 10 clinical subscales all fall within the normal range and indicate Mr. Sturgis to be a rather healthy person, psychologically."[43] Keeping in mind that Frank spent a month at the end of World War II at a psychiatric facility in Klamath Falls, Oregon, getting treated for "war neurosis," it appears that over the years he was able to adjust and cope with the scars that his war experiences had inflicted.

During his interview, Dr. Steinfeld asked Frank in depth about what motivated him to pursue a lifestyle and career that some described as being a "soldier of fortune." Frank told him about his childhood, the divorce of his parents, living on modest means with his grandparents, being raised with Catholic values, his World War II service, and the events leading to his involvement with and against Castro. Dr Steinfeld then offered this analysis of Frank's motivation:

> In talking about himself and discussing the possible reasons why he chose this kind of life of intelligence, espionage, penetration behind enemy lines, constantly placing himself in danger, he talked about the excitement, the feelings of mastery and the feeling of dedication to a cause. He was able to relate this back to feelings of insecurity that he experienced at a very young age. He talked about hero worship, the need to *be* [emphasis in original] the hero, the guy who gets the gal, and he seemed to have lived out this kind of existence. As mentioned, however, there was a kind of concern for the suffering of less fortunate people. This identification with underprivileged he attributed to the early training he received at a Catholic school. This sensitivity seems to be covered up by the aggressive, up-front kind of stance he has taken and a life where he has flirted with danger and finally gotten caught up in it as to lead to the present consequences . . . He placed himself in the hands of people he trusted, and he feels that if he needs to pay the consequences, then he would be willing to do that. Nevertheless, he feels used by those he trusted.[44]

The full report of the probation department's second PSI, including the psychological profile, was completed on July 2, 1973, and sent to Judge Sirica with a letter dated July 13, 1973, from Norman Carlson, director of the U.S. Bureau of Prisons.[45] As with the first PSI, there was detailed information about Frank's family, his military service record, his job history, and the Castro connection. As with the first PSI, Frank was found to have a strong and loving relationship with Janet and his stepdaughter—"The marriage continues intact and it is expected that it will remain so." Regarding Frank's proclivity for criminal behavior, the probation department found, "Mr. Sturgis is essentially a first offender" and "is not considered a criminally oriented individual and this can be seen as his first serious departure from the law." Frank was "friendly, gregarious and cooperative" during his interaction with the staff at Danbury and those doing the evaluation. As for the burglary, Frank was "fairly candid in detailing his participation." He told them how Barker had asked him to participate due to the suspicion that Castro was providing money to the Democrats. He understood that their mission "was sanctioned by very highly placed government officials and being done in the interests of national security." He said that E. Howard Hunt's involvement convinced him that theirs was a legal covert activity. Because of Frank's "long involvement in covert activities, the fact that he was asked to participate in what *might* be seen as an illegal act was not interpreted as an illegal act on his part."[46] Psychologically Frank was found to be "a fairly healthy individual" who would require little or no support services during any period of probation.

Based upon the "study" requested by Judge Sirica, the probation department concluded, "Mr. Sturgis is seen as an individual who would not be a custody risk and should function adequately in a camp or minimum security institution . . . Should a period of probation be considered, there is little reason to suspect that Mr. Sturgis could not function under this supervision."[47] As noted above, Judge Sirica received this report shortly after July 13, 1973. However, he took no action. The only thing Frank and his fellow burglars had not yet done was to testify before Senator Ervin's committee; they had already been in front of the grand jury that was pursuing criminal indictments. Frank and the others would have been more than happy to appear before Senator Ervin's committee that summer, but at that point the committee's focus was on the cover-up perpetrated by various Nixon aides, and Frank had nothing to offer or add to that issue. The earliest the committee could schedule them was during the week of September 12. In the meantime, Frank would continue to be held in the medium security facility at Danbury.

On August 22, 1973, while waiting to testify before Senator Ervin's committee, Frank got word that he had been indicted by a federal grand jury in Miami for conspiracy to steal cars and transport them to Mexico for sale. The criminal charges were the product of a federal prosecutor in Miami, William Northcutt, who appeared to be trying to find some way to be involved in Watergate. The indictments were filed one day before expiration of the statute of limitations and arose from Frank's last major operation against Castro in 1968, when Frank and two other anti-Castro fighters, Jerry Buchanan and Max Gonzalez, organized a group to launch a mission from Mexico to highjack a Russian freighter and try to exchange it for the USS *Pueblo*, a Navy intelligence ship being held by the communist North Koreans. Frank had advertised in newspapers for "adventurers" to participate in the mission. The ads attracted a lot of weird people, including a man who had no legs—"Just throw me on a horse," he said, "I'll lead the charge"—prompting Janet to dub the group "Fiorini's fuck-ups." It wasn't until a few years after the failure of the mission that Frank found out that several of his "troops" had driven two rental cars from the United States into Mexico and sold them for "drinking and gambling money."[48] Unknown to Frank, one of them had previously been convicted of a similar offense. Federal investigators had decided not to pursue charges until the notoriety of Watergate put Frank on the front page. Frank hired his friend and Miami attorney Ellis Rubin to represent him. As Rubin told the press, "If it had not been for Watergate, this case would never have gone to the grand jury for indictment."[49] The case was set for trial before U.S. district court judge C. Clyde Atkins in Miami on October 12, 1973.

During the second week of September 1973, Frank and his codefendants were transported by U.S. Marshals in a van from Danbury to the federal prison at Rockville, Maryland, and then to the old DC Jail. Under the grant of use immunity received from Judge Sirica, they testified before Senator Ervin's committee. According to a letter dated September 19, 1973, to Judge Sirica from Samuel Dash, who was chief counsel of the committee, Frank, Barker, Martinez, and González had "manifested their willingness to cooperate with the Committee." He went on to say, "Senator Weicker, who personally has spent more than ten hours interviewing these four individuals since the conclusion of the Committee's first phase of hearings in August, is particularly of the opinion that these men have cooperated with the Committee."[50] Additionally, Judge Sirica ordered Chief Probation Officer George W. Howard and his deputy, Frank Saunders, to re-interview Frank and the others. The interviews were conducted with the defendants as a group because of "the number of inconsistencies that had occurred in the past." The memo is divided into three sections—"planning phase," "operational phase," and "cover-up." Each of the burglars confirmed their belief that Hunt was recruiting them for a national security mission sanctioned by the White House. Again, they said that their motivation for breaking into the Watergate was Hunt's assurance that they were looking for evidence that Castro was giving money to the Democrats. Martinez finally openly admitted being on the CIA payroll while working for Hunt and the Plumbers. He continued to regularly receive biweekly checks in "unmarked envelopes" issued in the names of various CIA front companies. According to the Howard/Saunders memo to Judge Sirica, Martinez said he found it "inconceivable to believe that the CIA was not aware of his activities with Hunt."[51]

The evidence shows that Martinez is absolutely correct on this point. In sworn testimony before the House Select Committee on Assassinations on November 3, 1978, E. Howard Hunt revealed that he had ongoing contact with CIA employees during the time leading up to the Watergate break-in. "Yes, I sent occasional things to the CIA."[52] The CIA had supplied the disguises and the false identity documents Frank and the others received from Hunt just before the second break-in at the Watergate.

The "group" interview of the defendants conducted by Saunders and Howard did not include McCord. They therefore asked Frank and the others whether they thought McCord was a "double agent" who along with Baldwin "was working for the Democrats." In response, Martinez said that it was McCord who wanted to tape the doors at Watergate even though they did not have to do that with the first break-in because González was an expert lock-pick. When Frank and González made the initial entry into Watergate and radioed back that the tape was missing, Martinez and Frank wanted to abort the mission. McCord said "they had nothing to worry about" and it "was McCord and not Hunt who gave the final order that the mission would go ahead."[53] McCord was also the one who "took charge and gave them advice as to what they were to do," after they were caught. Based on all this, Saunders and Howard concluded that "none of the group could accept the possibility" that McCord was a double agent, "but now they [were] putting some of these items together and beginning to wonder themselves."[54]

As proof of their belief that the CIA had sanctioned the break-in, Barker stated during the interview by Saunders that after being released on bail in June 1972 and returning to his home in Miami he "received a telephone call from someone unknown to him." This person instructed Barker to go to the airport on the following day, where he would be met by "someone you know." The contact turned out to be Hunt's wife, Dorothy, whom Barker had previously suspected of being a CIA agent. Barker said that Hunt had told him that he met Dorothy "when they were both spies in China." According to Saunders and Howard, "everyone was quite convinced that Dorothy was the brains in the family so it is quite conceivable that she was working for the CIA." At that first meeting, Dorothy gave Barker a plain white envelope that contained $18,000 in cash. Until her death in December 1972 Barker received a total of "almost $50,000 from her." Barker said that just prior to their trial in January 1972, Hunt advised them that he was going to plead guilty and that they were "in a different sector and they have a different plan."[55] Barker and the others interpreted this to mean that they should also plead guilty. "Hunt did tell them that this was a decision which they must make on their own, but he had so convinced them that this was a mission of utmost security to the interests of the United States that they felt compelled to follow his leadership." They "assumed" that they would be taken care of "because they were working for the government."[56] However, by September 1973, when this third pre-sentence investigation report was sent to Judge Sirica, there was "an open split between these men and

Hunt." Hunt apparently stated point-blank that he had absolutely no interest in the men or what happened to them. Saunders and Howard ended the memo with the following statement:

> I sincerely hope that this draws some of the loose ends together in this most difficult and perplexing case. In effect, the men did plead guilty because of the psychological pressure exerted by Hunt and their belief that they were still working for the CIA.[57]

With the receipt of this third pre-sentence investigation report from Saunders and Howard, Judge Sirica had proof and confirmation that Frank and the others had cooperated fully with the grand jury and the Ervin Committee in testifying about their involvement in Watergate. They were candid and held nothing back, remembering that Judge Sirica had told them at the March 1973 sentencing that their degree of cooperation would go a long way in determining their final sentences. By September, when their attorney filed the motion to withdraw their guilty pleas, they had come to believe that they had been duped by the government they thought they were serving. In particular, Frank felt that the CIA, the organization he had done contract work for over the years, had betrayed him.

As mentioned above, Dan Schultz filed the motions to withdraw the pleas on September 14, 1973. With the motion, Judge Sirica required him to file detailed affidavits (sworn statements) from each of the defendants explaining why they had a good faith belief that they were doing legitimate government work at Watergate. (The same affidavits rescued from Schultz's briefcase.) Sirica scheduled a hearing on the motion for November 5, 1973, and indicated that he would exercise his discretion to not allow the defendants to testify but would decide based on the affidavits and the legal arguments of counsel, all of which would be part of the public court record. However, because these probation reports were kept in the judge's personal file, the conclusion reached by Saunders and Howard—that Frank and his fellow burglars believed in good faith that their mission was government sanctioned and top secret and for those reasons elected to plead guilty rather than disclose classified information—would not be filed in the criminal case or become an official part of the record, and Judge Sirica was free to ignore the PSIs with impunity. He scheduled final sentencing to take place on November 12, 1973.

While awaiting sentencing and the ruling on the motion to withdraw the guilty pleas, in mid-October Frank was taken by the U.S. Marshals to Miami for trial on the federal charges of conspiracy and transportation of stolen automobiles arising out of the 1968 mission in Mexico to ransom the *Pueblo*. Also charged were Jerry Buchanan and Max Gonzalez, longtime friends of Frank's who, over the years, had helped in the fight against Castro. The prosecutor presented three witnesses who testified that they each drove cars into Mexico, where they were sold in connection with the mission that Frank had organized to rescue the *Pueblo*. Frank's lawyer, Ellis Rubin, rested after the prosecution's case without presenting any evidence. He argued in closing that the government had simply failed to prove its case beyond a reasonable doubt as required by the law. The argument must have been effective because on October 20, 1973, after hours of deliberation, the jury informed Judge Atkins that they were deadlocked and therefore unable to render a unanimous verdict. As a result, Judge Atkins declared a mistrial. In criminal defense circles, a mistrial can be as good as an acquittal, especially if the prosecutor decides not to refile the charges. Unfortunately for Frank, the case was refiled, and on November 29, 1973, a jury of five women and seven men convicted Frank of conspiracy and illegally transporting stolen cars. Sentencing was scheduled for January 9, 1974, and Frank was sent to Eglin Air Force Base, which housed a minimum security federal prison in northern Florida, to continue serving the sentence he had received for Watergate.

Because Frank did not testify at either of the auto theft trials, his side of the story did not become public until in an April 1974 column political reporter Jack Anderson concluded that it was a "bum rap." Frank reiterated that he had no idea that three of the people who responded to his ads for "adventurers" had criminal records, including having served prison time for car theft. They were angry at Frank because the mission had failed and they had not been paid. Also, they were given immunity from prosecution in exchange for their testimony against Frank. Frank did tell the recruits that they would not get paid until the completion of the mission and suggested that they could raise money by driving their own cars into Mexico, where they could be sold for more than their value in the United States. Frank said they could use the profit to cover their expenses before being paid for their work with him and would still have cash to buy another car after the mission was over. However, at no time during the mission did Frank tell anyone to steal cars to sell in Mexico or know that they had done so. While Frank may have been resourceful in financing his various exploits against Castro, he never resorted to illegal schemes to raise money, except for the gambling tax money he skimmed from the Havana casino owners to use in his planned war against Castro and communism.

November 1973 was a watershed month for Frank. He was convicted of two felonies in Miami, and he would receive his final sentence from Judge Sirica unless the judge was willing to let him withdraw his guilty plea. As noted, the lawyers argued the motions on November 5, and two days later, without any written opinion or explanation, Judge Sirica issued an order denying the motions. He did shed some light on his reasoning thereafter when he filed "a statement of reasons for denying bail pending sentencing."

> [Judge Sirica] . . . noted that an extensive voir dire [cross-examination] was conducted before the guilty pleas were accepted; that the pleas were based on the Government's contentions in opening argument which furnished "ample evidence to conclude that there existed a factual basis" for the pleas; that appellants had been represented throughout by competent counsel; and that the motion to withdraw came many months after the pleas were entered.[58]

Dan Schultz appealed this ruling to the D.C. Circuit Court of Appeals. In the meantime, Judge Sirica proceeded with sentencing Frank and the others on November 12, 1973. He gave Barker eighteen months to six years, and Frank, Martinez, and González received one to four years each. McCord got one to five years. Each defendant would receive credit for time served. These final sentences were certainly more reasonable than the provisional sentences had been. Even so, given the fact that all the evidence from the PSIs showed that Frank and the others had cooperated fully with the ongoing investigations and were not hardened criminals or security risks, a sentence of time served would have been more appropriate. However, in addition to his reputation as a hanging judge, Judge Sirica was obviously angry because Frank and the other burglars had lied to him when he grilled them at the time of their guilty pleas. He saw this as impeding him from "getting to the bottom of Watergate," though, at the time, there were those who criticized Judge Sirica "for using the provisional-sentencing procedure as a device to get the defendants to cooperate with investigators." Chesterfield Smith, then president of the American Bar Association, said, "We must be concerned about a federal judge—no matter how worthy his motives or how much we may applaud the results—using the criminal-sentencing process as a means and a tool for further criminal investigation of others."[59] Other legal scholars compared his sentencing tactic to "the torture rack and the Spanish Inquisition" and stated, "Sirica deserves to be censured for becoming the prosecutor himself."[60] Even President Nixon was sympathetic to the plight of Frank and the others. He called them "these poor bastards," and told his aide Bob Haldeman, "God damn it, if they'd been communists you'd have the *Washington Post* and the *New York Times* raising hell about their civil rights."[61] Despite these concerns, *Time* magazine named Judge Sirica their Man of the Year for 1974 because of his judicial aggressiveness in the Watergate cases. It is, of course, ironic that those who believed that President Nixon and his kind had committed criminal and unethical acts would excuse dispensing with the constitutional rights of Frank and his fellow burglars to solve the riddle of Watergate—a classic example of the ends justifying the means. On the other hand, Judge Sirica deserves credit for his handling of the Nixon tapes issue. He correctly rejected the president's claim of executive privilege, thereby forcing Nixon to turn over the tapes to the Watergate prosecutor. In so doing, Judge Sirica was acting properly within his powers as a judge interpreting the applicable laws and issuing an order directing the president to comply, reinforcing the basic belief that ours is a government of laws and not men.

The appeal that Dan Schultz filed after Judge Sirica's refusal to allow Frank and the others to withdraw their guilty pleas was argued in the D.C. Circuit Court of Appeals on June 14, 1974. The case was heard by the court *en banc*—meaning that all seven judges would participate in the decision rather than just a panel of three judges. This type of treatment is reserved for cases involving "questions of exceptional importance."[62] In a decision published on February 25, 1975, five members of the court ruled that Judge Sirica had properly denied the motions. Two judges wrote dissents. The majority opinion by Judge James Skelly Wright noted that courts are generally inclined to grant such motions so as to be "fair and just." This is especially true when, as here, the motion to withdraw is filed before the judge has imposed the final sentence. However, the court was critical of the fact that there was a delay of eight months between the guilty pleas in January 1973 and the filing of the motions in September of that year. To allow pleas of not guilty at that point and force the government to reassemble and prove its case would be "prejudicial." Of greater importance to the majority was the fact that Frank and the others had lied—albeit to protect the CIA—to Judge Sirica when he grilled them at the guilty plea hearing. They found this to be a "flagrant abuse of the judicial process."[63] Instead of lying to protect their belief that they were involved in a legitimate national security operation, they should have gone to Judge Sirica before trial and disclosed what they thought was classified information. They failed to do that, so the guilty pleas and subsequent convictions were upheld.

Two judges, George MacKinnon and Malcolm Wilkey, dissented and would have allowed the guilty pleas to be withdrawn. To them, the defendants legitimately believed that they were carrying out a government sanctioned mission. As Judge Wilkey stated,

> They pled guilty because they believed national security interests precluded them from disclosing the nature of their activities, and because they interpreted the guilty plea of their supervisor, Hunt, as a directive that they follow the same course of action. Few facts were revealed in the months immediately following their pleas of 15 January, 1973 which could have given them reason to believe their assessment was incorrect.[64]

The other dissenter, Judge MacKinnon, agreed and noted that it took eight months following the guilty pleas for the true nature of Watergate to become manifest. It was not until August 1973 that Senator Ervin's committee heard testimony regarding Liddy's Gemstone plan as the genesis for Watergate. Once this became public, Frank and the co-defendants came to believe that they had been "duped" and that Watergate was a political operation, not a matter of national security. In light of this, an eight-month delay in filing the motion was excusable and explainable. As far as the fact that they lied to Judge Sirica and did not take him into their confidence, both dissenters found that the lies were not malicious and were, in fact, totally consistent with the defendants' belief that national security required them to not disclose whatever details they knew about the operation. Judge MacKinnon did not share the majority's belief that the defendants should have confessed all to Judge Sirica. "A federal judge is not necessarily any more to be trusted with, or authorized to receive, top secret material affecting national security than is any other unauthorized person."[65] He spoke highly of the defendants and their participation in the anti-Castro and anti-communism efforts over the years:

> All were, and are, bitter opponents of the Castro regime. They blame the Communists for the loss of their homes and livelihood. They exhibit a single-minded dedication to the cause of eradicating Communism in Cuba and preventing the spread of Communism in this country. They were willing in 1972 to give their full cooperation to any government operation which they believed was directed against traitors to this country or aiders and abettors of the Castro regime. . . . All but Gonzalez had taken part in the Bay of Pigs affair. Barker and Martinez were in the employment of the CIA even before that operation, and continued working for the Agency thereafter. (Indeed, Martinez was still working for the CIA and receiving a salary up until the night of his arrest in connection with the break-in.) They have known each other for over thirty years. Gonzalez is a longtime friend of Martinez's and was familiar with the CIA connections of his colleagues. He and Sturgis both had worked clandestinely against the Castro regime since its inception. They form a close-knit group bound by ties of personal friendship and common interest. Above all, they are loyal to each other, and to the cause of fighting Communism, in this country as well as in their native land.[66]

The dissenting judges therefore concluded that the defendants should be allowed to enter not guilty pleas and proceed to trial on the affirmative defense of good faith reliance on apparent authority. Unfortunately, they were never given this opportunity. If they had been, there is a good likelihood that a jury would have found Frank and his co-defendants not guilty. The evidence was overwhelming that Hunt and Liddy led Frank and the rest to believe that their work was sanctioned and legal. Hunt and Liddy were both working directly out of the White House. "They were told only that Hunt had information that Cuban Communist money was going into the Democratic campaign and that they were to photograph documents which would be analyzed to obtain evidence of this fact. Again, fake identification papers were provided by the CIA. The appellants had no reason to doubt Hunt's authority."[67]

Although Frank's Watergate conviction would stand, Dan Schultz had an opportunity to raise this affirmative defense again during the prosecution of Barker and Martinez for the break-in at Dr. Fielding's office. The case went to trial in July 1974, before Judge Gerhard Gesell of the D.C. District Court, the same court where Judge Sirica sat. The government's chief witness was E. Howard Hunt, whose testimony established beyond a reasonable doubt that Dr. Fielding's civil rights had been violated by an illegal break-in. Schultz asked Judge Gesell to allow him to present evidence about the defendants' good faith reliance on Hunt and Liddy's authority, but the judge refused to do so. This is the same type of defense Schultz would have used in Frank's Watergate case. Without the availability of this defense, the jury convicted Martinez and Barker. Schultz filed an appeal with the same appellate court that had rejected Frank's case and gave oral arguments on June 18, 1975, about three months after the court's decision in the Watergate case. This time the appeal was heard by a three-judge panel and not *en banc*. In a two-to-one decision, the court reversed and vacated the convictions of Barker and Martinez and remanded them back to the District Court for a new trial, at which they would be allowed to present their good faith reliance on apparent authority defense.[68] It should not be surprising that it was Judge Wilkey, one of the dissenters in Frank's Watergate appeal, who wrote the majority opinion and concluded that "a citizen should have a legal defense to a criminal charge arising out of an unlawful arrest or search which he has aided in the reasonable belief that the individual who solicited his assistance was a duly authorized officer of the law."[69] As it turned out, faced with having to deal with what appeared to be a good affirmative defense, the Watergate prosecutor decided to dismiss the case against Barker and Martinez and not refile the charges.

Looking back over these legal proceedings, Judge Sirica's real reasons for not allowing Frank to use the good faith reliance defense were twofold. First and foremost, he took great exception to the fact that Frank and the others had lied to him. In his book, *To Set the Record Straight,* he praises McCord for writing the letter that "broke the dam" of Watergate and furthered the judge's aim to get to the bottom of it. By lying about what they thought was the true nature of their mission, Frank and the other burglars impeded these efforts. The last thing Judge Sirica wanted to do was reward them for what he saw as duplicity. The majority in the Court of Appeals that upheld Judge Sirica's ruling was equally sanctimonious about the lying, which was characterized as a "flagrant abuse of the legal process." The other reason Judge Sirica overruled the motion was that by the time it was filed he had his hands full with other Watergate issues and prosecutions arising from the cover-up by Nixon and his aides and Nixon's refusal to honor the subpoena for the White House tapes issued by the prosecutor. More than thirty Nixon government officials, most of whom were tried by Judge Sirica, were ultimately convicted of various crimes. On August 9, 1974, President Nixon resigned. These are the things that Judge Sirica talks about in his book. He does not even mention or address the motion to withdraw the guilty pleas or why he overruled it. By the time the motion was filed, Judge Sirica had already gotten what he needed from Frank and the others by violating their constitutional rights and imposing maximum provisional sentences of fifty years, not just as a way to coerce them to talk but also as an example to others involved in Watergate who would be testifying during the ongoing probe.

Following the final sentencing on November 12, 1973, Frank continued to be held at the federal prison in Rockville, Maryland, and was then transported to Miami for the retrial of the auto theft conspiracy case at the end of the month. In the week prior to sentencing by Judge Sirica, he and the others had again testified before the Senate Watergate Committee. While he was incarcerated Janet wrote to him every day and he responded almost as frequently. He wrote about his Watergate Committee appearance in a letter dated November 10, 1973, just two days before final sentencing. He noted how well they were treated by the U.S. Marshals, who were "fascinated" by Frank's soldier of fortune lifestyle that predated his Watergate involvement. The marshals were nice enough to not use handcuffs or leg irons and even got coffee for the defendants. Frank testified from 10:30 A.M. until 2:45 P.M. Later, their attorney, Schultz, was allowed to take them to dinner Frank wrote to Janet, "We all had a large delicious steak and french fries. I drank a bottle of Coke. Honey, it was fabulous." When you're locked up in prison, little things like a tasty meal mean a lot.

He closed the letter by telling Janet that he was happy with the job Schultz had done for them and that there was a good chance he would be able to ask for parole when the board met in December at Eglin Air Force Base in the Florida panhandle. He told her how much he loved her and missed everyone, including "the animals." At that time, "the animals" consisted of two cats and two cocker spaniels, a female, Abigail, and a male, Chulo. Abigail was a totally pampered dog that Janet got as a puppy when she lived with her first husband in Brooklyn in the 1950s. Abigail was a registered purebred and did not eat regular dog food; rather, Janet would prepare special meals for her. Abigail was never spayed, and in 1962, at ten years of age, she somehow got loose and mated with another cocker spaniel. Her one and only offspring was Chulo, who was named by Frank. "Chulo" is a dirty Cuban slang term for a person who is "somewhere between a pimp and a whore, only worse." Frank never did explain why he chose this particular name for the dog, but for him it was a term of endearment; Frank truly loved his dog.

Following his conviction on the auto conspiracy charges on November 29, 1973, Frank and the other burglars were transferred to the federal minimum security facility at Eglin Air Force Base in northern Florida. Compared to Danbury and the DC Jail, Eglin was a veritable "Club Fed." No fences, no lockdowns, decent food, and plenty of recreation. Frank sent Janet copies of the prison weekly newspaper, *The Gazette,* which circulated to the 520 prisoners being held when Frank was there. The articles and information in the newspaper offer insight into the daily life of the prisoners. The weekly TV schedule shows that

they had their choice of three different channels showing such programs as *Hogan's Heroes, Perry Mason,* and *Mannix,* and movies such
as *The Secret of Convict Lake* and *In Cold Blood.* The menu for the
week is listed; a typical day's meals included "juice/cereals/oatmeal/
blueberry pancakes/coffee cake with topping" for breakfast, "onion
soup/fried fish/grits/macaroni with cheese/Jell-o/cornbread/vegetables"
for lunch, and "soup/swiss steak/whipped potatoes/squash and vege-
tables/iced brownies, etc." for dinner. The menu contains the reminder
"Coffee, cream, bread, butter, cold beverage, assorted salads at all
meals."

The November 30, 1973, edition of *The Gazette* contains several
pages of articles written in Spanish. One of them offers "Bienvenidos"—
"Welcome"—to Barker, Martinez, and González. Frank is not mentioned because he, of course was not Cuban. Barker et al are praised as
"great patriotic fighters accomplishing heroic feats" in "la causa Cu-
bana." During the interview of Macho Barker in 2007, he said he was
pretty miserable at Eglin. They made him work outdoors harvesting
vegetables in a short-sleeved shirt when the weather was cold, which
he claimed made him ill. He thought the guard who made him work
under these conditions "was probably a Democrat." There is another
explanation in one of Frank's letters to Janet. He wrote that Barker
"put this place down in front of one of the hacks. It was a bad move."
He also mentioned that Macho's face was disfigured due to Bell's palsy,
a usually temporary neurological disorder that can paralyze one side
of the face, making the person look like they suffered a stroke. No
wonder Macho was in such misery.

Along with the menu, TV schedule, and various inspirational articles, the November 30 edition contains an astrology column with
horoscopes offered for each of the signs and a "Spotlight on Sagittarius," which was Frank's sign:

"Symbolized by the Centaur, half horse, half man. Being a dual
sign, Sagittarians tend to have two personalities . . . Sagittarius is one
of the mutable signs in that it blends wisdom with understanding. Key
word for Sagittarius is inspiration."

All in all, this is a pretty accurate description of Frank and his personality. He always tried to keep separate his soldier of fortune life from his role as a family man. Watergate was one of the few times when the former significantly intruded into the latter. Frank's specific horoscope for the week of November 30 was prophetic—"New moon hitting you, making your personality shine. Things are looking up as you discover talents you never knew you had before." Frank appeared before the parole board during the middle of December and must have done an impressive job because on the twenty-eighth the board decided to grant his request for release on parole under the supervision of the probation department. However, Frank continued to be held because he was waiting to be sentenced by Judge Atkins in Miami for his conviction in the auto theft case. He was transported there by the marshals on Saturday, January 7, 1974, and appeared for sentencing on that Monday. Judge Atkins gave him nine months on each of the two counts to run concurrent with each other but consecutive to his Watergate sentence. Janet was in the court room and got to see Frank for the first time in over a year. The *Miami Herald* reported, "The marshals permitted the couple to kiss briefly before Sturgis was led back to a holding cell in the federal courthouse."[70] Because Frank's lawyer, Ellis Rubin, was appealing the conviction, Judge Atkins allowed Frank to be freed on bond in the meantime. Within hours Frank was released to his waiting wife. She expressed her feelings to a *Miami Herald* reporter who wrote an article, "Sleeping Beauty Wakes Up Tonight." Janet said that she felt like she had been in a trance and looked forward to waking up with a kiss from her "prince charming." At home she fixed Frank his favorite non-Italian meal—broiled steak and a baked potato. For dessert Frank had another favorite—vanilla cream soda over chocolate ice cream.

Although the appeal of Frank's Miami conviction was ultimately denied, Judge Atkins later agreed to reduce the sentence to time served. Frank remained out on parole for Watergate until July 11, 1975, when Judge Sirica granted a motion filed by Schultz to reduce the Watergate sentences of Frank, Barker, González, and Martinez to time served, officially ending Frank's punishment for Watergate. Three years later, in 1978, Frank applied for a pardon from President Jimmy Carter. That same year President Carter had used the pardon power to free G. Gordon Liddy from the prison term he was serving. During his presidency, Jimmy Carter granted a record 536 pardons, but Frank's was not among them. In preparation for this book we wrote to President Carter asking if he could recall why he turned Frank down. The former president was kind enough to reply and candidly stated that he did not remember Frank's request. This is not surprising, since all pardon requests go through a screening process in the Justice Department and many of them do not even reach the president's desk. Frank never did renew his request during subsequent administrations, though in 1986, his lawyer Ellis Rubin filed a motion requesting a new Watergate trial based upon a claim that FBI investigators had failed to find any "bugs" at the DNC offices other than one that was a fake and could have been planted by the Democrats to keep the case alive during the 1972 presidential race.[71] Rubin also argued in his brief that "John J. Sirica, now dead, coerced Mr. Sturgis and his co-defendants into guilty pleas." In fact, Judge Sirica was still very much alive, as he told a UPI reporter. Not surprisingly, Rubin's motion for a new trial was turned down. Frank's Watergate conviction would stand. Of the forty-plus people caught up in the Watergate debacle, only two ever received presidential pardons— former president Nixon, pardoned by his successor, Gerald Ford, within the month following the resignation, and Rolando Martinez, whose petition was granted by President Reagan. Nixon's pardon was negotiated before he left office and was probably the right thing to do. Otherwise, the nation would have faced a potential political and governmental crisis due to the impeachment proceedings that were in the works for Nixon. The resignation and pardon allowed this country to move beyond Watergate. Martinez certainly deserved his pardon. He had been a loyal longtime CIA agent and was a true patriot. The same can be said for Frank, who remains a convicted felon for participating in what he thought was a legal national security mission.

Even former president Nixon acknowledged the legitimacy of this mistaken belief. He told interviewer David Frost in 1978, "If the President says 'do it,' that makes it legal, doesn't it?"

In addition to representing Frank and the other Watergate burglars in the criminal case, Dan Schultz filed a civil action for damages against CREEP based upon the same legal theory—good faith reliance on apparent authority—he attempted to use in their defense. The trial was scheduled to begin in Washington, D.C., on February 24, 1977, but the day before, they reached a financial settlement requiring CREEP to pay $200,000 in damages. The majority of the money went to Schultz for his legal services, with no complaints from the defendants. As Martinez told the *Miami Herald,* "The money is not the important thing. In fact, I don't think I'm going to get a penny. Money, money, money. Proving one's innocence in this country is expensive."[72] After payment of legal fees, Frank and the others received approximately $15,000 each. The attorney who represented CREEP and negotiated the settlement, Richard Galiher, on his own volition wrote a letter supporting Frank's pardon request, which was still pending with President Carter. In that letter of June 28, 1977, to the U.S. pardon attorney, Lawrence M. Traylor, Galiher stated:

> I took the depositions of these men in Miami prior to working out a settlement. On the basis of the depositions of these men, other depositions which were taken, and my own investigation, I reached the conclusion that these men were misled, that they were acting, they believed, in the service of duly authorized representatives of our government and consequently I worked out a fair settlement of their damages.[73]

Despite this support, Frank's pardon application was denied. It was actually the second time Frank had made such a request, the first having been submitted to President Ford, who had pardoned Nixon. Frank was especially bitter toward Ford for not granting a pardon. "He pardoned that traitor Tokyo Rose and here I have three honorable discharges and two Purple Hearts." Throughout the rest of his life

Frank remained a patriotic, loyal American, but his Watergate experience left him disillusioned, especially with the CIA. After Watergate, Frank refused to do any more contract missions for the CIA.

After his release, Frank was extremely careful about not doing anything illegal, while at the same time carrying on the fight against Castro and Communism. On a personal level, Frank did not think he deserved any ridicule or criticism for the botched job that was Watergate. President Nixon's press secretary, Ron Ziegler, dismissed the break-in as "a third-rate burglary"; Frank and the others were described as "Watergate bunglers." Frank pointed out that he and Martinez wanted to abort the fateful mission due to the tape's not being on the door. If the others had listened to Frank and Martinez, they would not have been caught that night. However, because Frank and the burglars thought McCord was a double agent, it was probably just a matter of time before they would have been caught doing something. Frank believed that the break-in itself had been hatched by individuals in the CIA who were concerned that Nixon was becoming too powerful and too easily influenced in foreign affairs by special interest groups.[74] Frank also thought that much of the tension between Nixon and the CIA had to do with certain CIA classified files, particularly those dealing with JFK's assassination that Nixon had requested. "Nixon was lucky he wasn't killed—assassinated like President Kennedy." Instead, Frank said individuals in the CIA worked through Hunt and Liddy to foment the break-in scheme and then deliberately sabotaged it through their "mole" McCord so as to discredit Nixon and his administration. All of these claims were, of course, denied by the CIA. There is no question that in the year before Watergate, Nixon requested a number of CIA secret files. The Rockefeller Commission concluded in 1975 that Nixon asked for "highly classified files relating to the Lebanon landings, the Bay of Pigs, the Cuban missile crisis, and the Vietnam War."[75] These were supposedly turned over, but only after CIA director Richard Helms conducted an "internal review" to assess the possible impact of declassifying them for Nixon. That certain files were turned over to Nixon cannot be doubted. Whether they underwent significant editing by the CIA before disclosure is a legitimate question. It was Helms who, after being asked by Senator Mike Mansfield in January 1973 to preserve any and all evidence pertaining to Watergate so as to assist in the Senate investigation, decided to destroy all tapes of conversations in his office and in two conference rooms that had been maintained over the prior three years in a taping system similar to the one in Nixon's White House.[76] Helms obviously had something to hide. There is no reason to believe that Helms would have willingly turned over information that might be critical of the CIA to President Nixon.

The Rockefeller Commission concluded that Nixon had improperly asked for these files to use for his own political ends. He apparently hoped to find information that would be damaging to previous Democratic presidents. However, there are those, including Frank, who believe that there was a more sinister struggle going on, having to do with the possible involvement of the CIA in the assassination of President Kennedy. They believe that the file designated "Bay of Pigs" actually contained this information. This observation has been seconded by Nixon's top aide, Bob Haldeman, who said that when Nixon talked on the White House tapes about the Watergate investigation opening up "the whole Bay of Pigs thing" he was understood to be talking about the Kennedy assassination material, not just the ill-fated invasion attempt. As we will discuss in chapter 14, Frank believed that there was participation by agents of the CIA in the assassination. He pointed out that the CIA had recruited heavily and not always carefully from the Cuban exiles in Miami in 1960 and '61. Frank believed that some of them were double agents actually working covertly for Castro.

If, in fact, the CIA had classified information implicating its employees in the assassination plot, one can understand the reluctance to disclose it. It is also understandable that, under these circumstances, people in the CIA would do what they could to discredit and neutralize President Nixon to prevent disclosure. Frank believed that the actual genesis of the Watergate break-in came from agents in the

CIA. On the other hand, the historical record shows the plot was probably hatched by Nixon and his kind to further their political aim of dominating the Democrats. Upon learning of these plans, certain individuals in the CIA simply seized the opportunity to go after Nixon. In 2003 Haldeman stated publicly that President Nixon knew all along about the planned break-ins and approved them. From Nixon's standpoint he was just carrying out the political espionage that both parties engaged in to varying degrees.

There is substantial evidence proving that individuals in the CIA knew a lot more about Watergate than was ever admitted publicly. Some of the evidence is contained in various documents that the CIA declassified and made available in June 2007. With great fanfare the CIA announced the release of files and documents code-named "Family Jewels" listing potentially illegal and clandestine activities going back to the 1960s or, as described by the CIA, "situations or associations that might appear to be irregular on the surface."[77] However, of the 693 pages that were released, well over half of them have been completely expurgated. These documents may be of more interest for what has been erased than what is disclosed. Further, much of this information had previously been produced for the Rockefeller Commission in 1975 and is discussed in chapter 14 of the report, "Involvement of the CIA in Improper Activities for the White House," which has been declassified and made available to the public for a number of years. Both of these sources detail the contacts that Hunt and McCord (both ex–CIA employees) had with people in the CIA in the year leading up to Watergate. In early July 1971, after Hunt had been hired by Nixon to head up the Plumbers, White House aide John Ehrlichman called the deputy director of the CIA, General Robert Cushman, and asked the CIA to help Hunt with "a highly sensitive mission" involving national security.[78] Thereafter, on July 23, 1971, at Cushman's direction, the CIA gave Hunt various "alias" documents including driver's licenses, social security cards, and membership cards in the names of Edward Joseph Warren and Edward V. Hamilton. Hunt was also given a wig, glasses, and a voice-altering device. At a subsequent meeting with the CIA, Hunt was given a commercial Tessina camera disguised as a tobacco pouch and a commercial tape recorder. On one of the visits, Liddy was with him and received a wig, glasses, and alias documents in the name of George F. Leonard.[79] After obtaining the camera, Hunt and Liddy traveled to Los Angeles to "case" the office of Dr. Fielding, Ellsberg's psychiatrist. On August 27, 1971, Hunt gave the film to the CIA's technical division for processing, which they did even though Hunt was no longer employed by the "Company." Some of the photos clearly depicted Dr Fielding's name and office address. Before giving the prints back to Hunt, someone at the CIA made Xerox copies and put them in a file marked "Mr. Hamilton," Hunt's CIA alias.[80] There is no documentation of who, if anyone besides the person processing the film, saw these photos at that time or looked into them to find out what Hunt was up to.

Certain people at the CIA supposedly became "concerned" because of the assistance that was being given to Hunt, who they thought was involved in domestic issues and therefore not within the jurisdiction of the CIA. Under Section 102 of the National Security Act of 1947, subparagraph (D)(3), "The agency shall have no police, subpoena, law enforcement power or internal security functions." This was probably a legitimate concern because the contact with Hunt was just one of a number of domestic operations the CIA had been involved in. As early as 1962, the CIA tapped the telephones of several U.S. newspaper reporters at the request of then–attorney general and brother of the president, Bobby Kennedy. In the 1970s the CIA actively engaged in spying on radical groups in the United States, particularly those promoting black minority interests like the Black Panthers. The Agency spied on and kept files on such youth icons as Beatle John Lennon. A February 23, 1972, memo notes that Lennon had been giving financial aid to Project Yes to support antiwar activities.[81]

CIA documents in the "Family Jewels" indicate that on August 27, 1971, the very same day that Hunt gave the CIA the Fielding film, General Cushman called Ehrlichman at the White House and said that the CIA would offer no more assistance to Hunt. This was obviously in response to Hunt's having used the CIA to develop his film. The fact that a chief deputy director like General Cushman would hear about the Hunt contact so quickly is proof that there was knowledge of and interest in his activities at a high administrative level. Keep in mind, too, that Hunt did not have the best reputation in the spy business. He was known within the CIA to be the proverbial loose cannon. He was assessed by one coworker as "Totally self-absorbed, totally amoral and a danger to himself and anybody around him."[82] He was remembered as the person who led the failed Bay of Pigs operation. Under these circumstances, it is conceivable and likely that there was a great deal of interest in Hunt and his activities beginning with his first contact with his former employer in July 1971.

Despite the assertion of General Cushman on August 27 that the CIA would no longer provide assistance to Hunt, in fact they did. Hunt's immediate superiors in the Plumbers were Egil Krogh and David Young. In July 1971 the three of them wanted to obtain a "personality assessment" of Daniel Ellsberg. Hunt knew that the CIA psychiatrists had prepared such reports in the past. Young therefore asked the director of security for the CIA to prepare such a report on Ellsberg. The director of security went directly to the head of the CIA for approval of the request. A few days later Director Helms told Security to go ahead, based on a belief that it related to a major security leak; that is, *The Pentagon Papers*.[83] The profile was prepared under the direction of the "Chief of the Psychiatric Staff, who had had prior experience along these lines." He also "had known Hunt when he was with Agency and had rendered services to his family." A copy of the report was sent to Young on August 11, 1971, and on the following day Young, Hunt, and Liddy met with the psychiatrist. They complained that the profile was "inadequate" The psychiatrist pointed out that it had been prepared on the basis of very limited biographical information on Ellsberg that had been provided by Hunt.[84] At the end of the meeting Hunt took the psychiatrist "aside and asked him not to tell anyone at the Agency of his presence." Several days later the psychiatrist telephoned Hunt and told him that he "could not conceal his presence" and therefore had discussed it with the other doctors involved. Hunt sent additional material on Ellsberg to the psychiatrist. No further contact occurred until September 30, 1971, several weeks after the Fielding break-in, when Young telephoned to set up another meeting with the psychiatrist, which was scheduled for October 27.

In the meantime, Hunt sent "additional materials of the same kind as before" but "as far as could be ascertained" they did not include any psychiatric reports."[85] At the meeting, Hunt and Young asked for an updated profile based upon the recently provided "materials." A second profile was prepared and sent to Director Helms for his review on November 8, 1971. On the following day Helms wrote to Young:

> I have seen the two papers which [the psychiatrists] prepared for you. We are, of course, glad to be of assistance. I do wish to underline the point that our involvement in this matter should not be revealed in any context, formal or informal. I am sure you understand our concern.[86]

In other words, never mind that what the CIA is doing is illegal— just don't let us get caught. Given this attitude on the part of the director of the CIA, is it any wonder that Frank and the others had no trouble believing that the CIA was behind the Watergate operation, illegal as it might have appeared to be? On November 12, 1971, a little over two months after Deputy Director Cushman ordered that the CIA provide no more help to Hunt, the CIA psychiatrist personally delivered the updated Ellsberg profile to Young, Hunt, and Liddy "and a brief discussion of its contents was held." A few weeks earlier, in October 1971, Hunt had lunch with the CIA's deputy director for Plans, ostensibly to discuss Hunt's continued employment with the Mullen Company, which did undercover work for the CIA. Prior to the meeting, the deputy was shown copies of the Fielding photos and was briefed on the technical support previously given to Hunt. Nevertheless, the CIA maintained that the photos were never discussed at the lunch meeting.[87] It is obvious that the CIA is not being honest about this claim. To put this meeting and the various other contacts Hunt had with CIA employees in the months leading up to Watergate in context, remember that Hunt had, essentially, left the CIA in disgrace. At the same time, he was a very egotistical person whose self-image was, no doubt, grandiose. After all, he was educated at an eastern college, he had been in charge of spying in Mexico City, he was the author of numerous spy novels and other books, he lived in a good neighborhood in suburban Virginia and sent his children to private schools. Given this mind-set, it is likely that Hunt talked "off the record" about the important national security work he was then doing for the president in an attempt to salvage his reputation with his former colleagues at the CIA. Frank stated privately that one of the reasons that Hunt had a bad reputation as a spy is that he sometimes talked too much. Barker, who continued to profess his devotion to Hunt, also believed that Hunt and Liddy were both too "rash" and that this contributed to the failure of their mission.

Following these contacts in October and November 1971, the Rockefeller Commission concluded that "Hunt had what appeared to be only a few sporadic and insignificant contacts with Agency personnel."[88] However, in the same report, the commission found that "Hunt frequently played tennis with a long-time friend who was a CIA officer and may have had other social contacts with CIA employees." Is there really any such thing as a strictly "social" contact in the spy business? The commission also determined that "on a few occasions" after November 1971, Hunt contacted the CIA's External Employment Affairs branch looking for persons with skill at picking locks and expertise in "electronics" and asked for referral to a company that could provide him with "hostile listening devices."[89] This same arm of the CIA provided McCord to Hunt and Liddy in April 1972 as a purported electronics expert, several months before the ill-fated break-in. Despite these contacts, the Rockefeller Commission concluded that there were "no records" establishing that some people in the CIA had advance knowledge of the mission. Considering the fact that Helms and others in the CIA destroyed tapes and documents and that the declassified "Family Jewels" has had half of its contents erased, it is not surprising that there is no such documentation that has been produced.

However, there is one memo in the "Family Jewels" that, indirectly at least, shows advance knowledge by higher-ups in the CIA, including Director Helms. As part of his office routine, Helms started each day with a "Morning Meeting" at which he was brought up to date on events that had occurred the previous evening. At the top of the list of topics discussed on June 19, 1972, the morning after the break-in, was the arrest of Frank, Barker, Martinez, González, and McCord and the notation, "Howard Hunt may be implicated."[90] If there was not some suspicion or knowledge on the part of Helms and his underlings about Hunt's plan to bug the Democrats and burglarize their national office, how did they know within hours about his involvement? There was not a word about Hunt in the press until sometime later. Hunt's name came up again during the meeting on June 20—"highlighted developments over the past 24 hours with respect to the McCord/Hunt, et. al. situation." Again the focus was on Hunt, who still had not been publicly identified as being connected with Watergate. It would be a few more days, until the FBI tracked down Alfred Baldwin, the Democrat that McCord had hired to assist with the electronics, who immediately turned state's evidence and implicated Hunt and Liddy. The CIA's knowledge of Hunt's involvement could therefore not have come from some information shared by the FBI. All the evidence suggests that Hunt had been on the CIA director's radar screen for almost a year before the Watergate break-in. It is no wonder that Helms and others knew as soon as they heard the news about the break-in that E. Howard Hunt was behind it.

Another piece of evidence that points to more knowledge on the part of the CIA of Hunt and Watergate than is being disclosed concerns the phony ID documents Frank and the others received from Hunt, who said they came from the CIA. Frank's alias documents included a passport in the name of Frank Hamilton, which did not surprise him because it was an alias he had used while doing previous contract work for the CIA. McCord and the Cubans were each given similar sets of documents. According to the "Family Jewels," the only documentation of Hunt's receiving alias IDs from the CIA was in July 1971 when he and Liddy received such documents, eleven months before Watergate. Hunt's alias was Edward Hamilton, not Frank. Martinez said that in the spy business when selecting an alias the usual practice is to use your real first name to avoid confusion; Edward is Hunt's real first name. Sometime between July 1971 and the June 1972 break-in, Hunt must have had further contact with someone at the CIA to obtain the phony ID documents he passed out to Frank and the others. Yet, neither the "Family Jewels" nor the Rockefeller Commission report mentions any such contact. That the CIA was aware of Frank's use of the Frank Hamilton alias is documented in a memo dated December 13, 1972, that references a newspaper article that left "the impression" that the CIA was involved in Watergate because of the Frank Hamilton passport Frank was caught with and the fact that he had used it in other CIA contract operations.[91] The author of the memo states that any inquiries from the press be deflected with the comment, "This is nonsense." What did the CIA have to hide in avoiding this question?

The CIA had another potential source of information about Hunt in the form of Rolando Martinez. Shortly after he had been recruited by Barker and Hunt for the Fielding burglary he mentioned to his CIA case officer during one of their regular biweekly meetings that he was doing "some work" with Hunt. He did not, however, disclose the nature of the work, and the officer said he was not aware of anything Hunt was doing. At that time Martinez thought that Hunt's work and connection with the CIA was probably on a top secret basis and, consistent with "compartmentalization," his officer did not need to know what Hunt was doing. In March 1972 Martinez met face-to-face with the Miami CIA station chief on an intelligence mission unrelated to Hunt. Martinez said that he told the station chief that Hunt had made several trips to Miami and wondered if the station chief was aware of all the CIA activity in Miami.[92] This prompted the station chief to contact the associate deputy director for Plans at CIA headquarters asking that Hunt be "checked out." The associate director said he had previously learned from the deputy director that Hunt was "engaged in domestic activities" and the CIA, therefore, should not "check into Hunt's activities." What happened next is described in the Rockefeller Commission report:

> As a result of this advice from the Associate Deputy Director, premised not only on concern that the Agency should not become involved in domestic political activity *but also on his estimate of Hunt's erratic judgment,* a strongly worded letter was sent to the Miami Chief of Station advising that Hunt "undoubtedly is on domestic White House business, no interest to us, in essence, cool it" [emphasis added].[93]

However, the station chief persisted in his interest in Hunt's activities, instructing the case officer to tell Martinez to make a written report of the Hunt contacts. At the next meeting, the case officer relayed the request and told Martinez to "write something that he would not be afraid to have shown to him later on." This reinforced Martinez's belief that Hunt's operation was top secret and "compartmentalized" from the officer and station chief in Miami and he should not disclose the true nature of what he had been doing with Hunt. The last thing he wanted to do was leave a written trail, so he made up a completely fabricated story. He wrote that Hunt had been in Miami with his daughter, who was meeting with one of the Somoza brothers regarding a business deal to build a canal through Nicaragua to compete with the Panama Canal. Martinez said there was a grain of truth in this because Hunt's daughter did know Somoza, who was then living in Miami, and a possible Nicaraguan canal had been a well-known topic in Latin America.

Does the fact that Martinez did not tell the truth and that the CIA in Miami had been instructed to "cool it" mean that there was no continuing interest on the part of CIA administrators in Hunt and what he was doing as of the spring of 1972? Is it coincidental that it was around this time that McCord had been hired by Hunt and Liddy at the recommendation of the CIA's External Employment Branch? Liddy's involvement with Hunt was probably another reason individuals at the CIA wanted to keep tabs on Hunt. Liddy had a reputation for being "over the top," as demonstrated by Liddy's recounting in his book, *Will*, how he would practice self-control by holding a hand over the flame of a cigarette lighter. It was Liddy who, in his Gemstone plan, initially suggested using the type of political espionage and "bugging" missions that occurred at Watergate. Whatever his reputation, of all the people in Watergate, Frank admired Liddy the most because he kept to his convictions by remaining silent and suffered the consequence of prison. Frank always referred to Liddy by his first name, George.

As noted in the September 13, 1973, memo from U.S. Probation Officer Frank Saunders to Judge Sirica, at that point Frank and the Cubans were beginning to wonder if McCord was some kind of double agent. Frank, Martinez, and Barker have all since publicly stated that they have no doubt that McCord was a double agent working with certain individuals in the CIA who saw an opportunity to bring down Nixon. Frank elaborated on this in the 1977 interview with *High Times* magazine in response to a question about the Bay of Pigs file. Frank said the file contained "intelligence information" on communist activities in the western hemisphere, and "pertinent intelligence information pertaining to the assassination of the president of the United States, the Cuban Missile Crisis and all that."[94] He said that Director Helms did not want to give Nixon this file because he knew it could be used against the Agency. Frank believed that Nixon belonged to what he called the "Club," or "the military-industrial complex." Frank said the Club wanted Nixon to appoint Nelson Rockefeller (also a member of the Club) as vice president to replace Spiro Agnew, who was found guilty of taking bribes while a county commissioner in Baltimore, forcing him to resign. Nixon defied the Club and appointed Gerald Ford instead. After Watergate and the elimination of Nixon, the new president, Ford, appointed none other than Rockefeller as vice president. Helms, who was fired by Nixon due to the dispute over the Bay of Pigs files, was later made ambassador to Iran, a very good post because the Shah was a big supporter of the United States and there was none of the religious intolerance or outright terrorism that exists in Iran today. Frank believed that Nixon wanted to use the Bay of Pigs file as a "lever against the same people who were harming him." At the same time, believing the Club was using Watergate as a lever against Nixon, Frank was prompted to conclude, "So here we have a conspiracy within a conspiracy within a conspiracy."[95] The burglars alleged that McCord was a "mole" planted by those in the CIA who wanted to get rid of Nixon.

Frank pointed to other specific things that led him to believe that McCord was a double agent. He said that during Watergate McCord was "in constant touch" with a CIA officer whom Frank identified as "Pennington." He noted that while McCord was in jail and being tried for Watergate, Pennington went to McCord's house, where he and Mrs. McCord burned and destroyed files and tapes McCord had been maintaining.[96] This was described in the Rockefeller Commission report. The commission found that in August 1972 the FBI contacted the CIA regarding "information about one Pennington, said to have been an employee who may have been McCord's supervisor a number of years ago."[97] The request was given to the CIA Office of Security for a response. Even though individuals in Security should have known that Lee Pennington was the person the FBI wanted, they sent information about "Cecil Pennington," who had no connection with McCord at all. This mix-up (wherein information and evidence was allegedly deliberately withheld from the FBI until brought to light by the Senate Watergate Committee in January 1974, well after Helms destroyed all his office conversation tapes and Pennington and Mrs. McCord destroyed documents and tapes) points to the efforts of the CIA to conceal McCord's true role. If there was nothing to hide about McCord and Pennington, why keep it secret from the FBI? Frank's answer is the one he gave to *High Times*—"There's a link between McCord and the CIA staff through Pennington."[98] Frank always believed that McCord sabotaged the Watergate mission.

Other things Frank pointed to that tied McCord to the CIA were: At the initial court appearance, McCord volunteered that he had worked for the CIA; according to Martinez, McCord lied about removing the tape on the door; he deposited $10,000 in his bank account during the week before Watergate; he was obviously not an electronics "expert" as billed by the CIA; according to Martinez, he gave the order to go ahead that night even though Frank and Martinez wanted to scrub the mission; he left the Howard Johnson motel for approximately one and a half hours just before the break-in saying he had to buy batteries; he wrote the letter to Judge Sirica prior to sentencing that "broke the dam." Then there is the fact that between August 1972 and January 1973, just before trial, McCord sent seven letters to individuals in the CIA which related to "McCord's involvement in the Watergate affair."[99] Although they are referenced in the "Family Jewels," the letters themselves were not produced. The CIA deliberately withheld the letters, citing an opinion of their legal counsel that disclosure was not required. Nor did CIA officials testifying before the House Armed Services Committee Subcommittee on Intelligence in 1972 reveal anything about the McCord letters. It was not until an internal investigation by the CIA inspector general under the auspices of the new director, James Schlesinger, who had replaced Helms, that the letters came to light. The CIA officials who had testified in 1972 said when interviewed by the inspector general that they must have "forgotten" about the McCord letters when they were asked about possible CIA ties to Watergate.[100] Again, if there was not some sinister connection between McCord and the CIA why go to such lengths to hide things?

Adding all of this up, it became clear to Frank and his fellow burglars that there were people in the CIA who were all over Watergate and that McCord was their operative. Frank said that after Watergate he felt betrayed and used by the CIA. Rolando Martinez believes the lesson of Watergate is that the United States has a strong government of laws and not of men in which the power to govern is divided. Even the president must answer under the law and the authority of the judicial branch of our government. Dan Schultz gave much the same response. On that level maybe the Lynyard Skynyrd boys were right, maybe Watergate should not bother us since ultimately the system worked. The most concise analysis of the meaning of Watergate was provided by Macho Barker, who said, "Watergate. We went in. We got caught. Nixon lost his job."

While the system may have worked at the presidential layer of Watergate the same cannot be said for the layer involving Frank and the burglars. They were made scapegoats, most likely by the CIA. Their constitutional rights were trampled by an activist, aggressive judge who took on the role of prosecutor. The initial fifty-year sentences were used as object lessons to others involved in Watergate and the ensuing cover-up to force their cooperation. On the other hand, Frank received a certain notoriety from Watergate that enhanced his standing in the Cuban exile community in Miami. He was able to continue the fight against Castro, though not always as directly as he had before. He did undercover work for the FBI and the DEA. He became a licensed private investigator under Florida law. He was an advocate for the homeless in Miami and even became an ordained minister, performing a number of marriages. There is no question that Frank survived his Watergate ordeal. But there was another consequence of Frank's Watergate notoriety that was not immediately apparent after he got out of prison. Were it not for Watergate and his having his picture and his association with Hunt all over the national media, it is unlikely that in 1974 A. J. Weberman and Michael Canfield would have fingered Frank and Hunt as two of the bums on the grassy knoll in Dallas who helped assassinate President Kennedy when they published their book, *Coup d'État in America*. In the years following Watergate until his death in 1993, Frank constantly faced questions about his alleged role as part of a plot to kill Kennedy.

10

The Assassination of a President

They say I shot him from the grassy knoll . . . but I never took the time.

—**Frank to his nephew Jim Hunt, April 1975**

FRANK'S ALLEGED INVOLVEMENT IN THE KILLING OF PRESIDENT Kennedy is probably the most controversial aspect of his life. Not surprisingly, the authors reached somewhat different conclusions and interpretations of what role, if any, Frank played in the assassination. Both of these are presented.

BOB'S ANALYSIS

For much of his life Frank was associated with anti-Castro Cubans, right-wing CIA operatives, and crime syndicate figures. These three groups were responsible for much of the western hemisphere's more shadowy escapades: espionage, disinformation, illegal domestic and international business deals, assassinations—the list is as nefarious as it is long. The CIA asked him to liquidate people; the mob asked him to hit people. These groups used assassination as a means to their ends, and Frank was in the mix. He did a lot of things most of us would not do, but he had a moral code, and it wasn't complicated. It was founded on his love of country, freedom, democracy. He hated Communism, and he hated those who lied to him or hurt the ones he loved. His allegiance and fierce loyalty could change if its objects did. Two clear examples are Fidel Castro and John Kennedy.

When Frank first met Fidel, the courageous and ill-equipped rebel fighting against the dictatorial Batista, Frank totally committed himself to the cause. Frank had a lifelong love affair with Cuba and Cubans, but he hated communism. He risked everything for Fidel in the beginning. He almost lost his life, and he did lose his citizenship, to help Castro. But when the revolution was co-opted by the communists, he turned against Castro with the same energy with which he had supported him. He worked tirelessly to overthrow him and was involved in plots to assassinate him.

As for Kennedy, Frank loved him as the president. He met him in Miami in 1962 and pledged to support his presidency and help with campaigning. But when Kennedy decided not to supply the promised air support for the Bay of Pigs invasion and did not tell the invading force of the decision, Frank's admiration turned to hate—a hate so pronounced that some have used it to link him to the president's assassination. Frank's method of operation was one of single purpose. He would establish a goal and go after it without letting much cloud his vision, including fear or remuneration. Castro called him "the most dangerous CIA agent." An FBI investigator said, "Frank, if there's anybody capable of killing the president of the United States, you're the guy who can do it." A New York reporter told him he was a real-life James Bond. There's no question Frank's training, begun in the early 1940s in the Solomon Islands as an Edson Raider, was put to murderous use. Frank killed so many people in combat, he began to lose it. The compunction was gone. That something that's in most of us that keeps violence in check was eroded. Frank was a killer.

On March 3, 1975, in his testimony before the Rockefeller

Commission on CIA activities within the United States, Frank testified to the following concerning assassinations.

> ... and knowing that Captain Devereau [a captain in Castro's intelli-
> gence operation] was crazy, and closely associated with Raoul [sic] Cas-
> tro and Che Guevara, known Communists, I had a confrontation with
> him and two of his bodyguards in a jeep one night when he stopped me
> and I told him mainly that he better step lightly, that I would kill him
> right then and there. And I would have done it except for one thing only,
> that I spoke to Nichols [CIA] about this—and Nichols told me to leave
> him alone at the present time. Other things that I discussed with Colonel
> Nichols was the attempted assassination on two occasions of Fidel Cas-
> tro and all the top military commanders that used to come to the Air
> Force Base. And remember that I had another job at the Air Force Base,
> training the military police. And I also was still Chief of Security.
>
> OLSEN: Let me ask you, are you telling us that while you were a Cuban
> Air Force officer and chief of training military police and security and
> intelligence operations in the Cuban Air Force, that you participated in
> an attempt to assassinate Castro?
>
> STURGIS: Yes, on two occasions, plus other military officials.
>
> OLSEN: When did those attempts take place, during [the] early part of
> 1959?
>
> STURGIS: Yes sir, I would say the first attempt—and I set it up as an
> exercise, that if I was to get the green light—which I did not anticipate
> that I would, because there is such a thing as getting a green light—and
> there is another thing about doing something without the green light, in
> other words they do it—but they don't get caught—but I did set it up as
> an exercise, and I did have the men on several occasions, like I said, as a
> training exercise, stationed at the gate with me there, with men sta-
> tioned on the rooftops on the homes—my excuse was for the protection
> of the entourage. Fidel and the military commanders he had with him.
> He had a hometown bunch with him when they came to the Air Force,
> even with General Bayo. And I felt that if I would get the nod to assas-
> sinate them. I could do it within 30 seconds, hightail it and everything.

Later in Frank's testimony another assassination is discussed.

STURGIS: *I was asked to do an assassination.*

OLSEN: *By whom*

STURGIS: *Can I hold back on that?*

OLSEN: *Is this in Miami?*

STURGIS: *Yes*

OLSEN: *First of all, can you go back and tell me when you were approached by this friend of yours?*

STURGIS: *I can't remember the year.*

ROETHE: *This is after you got back from Cuba, obviously?*

STURGIS: *Yes, it had to be . . . It had to be either before the Bay of Pigs, which is 1961, or after, which again could be 1961 . . . so I would say approximately 1961 . . . he asked me if I wanted to do an assassination for the outfit. And I looked him square in the face and asked him, why did you come to me? And he says . . . well Frank, who else? You are a man the chief knows your background, and I know your background, and I know you are capable . . . and if anybody can do it, you can . . . but the thing is, would you be interested? And I said yes, I would be.*

OLSEN: *Who was the target of this assassination? Was it Fidel?*

STURGIS: *No. I don't know . . . I had a second meeting with him at the Ranch House and he told me, he says well, this is interesting Frank. He said, about his assassination, and I said, fine. I did. And then he started to questioning, how would you do it? And I said, how do you mean how I would do it? There are several ways of trying to do an assassination. The things I have to know is who the person is, that is number 1. It is important, and where the person is at, which is important. And then, I will have to go ahead and go to the place where this man lives or what have you, after I know this information. And I said then, I can go ahead and tell you how I can do it. And he said, with a body, this and that, he will be discovered. You know we can't be connected with it. And I said, well, if you are worried about that, you do it. And he said, well, I can't do it. And I said, Okay, beautiful, and I want—I wanted to tell you something, I will do this, because you are a friend of mine, and because you*

*asked me. But I will want more than that. And he said what is that? I said
I want it from somebody higher than you, from somebody with authority.
If you tell me—and you are my friend, and I believe you—but I want it
more from somebody that has some authority. You have a case officer. I
want your case officer to tell me to do an assassination plot, and I will do
it. But coming from you, you are my friend, my buddy, but I have got to
have more than that for my protection.*

ROETHE: *Did you have any idea that this had anything to do with
Cuba.*

STURGIS: *It always had to do with Cuba.*

ROETHE: *What was your motivation for saying that you would do this?*

STURGIS: *Do you know what a whore is?*

ROETHE: *Do I know what a whore is?*

STURGIS: *Yes.*

ROETHE: *I guess I do*

STURGIS: *I don't mean to . . . embarrass you. I am sorry. But in intelligence, a whore is an agent that they would want to do anything. But he
has got to be motivated by patriotism and that he would do anything for
his country, regardless of what is was.*[1]

Michael Canfield, co-author of *Coup d'État in America,* claims
Frank told him that this was a domestic assassination. The leverage for
Frank in JFK's death was to blame it on Castro in hopes the reaction
would lead to Fidel's demise. Every time Frank was questioned about
the assassination, and the instances are legion, he blames Castro. A
good example is the April 1977 interview in *High Times* magazine.

*I told The Senate Intelligence Committee this: there were documents
detailing the assassination of John F. Kennedy and plans for an early
attempt on his life in Wisconsin in September 1963. Security on JFK was
very tight. We have documents and notes stating that Castro had JFK
killed . . . a few months before the assassination . . . there was a meeting
in Havana—exactly where I do not know . . . at this meeting were Fidel
Castro, Raúl Castro, Ramiro Valdés, the chief of Cuban intelligence, and*

an American by the name of El Mexicano . . . Che Guevara was present. Tanya, Che's secretary, was present . . . Jack Ruby was present at the meeting.

Some of what Frank told this committee was less than truthful. Part of being good at espionage is to be flexible with the truth. Your life may depend on it. If Frank was going to make the president's death count for something, Castro would have to take the fall. If you read only a sampling of the mountains of material on the assassination, you will find those who think that JFK was trying to kill Castro and vice versa. You will find an equal number who think that JFK was the last person Castro wanted to kill. He feared reprisal, and there were indications that the ice was thawing between the two countries. Assassination literature is riddled with mutually exclusive explanations and paradox.

For example, in his testimony to the Select Committee on Assassinations on November 3, 1978, E. Howard Hunt relates a story of a woman who was supposedly in the Castro household when the news of the president's assassination came over the radio. Hunt says this story was told to him by Rolando Martinez. The woman allegedly said that "a pall of gloom had settled over the Fidel Castro household," because according to what she heard, President Kennedy and Castro were on the verge of working out an agreement that would permit both countries to live without the tensions that had existed. This would certainly lead one to believe that, indeed, some détente may have been in the air. Rolando Martinez, the alleged source, claims that this story was simply not true. The woman was the daughter of a ship captain and was one of Fidel's mistresses. Those in the Castro household had reported that Castro's mood was "celebratory" upon hearing the news. There was no pall. The reasons are unclear, but the fact that Mr. Hunt misled investigators about this incident is certain.

An example of the United States going after Castro (that would lend credence to the theory that Castro was going after JFK) is exposed in Operation AMLASH—a CIA operation that was in process at the time of the JFK assassination. In fact, on November 22, 1963, AMLASH met with CIA officials. AMLASH was Rolando Cubela, a high-ranking Castro military and government official. On that day he was given a fountain pen full of poison to be used on Fidel. In 1966 Cubela was arrested by Fidel's police for attempting to assassinate Castro. He was sentenced to death but the execution was never carried out. Eventually he was released and exiled to Spain.

Perhaps the least difficult lie to tell, and one that Frank utilized with some frequency—even under oath—is that one cannot remember names and dates. This way he would not inadvertently poke holes in anyone else's alibi. In 1975 A. J. Weberman and Michael Canfield wrote *Coup d'État in America,* wherein they set out to prove that the president was assassinated by E. Howard Hunt and Frank Sturgis and others. One result of the book was a lawsuit by Hunt in 1976. In his testimony in that case, Frank talks about an assassination plot to kill Henry Kissinger in Venezuela. Because of his connections and his travel, Frank was in a position to hear such things. Assassinations were not a rare occurrence in his circles. Weberman and Canfield make the case that Frank and Hunt were two of the "tramps" photographed on Dealey Plaza. Frank testified that he was not in Dallas on November 22, but his alibi is less than solid.

On at least two occasions, to two different interrogators, Frank told somewhat different versions of his whereabouts on the day of the assassination. To one he said he was at work as a car salesman on NW Twenty-seventh Avenue in Miami. On another occasion, he remembered being at home with his wife, mother-in-law, and nephew (Jim Hunt, co-author of this book) watching TV when the news of the assassination broke.

The House Committee on Assassinations reported in October 1977 that John Martino (a CIA operative then deceased) had alleged JFK was killed by *anti*-Castro Cubans. He supposedly also said that Oswald wasn't the hit man, that anti-Castro types put Oswald together, that Oswald didn't know who he was working for, that he was there to meet his contact at the Texas Theatre and the contact was to get him out of the country and then eliminate him. When that didn't work, they had Ruby kill him. Martino told his wife that when they went to the theater and got Oswald, they blew it. There was a Cuban in there. They let him go. He was the other triggerman. There are countless other examples of Cubans allegedly being involved in the assassination. The anti-Castro Cubans, of course, had no use for Kennedy after the Bay of Pigs.

In the 1992 book *Double Cross,* which purports to be the memoirs of Sam Giancana (an associate of Frank's from the early Cuba days when Frank was Castro's casino czar), Frank is described as "the mob's inside man when he was Castro's Minister of Games of Chance" and also as being present in Dealey Plaza on November 22, 1963, with Charles Harrelson (father of the actor Woody Harrelson), Jack Lawrence, two of Santo Trafficante's Cuban friends, Richard Cain, Milwaukee Phil, Chuckie Nicolleti, Officer Roscoe White and Officer J. D. Tippit (both of the Dallas Police Department), and Oswald. The crime syndicate folks had no love for the Kennedys. Bobby Kennedy had declared war on them. His battle with some of them got personal.

A prime example of Bobby's personal vendetta against the mob is a story in and of itself. On December 27, 1960, Kennedy, who had not yet been confirmed as attorney general, announced two priority candidates in his war on organized crime: Jimmy Hoffa and Carlos Marcello. The Kennedy-Hoffa confrontations were headline news, the Marcello caper less so, but perhaps more significant in the long run. On April 4, 1961, at Kennedy's direction, Marcello (the crime boss of New Orleans) was picked up by INS agents, put aboard a United States Border Patrol aircraft, and deported to his "native" Guatemala. Some ten years earlier the Justice Department had attempted to deport Marcello and had found that his birth records in Guatemala had been forged. It seems that Marcello had rejected the notion of being deported to far-off Italy, so in order to prove he was not Italian, he had his "birth" recorded in a Guatemalan church registry, antique ink and all. Based on this counterfeit entry, the Guatemalan government was bribed into issuing him a birth certificate. In 1961 he was received by Frank's friend President Miguel Ydígoras. But his deportation to Guatemala was short-lived. Public outcry forced his deportation from Guatemala to the El Salvador border on May 3, 1961. The El Salvadorans, not too happy with this turn of events, promptly deposited Marcello in the Honduran wilderness. The United States was faced with the fact that no country wanted the deported mob figure. A New Orleans jury took only an hour to find Marcello not guilty of conspiracy to commit fraud (by obtaining a fake birth certificate), despite overwhelming evidence to the contrary. The mob was holding its own, but the attorney general had declared war on them. Allegedly, when someone at a mob gathering suggested taking out the attorney general, the answer was, "If we kill him, his brother will send the Marines after us . . . but if you cut off the head . . . the whole snake dies." The mob had motive and means.

A third group with which Frank was affiliated was the CIA. In his testimony before the Rockefeller Commission and in other interviews and testimony and conversations with his family, Frank admitted working for the agency. It is interesting that Frank and E. Howard Hunt, however, were not truthful about when they knew each other. They went to great pains to tell everyone they did not know each other in 1963. Hunt publicly claimed not knowing Frank until at least the late 1960s, and Frank told anyone who would listen that he had never met Hunt until Macho Barker introduced them in Barker's office in Miami in 1971 or '72 in connection with the Plumbers and Watergate.

In a recent article written by Erik Hedegaard in *Rolling Stone*, Saint John Hunt, Howard's eldest son, relates a conversation he had with his father not long before Howard's death on January 23, 2007. The article is titled "The Last Confessions of E. Howard Hunt," and in it Saint John claims that his dad told him that Lyndon B. Johnson, Cord Meyer (a CIA agent whose murdered wife allegedly had an affair with JFK), Bill Harvey and David Morales (CIA), and a "French gunman" (presumably "the Corsican Mafia assassin Lucien Sarti") were involved in JFK's assassination. In the article is this passage:

Sturgis, like Saint's father, is supposed to have been one of the three tramps photographed in Dealey Plaza. Sturgis was also one of the Watergate plotters, and he is a man whom E. Howard, under oath, has repeatedly sworn to have not met until Watergate, so to Saint the mention of his name was big news.

In the next few paragraphs, E. Howard goes on to describe the extent of his own involvement. It revolves around a meeting he claims he attended in 1963, with Morales and Sturgis. It takes place in a Miami hotel room. Here's what happens:

> Morales leaves the room, at which point Sturgis makes reference to a "Big Event" and asks E. Howard, "Are you with us?"
>
> E. Howard asks Sturgis what he's talking about.
>
> Sturgis says, "Killing JFK."
>
> E. Howard, "incredulous," says to Sturgis, "You seem to have everything you need. Why do you need me?" In the handwritten narrative, Sturgis' response is unclear, though what E. Howard says to Sturgis next isn't: He says he won't "get involved in anything involving Bill Harvey, who is an alcoholic psycho."

After that, the meeting ends. E. Howard goes back to his "normal" life and "like the rest of the country . . . is stunned by JFK's death and realizes how lucky he is not to have had a direct role."[2]

So, what do we have so far? Frank is connected to three groups: anti-Castro Cubans, the mob, and the CIA (especially its right wing, those who were invested in the Bay of Pigs invasion). Those interviewed for this book (some of whom have spent considerable time investigating the assassination—some for themselves, some for government agencies) had many stories connecting Frank to Dallas and the assassination. Many of these were found to be not true. In several instances the stories appear to have been concocted to discredit another story (perhaps very close to the truth) that had surfaced at about the same time. One story was offered by Marita Lorenz, Fidel's mistress who met and became a very close friend of Frank's when he helped her escape Cuba in 1959. She and Frank were an espionage team doing work for the CIA up to and including an assassination attempt on Castro and supplying intelligence such as where the Russian missiles were eventually going to be located. The reports of the day would have us believe that Marita and Frank became enemies and that at one time Marita's daughter was literally gunning for Frank. There isn't much doubt that Marita did have her delusional moments, but her shenanigans may have been an effort to cover up what was really going on. To explain: Marita's story to the authorities was that she and Frank had driven from Miami to Dallas in two beat-up cars with a group of men, including Oswald, Orlando Bosch, Pedro Diaz Lanz, and two Cuban brothers, and that in the trunk was what she called Frank's "baby," a high-powered rifle with a scope and a silencer. Before they left, they were briefed. There would be no phone calls, no speaking Spanish, no leaving the motel room for restaurants, and complete obedience. Supplies and food were put in the trunks. They all wore dark clothes. They drove all night along the coast and nobody spoke much. Frank drove; Marita sat in the back. It was hot and crowded. They drove through Dallas to the outskirts, to a motel where Frank and Pedro Diaz Lanz registered. There were two rooms; each room had two double beds. Oswald brought in a newspaper and everybody read it. Marita fell asleep in her clothes. Frank brought in sandwiches and soda. Only Frank or Bosch was to answer the phone if it rang. Ruby showed up, and Frank spoke to him in the parking lot. Marita started questioning Frank about Ruby and why they were all there. Frank told her it was too big, that he had made a mistake by bringing her and that he wanted her to go home. E. Howard Hunt drove up as Marita was about to leave and there was a discussion about who would drive her to the airport for the flight back to Miami. Frank and Orlando Bosch drove her to the airport. She flew under the name Maria Jimenez.

There were a lot of elements of this story that did not check out. It was easily disproved. Did Marita tell this story to move the limelight away from something else? Perhaps what really happened? Were Marita and Frank working this together? As Gaeton Fonzi says in his

book, *The Last Investigation,* "Frank Sturgis hasn't survived a life cob-
webbed with dangerous, clandestine missions by being naïve."

"If you believe that someone other than Oswald had anything to
do with the death of the president, then you'd have to look at Frank,"
Fonzi said in a 2007 telephone interview. And as he said in his book in
1993, "A character like Frank Sturgis illustrates some of the dilemmas
in investigating the Kennedy assassination. He can't be ignored. He is,
by his own admission, a prime suspect. He had the ability and the motivation and was associated with individuals and groups who considered, and even employed, assassination as a method to achieve their
goals." When asked if he thought Frank had anything to do with the
death of the president, he answered, "There is some gap in his alibi . . .
same with Howard." He added that "it would have been impossible for
Oswald to have killed the president by himself." And then he said
something that at the time seemed rather far-fetched: "I doubt that
Oswald even fired the rifle." To many, Gaeton Fonzi is the gold standard when it comes to investigating JFK's assassination and is recognized as an authority on those aspects of the assassination involving
anti-Castro Cubans and the intelligence agencies. He is a first-class
investigator and writer. Independent corroborations are his stock-in-
trade. When asked what convinced him there was a conspiracy, he
answered the same way he had in an earlier interview with two other
gentlemen when he lived in Miami in 1996 and the way he wrote
about it in his book.

> I was working for *Philadelphia* magazine at the time and Arlen Specter
> happened to be in Philadelphia. Vince Salandria was the local lawyer
> who wrote an article in *The Legal Intelligencer* about the Warren Com-
> mission report, specifically about the shots and trajectories and the
> head hit, which was the area in which Arlen Specter worked. I remem-
> ber thinking that Salandria has to be some crackpot, telling everybody
> that the Warren Commission report might be wrong. So I decided to
> do an article for *Philadelphia* magazine about this crackpot lawyer
> who said the Warren Commission might be wrong. And that's how I

got involved. After I interviewed Salandria and studied the Warren Commission report I became convinced that Salandria wasn't a crackpot and, then, after interviewing and questioning Arlen Specter, I also became convinced that the Warren Commission report was in fact not the truth.

It wasn't long before he developed knowledge of the "bureaucratic charade" covering up the facts of what certain people knew. He discovered and picked through "layer upon layer of irrelevancies piled on top of each other." At the end of his 1996 interview, Fonzi was asked if he thought we'd ever know the answers. His response was, "I think we already know the answers. We just don't know the details."

To me "the answers" include the fact that, unfortunately, there were multiple parties that wanted to see the president dead, and there were probably plots to make that happen. Each of the three groups mentioned had the means and the motive to do the job, and it appears that in some of the scenarios the groups were working together. Between planners and spotters and shooters and those who would spirit the shooters in and out of the country and those who would make sure some of those involved never talked, we're talking about more than just a few people. It was a murderous exercise, and more deaths than the president's were part of the scheme. Was Frank Sturgis involved? As Gaeton Fonzi says, "There is some gap in his alibi." Yes, I think he was involved. Did he pull the trigger? No, I don't think he pulled the trigger. If he was in Dallas, it was in another capacity. There is some evidence that an assassination plot had been put together for Miami just one week before. The plan was scrubbed in favor of Dallas. Had the Miami plan been put into play, perhaps Frank would have had a different role. Much has been made of the "tramp photos" (the picture of the three men described as tramps who were on Dealey Plaza behind the fence, who were questioned and released). The comparisons of E. Howard Hunt and Frank Sturgis to the two corresponding tramp photos are included in the photo pages. I think the two "tramps" in question are Gus Abrams and Harold Doyle (as the investigators have identified them) and not Hunt and Frank. If the book *Double Cross* is in fact Sam Giancana's memoirs, and if he in fact was in the know, and if in fact he was telling the truth, then there was a raft of people, capable killers, all with means and motive in Dealey Plaza that day.

Frank was not a stranger to assassinations. As he told New York *Daily News* reporter Paul Meskil in 1975, "I was involved in assassination plots and conspiracies to overthrow several foreign governments." He had the training. The Marines taught him many ways to kill, the Navy put him in boats and planes, and the Army put him into the shadows of espionage and intrigue. These are the reasons Castro called him dangerous and the FBI said he was capable of assassinating the president. Frank had the means, and his motive was strong enough to spark the deed. It is possible he was in Dallas on November 22, and for sure he was connected to the groups who probably had a hand in JFK's death. But even if he were on Dealey Plaza that day, Gaeton Fonzi notes,

> I agree that the three entities you mention (the Mob, the anti-Castro Cubans, and the CIA agents invested in the Bay of Pigs) were "involved" in the JFK hit, but I believe for the most part the involvement was limited to hazy or a bit less than hazy foreknowledge or postknowledge of some aspect of it. But I think that included a very few individuals as far as hard, valid information goes, perhaps Frank among them. I think this statement is true: The government killed JFK. By the government in this case I think it was orchestrated by a small group of individuals linked by their positions at key power points. I was never much interested in "the apparatus," meaning the shooters, but I suspect they were brought in from abroad and quickly departed, to be disposed of later. All the other activity of individuals floating around Dealey Plaza that day was designed to take investigators around in circles for decades. And we're all still spinning.[3]

It is also significant that Bobby Kennedy, later on the very day his brother was assassinated, had three discussions (two on the telephone and one in person) with the CIA, the anti-Castro Cubans, and a Justice Department employee regarding the mob. Only hours after the assassination he evidently called Langley and spoke to a "ranking official," confronting him with, "Did your outfit have anything to do with this horror?" Also on the afternoon of November 22, he spoke to Enrique Ruiz Williams, a Bay of Pigs veteran who was the attorney general's trusted ally among exiled political leaders. "One of your guys did it," he accused. In a conversation on the same afternoon at Kennedy's Virginia estate, Bobby told one of his Justice Department lieutenants, referring to the mob bosses, "I thought they would get me, instead of the president."[4] So we have the one person arguably closer to the assassination than anyone else linking the CIA, the Cubans, and the mob to his brother's death only hours after the events in Dallas.

Taking everything into consideration, it would seem that an assassination apparatus had been in place for a long time. In fact, Frank had been involved with this machinery earlier in his career when he took part in assassination attempts (some successful, some not) in Cuba, Panama, Haiti, and the Dominican Republic. As Gaeton Fonzi noted, "assassination was a method these groups used to achieve their goals." When Frank had assisted in hooking up his contacts in the CIA, anti-Castro Cuban community and the mob, the assassination instrumentation took on another dimension. For whatever reason (good candidates would be the president's failure to follow through with his promised support for the Bay of Pigs and his administration's war on the mob bosses), the assassination contrivance that had been aimed at various figures at different times in the past was now turned on JFK.

President Nixon may have also found himself on the wrong side of some of the same players and was disposed of in a less violent, if more involved, manner via the Watergate scandal.

In summary, Frank was connected to the entities that many students of the assassination think collaborated on the deed. His alibis for November 22, 1963, were suspect at best. Among Frank's skills was the ability to clandestinely move individuals in and out of tight spots, cities, states, and countries. Frank, in my opinion, was involved in some aspect of the assassination, including foreknowledge, planning, and perhaps the task of exfiltrating one or some of those involved.

JIM'S ANALYSIS

I moved in with Frank and Janet in June 1963 after graduating from high school to attend Miami-Dade College. On Friday, November 15, just before I left that evening, there was a knock at the door. I opened it and saw two men dressed in dark suits who asked to see my uncle. I called Frank to the door, and he seemed to know one of them, whom he called Bob. They said they wanted to talk to him and suggested they sit in the nondescript gray sedan they had parked in front of the house. The next day I asked Frank who these two men were and he said they were FBI agents who were doing advance work for the visit of President Kennedy that was scheduled for Monday, November 18. The president would be addressing the Inter American Press Association at the Americana Hotel on Miami Beach. Frank said the agents were concerned that there would be anti-Kennedy demonstrations by the Cuban exiles, who still blamed the president for the failure and humiliation at the Bay of Pigs. Frank told them that he intended no such activity but he had heard that some dissidents in the Cuban 2506 Brigade might be planning an unsanctioned demonstration to demand that the president return their battle flag, which had been presented to him at a ceremony at the Orange Bowl earlier that year. Frank showed me an article in the Sunday *Miami Herald* that said the president would land at Miami International Airport at 5:00 P.M. and would make a brief speech there before being flown by helicopter to Miami Beach for a short ride down Collins Avenue to the Americana. I decided that I would go to the airport the next day to see him.

According to a report about the presidential visit prepared by the Secret Service, Frank was not the only person who was interviewed. In addition to other members of the 2506 Brigade, federal agents also spoke to Manuel Artime, head of the Revolutionary Recovery

Movement (MRR), and Orlando Bosch, leader of Movimiento Insurrecional de Recuperación Revolucionario (MIRR). Both gave assurances that there would be no anti-Kennedy demonstrations. Federal agents were also concerned about Frank's friend and compatriot Pedro Diaz Lanz, who "might attempt to approach President Kennedy verbally at a Cuban rally."[5] As it turned out, Diaz Lanz had flown to New York earlier in the day on November 18, 1963, and therefore posed no threat. However, there were still concerns about the president's safety. Originally the president was to ride in a motorcade from the airport to Miami Beach, but that was scrapped because of the increased security risk, especially in a route that would, of necessity, carry the president over causeways and bridges that could not readily be defended. On the morning of the president's arrival, the Miami-Dade police received an anonymous postcard specifically threatening to kill him. Supposedly, there would be an anti-Castro rally at Bayfront Park, where volunteers would pick up bombs to be used in the assassination. While this was probably an empty threat, it illustrated the fact that many Cuban exiles were angry enough to take such action because of the Bay of Pigs and the withdrawal of U.S. support for their activities that followed the Cuban Missile Crisis. For those same reasons, Frank had no love for the president, even though he had once been a supporter. By November 1963 Frank considered Kennedy to be a "phony" who had gone back on promises made. He was definitely not going to the airport with me to see the president.

I arrived early at Miami International Airport that Monday to get a good view of the president. An area had been set up on the tarmac of the Delta Airlines concourse with a raised stage and podium. A chain-link fence had been temporarily erected approximately ten feet in front of the speakers' platform to separate the crowd from the president. There were no signs of a Cuban exile protest among the spectators. Seated on the platform were Florida's governor, C. Farris Bryant, Frank's friend Senator George Smathers, Miami mayor Robert King High, and various other local Democratic politicians. A few minutes after 5:00 P.M., Air Force One rolled up behind the platform and the president came down the gangway and walked up the steps to the platform. After his speech, instead of going to the helicopter waiting for him behind the speakers' platform, the president walked down the steps on the front of the platform and headed straight for the crowd behind the fence and began shaking hands. It would have been very easy for someone to attack him with a weapon. Just four days later some person or persons did just that in Dallas.

Many of us who were alive in November 1963 have a vivid recollection of where we were and what we were doing when the president was shot. On the other hand, writing this book more than forty years later, it is possible that time has clouded some of my memories of the events. For instance, until I recently checked, I thought JFK had come to Miami on Friday, November 15, 1963, a full week before Dallas, instead of on Monday. The first time I was asked to recall the events of that day was on April 1, 1975, when I was contacted at my law office by Peter Clapper, an attorney with the Rockefeller Commission, who asked about Frank's whereabouts at the time of the assassination. Before going further, I told him I wanted to talk to Frank about this request. I called Frank to find out what was going on. Except for one contact by the FBI within a week of the assassination, I was not aware of any issue concerning Frank as a suspect. Frank told me that "two idiots" had written a book accusing him of being one of the three "bums" seen near the grassy knoll in Dallas when Kennedy was shot. He said that they "and that former comedian phony, Dick Gregory," had launched a speaking tour publicizing their allegations. I asked Frank what he had told the investigators. He laughed and said, "I told them I was in Miami that day, but it was only a two-hour plane flight from Dallas to Miami across the Gulf of Mexico, so if they think I shot him from the grassy knoll, all I can say is I never took the time." I told him that I definitely remembered seeing him in Miami that day and would confirm that for the investigator. I called Clapper back and told him I would be happy to provide an affidavit to the commission stating what I recalled about Frank that day. According to a memo Clapper prepared regarding our conversation, I told him that I had an early class at Miami-Dade College, probably starting at 9:00 A.M.[6] Before I left I recalled seeing Frank, who was also about to leave the house. At the time, Frank was working as a used-car salesman at a lot a few blocks away on NW Twenty-seventh Avenue and usually did not leave for work until closer to 11:00. I thought that maybe he had some business to take care of before going to work.

I returned home mid-morning, probably between 11:00 and 12:00, and ate breakfast. My aunt and my grandmother Hunt were there. After eating, I went to my room to read and take a short nap. Sometime around noon my grandmother woke me up and said that the TV news was reporting that there had been an attempt on the life of President Kennedy. Like most Americans, my aunt, my grandmother, and I watched the events unfold, leading to the emotional announcement by CBS news anchor Walter Cronkite that President Kennedy had died. My aunt was extremely upset. She wondered if "those right-wing goofballs in Texas" could have been behind the killing. Dallas was certainly not Kennedy country. I had a class scheduled for 3:00 P.M. that afternoon, which I thought would probably be canceled, but I drove to the school to be sure, leaving the house at around 2:30. When I left, as I recall, Frank was not yet back home, although my aunt believes that he was. Upon arriving at the school I found that the class had, in fact, been canceled. Before going back home I spent an hour or so driving around Miami thinking about the significance of the events of that day. When I got back home at 3:30 or 4:00 Frank was there watching TV with my aunt and grandmother and my cousin Gale, a grade school student. I recall that he was very sympathetic with my aunt, which was a little surprising given Frank's negative feelings about President Kennedy. We spent the weekend watching the CBS news coverage of the assassination and the apprehension of Lee Harvey Oswald. I do not recall any particular discussion with Frank about why Oswald would have done such a thing, other than the speculation about right-wing groups being responsible. However, things changed on Sunday as we and millions of other Americans watched on TV as Jack Ruby shot and killed Oswald, prompting Frank to say, "Now it's really getting interesting." He said Ruby's actions showed that there probably was some sort of conspiracy behind the killing.

Several days later the same FBI agents who visited Frank before JFK's trip to Miami came to the house again. This time Frank left with them and returned several hours later. When he came back he said they had interrogated him about the assassination. When he asked them why they wanted to talk to him, one of them said, "Frank, you are one of the few people in this country who could pull off something like this." Frank told them he'd had no part in the killing and that he was in Miami on the day of the assassination. Frank believed from the start that there was a conspiracy to kill the president. He said that it probably started with the Russian KGB working through Castro's G-2 agents. He believed that coordinating such a project would require the help of people in the CIA who would have knowledge of the details of Kennedy's travel plans. He believed there were Cuban communist counterspies working inside the CIA. He said that during the exodus of anti-Castro Cubans to the United States the CIA began hiring these exiles in large numbers without always checking carefully to see if they might be spies. Frank thought that the idea for assassination might have originated with Fidel as revenge for the various assassination attempts President Kennedy and his brother the attorney general had authorized against Fidel. He said that Ruby's killing of Oswald smacked of a mob tactic and it looked like Oswald might have been a patsy. On the other hand, he acknowledged that there were plenty of Cuban exiles in Miami who would have wanted President Kennedy eliminated.

Over the years, Frank advanced various theories of who killed Kennedy and why it happened. In 1975 he told the Rockefeller Commission that he believed that Cuban double agents in the CIA who had ties to the Cuban Mafia had been behind the plot. He said the motive was twofold—to eliminate Kennedy because he was no longer pursuing an aggressive policy to oust Castro, and to do it in such a way that Castro would be blamed, thereby increasing the likelihood of U.S. intervention in Cuba. The Cuban Mafia hoped to reestablish its gambling interests in Cuba. He also suggested that the American mob might have been involved because the real target was likely the president's brother Bobby. In his capacity as the top law official in the country, Bobby had been waging a war against the Mafia. As Frank said,

> I believe from the information and discussions that I have had in the Cuban colony that the thing was more against Bobby Kennedy because he was the top law enforcement official in this country, that—you know like 'Hey, if you get rid of Bobby Kennedy, you still got his brother which is President Kennedy.' So the thing was to—the hostility was then put off against President Kennedy.[7]

Two years later, in 1977, he told the *High Times* reporter who interviewed him that he had proof that Castro had been the instigator and that the plot was hatched at a secret meeting in Havana some months before the assassination attended by Fidel and his brother Raúl; Che Guevara and Che's secretary, Tanya; Ramiro Valdés, the chief of Cuban intelligence; and Jack Ruby.[8] Frank said that Ruby traded in guns and drugs with the Castro government, and in addition to discussing that topic, the group made plans to assassinate Kennedy. Frank claimed to have seen FBI documents containing a letter that had been written by a Cuban who was also at the meeting confirming this information. Other portions of the FBI file included proof that Oswald and Ruby had met in New Orleans and Mexico City before the assassination. As far as Fidel's motive, Frank offered the following analysis:

> Now here we have the president of the United States who has unleashed our Intelligence Service against him, to remove him at any cost. What do you think Fidel is going to do? Fidel actually killed people himself personally. JFK never killed anybody like that, but Fidel has. So I can't see anyone telling me that Castro wouldn't kill the president of the United States. Like hell he wouldn't.[9]

Frank told essentially the same story to Gaeton Fonzi, who interviewed Frank in connection with *The Last Investigation*. However, initially Frank talked about the "possible motivations of the anti-Castro people" who used Oswald as a patsy. At the same time, Frank believed that Russia's KGB, Cuban intelligence, and moles in the CIA actually carried out the assassination.[10] A few months later, Frank contacted Fonzi and related the story of the Castro/Ruby meeting, thus pointing the finger back at Castro and not at the Cuban exiles. Fonzi writes that Frank set up a meeting with a man he identified as "Paul" who could confirm the Ruby/Castro connection. Frank introduced Fonzi as a friend with "the Government committee that's looking into the assassination of John F. Kennedy."[11] In response, Paul said, "Oh, you mean the guy you killed?" Fonzi does not indicate if he thought this statement was a joke. He concludes that Frank cannot be "ignored" as a possible suspect. Speaking as Frank's nephew who was with him for at least part of the day on which Kennedy was shot, I can agree with Fonzi that Frank has to be considered a suspect, but a suspect of what?

There are three basic issues concerning Frank's alleged involvement in the assassination. First, was he one of the bums on the grassy knoll, and if so, what was his role? Second, if he was not in Dallas that day, was he still a part of the conspiracy apparatus that had allegedly been assembled to carry out the assassination? Third, even if he wasn't directly involved, did he have information or knowledge about the plot that for one reason or another he did not completely divulge?

The evidence shows that Frank was not in Dallas on November 22, 1963. Based on my personal knowledge, I saw him at approximately 8:30 that morning. I next remember seeing him between 3:30 and 5:00 in the afternoon. President Kennedy was shot at 1:30 P.M. Miami time, which is when my grandmother woke me from a nap. He was pronounced dead at 2:00 P.M., and I distinctly recall that news being delivered by Walter Cronkite before I left to see if my afternoon class had been canceled. When I returned later that afternoon, I remember

Frank being there. Thus, at most, he had an eight-hour window to fly to Dallas, participate in the assassination, and fly back to Miami. When author Gaeton Fonzi says there are "some gaps" in Frank's alibi, I assume he is referring to this time span and not some claim that I, as a family member, would join in the JFK assassination conspiracy and lie about Frank's whereabouts that day. It is true that the Opa-locka airport is just five minutes from where we were living, and Frank did fly planes out of that facility. Could he have been the pilot that flew E. Howard Hunt and possibly others to Dallas that day? Based upon what is known about the three Dallas "bums" and their apprehension by the Dallas police the answer is no. According to an FBI report prepared in 1992 and based on an interview with former Dallas policeman Marvin Wise, Wise was called to Dealey Plaza due to the shooting at 12:30 Dallas time (1:30 in Miami).[12] Shortly after arriving, he was told to go to the nearby railroad control towers located just to the west of the Texas School Book Depository and see the supervisor, who had information about the shooting. The supervisor told Wise and two other officers that he had seen three men running down the tracks from the area of the grassy knoll. He saw them climb into a coal car, and he directed the officers to that location. Wise and the other officers found the three "bums" hiding in the coal car and ordered them to exit. Wise recalled that they were "dirty and smelly."[13] They said their names were Gus W. Abrams, Harold Doyle, and John Forrester Gedney. Gedney was wearing a hat. They were searched, and the only one who had any personal belongings was Gedney, who carried a bag containing a bar of soap, a shirt, a towel, a can of SPAM or Vienna sausages, and a bone-handled jackknife. Wise remembered that the knife looked new and shiny and he confiscated it, thinking it might have been recently stolen.

Wise escorted the three bums to the sheriff's office, which was located across the street from the rail yard and the Book Depository building. He watched as another officer took them to the sheriff's office, where they stayed for approximately five minutes, talking to the sheriff. Wise could not hear the conversation. He was then ordered to take the three men in his patrol car to Captain J. W. Fritz, who was in charge of homicide. Wise made the short drive and waited for thirty minutes to an hour, maybe longer, while the three were interviewed. He was then told that the men were not going to be booked and should be returned to the sheriff. They were again escorted into the sheriff's office but did not speak to him. Wise was told that he could return to his patrol car parked across the street in front of the Book Depository building. After five or ten minutes he called on his radio to see if the men had been incarcerated, since he would get credit for it. He was told by a deputy that they had just been released. Assuming that Wise originally apprehended them at 12:30 P.M. (1:30 P.M. Miami time), they had spent at least another hour and a half to two hours in custody, meaning their release came at around 2:30 p.m. (3:30 p.m. Miami time). Given this time frame and my recollection that I saw Frank sometime between 3:30 and 5:00 P.M. that day in Miami, there is no way he could have made it from Dallas back to Miami. The distance between those cities in air miles is 1,099. Even if they had traveled in some kind of jet (Frank was not qualified to fly jets) capable of going 500 mph, there simply would not have been sufficient time to find transportation to some airport from the sheriff's office in downtown Dallas and then fly to Miami, even if they landed at the Opa-locka airport just minutes from Frank's house. Frank was obviously talking tongue in cheek when he told me and the Rockefeller Commission that it was just a two-hour flight from Dallas to Miami.

There is other evidence that shows he was not in Dallas when the president was killed. In April 1975 the Rockefeller Commission submitted a number of photos of Frank for analysis by FBI agent Lyndal L. Shaneyfelt, "a nationally-recognized expert on photo identification and photo analysis."[14] He was asked to compare them to the several photos of the bums in Dallas. He was also provided with Frank's height (five feet, eleven inches) and that of E. Howard Hunt (five feet, nine inches, for a net height difference of two inches). Agent Shaneyfelt went to Dallas and re-created the photos taken of the three bums, using the same camera. He calculated that the person purported to be Frank in the photo was six feet two inches tall and the Hunt person was five feet seven inches, for a net height difference of seven inches, not two. He measured Frank's facial features, including the ratio between nose length and forehead height, then compared it to the bum photos, and found that the ratios were markedly different. He concluded that Frank looked like a Latin while the "derelict" had the general appearance of a Nordic. Frank's hair was dark and wavy while the derelict had light or blond hair that was straighter. I am no expert, but I have seen the photos, and while there might be a slight resemblance to my uncle Frank, I do not think it is him. In particular, the picture that shows the three bums from head to toe depicts someone who is clearly taller and thinner than Frank. Based on the expert analysis of Shaneyfelt, the Rockefeller Commission concluded that the photographs do not depict Frank.

When it comes to the bum who was supposed to be Hunt, the person does look a lot like him. Hunt's son Saint John has stated publicly that it looks like his father in the photo. To see a clever morphing of Frank and Hunt into the bums in Dallas, visit A. J. Weberman's Web site, http://ajweberman.com. While entertaining, the morphing proves nothing. Also, Weberman's claim that I told him my aunt asked me to say that Frank was at home all day the day of the assassination is not true. She simply recalls that Frank was there during the entire period of time while I only recall seeing him that morning and then again later in the afternoon. The other issue that Weberman and his fellow conspiracy theorists ignore is whether anyone has ever come forward claiming to be one of the Dallas bums. When the Rockefeller Commission issued its report in 1975, it was noted that no such persons had turned up, even though the photos "were displayed in various newspapers in the United States, on national television programs, and in the April 28, 1975, issue of Newsweek magazine." However, in 1992 a journalist, Mary La Fontaine, reviewed documents released by the Dallas City Council pertaining to the assassination.[15] Among them she found the original arrest records of the three bums, Doyle, Gedney, and Abrams. Using that information, she was able to locate Doyle, the one who was supposed to be Frank. He was living in Klamath Falls, Oregon. Doyle was also interviewed by the FBI and confirmed that he had been in Dallas that day and was one of the bums. Following the discovery of Doyle, the tramp identified as Gedney (allegedly Hunt) was found living in Melbourne, Florida, and was employed by the city. He was apparently embarrassed about his former life as a vagabond and had never spoken publicly about it. Both he and Doyle stated that they had been at a rescue mission that morning where they had gotten fresh clothes and a meal. They were headed to the rail yard across from the Book Depository building to hop a train when they heard that the president had been shot. In addition to the embarrassment, both Doyle and Gedney were afraid they would have somehow been blamed if they had come forward. By 1992 the other bum, Abrams, was deceased, but his sister identified him in the photo taken in 1963 and confirmed that he had lived a hobo's life. It is not surprising that Weberman and his fellow conspiracy theorists never address the discovery of the actual three bums.

Another person who has attempted to put Frank in Dallas to assassinate the president is Marita Lorenz, Castro's ex-lover who had worked with Frank on several plots to kill Castro. On September 20, 1977, prior to appearing before Senator Church's Select Committee on the Assassination of the President and while planning to publish a book about her life, she went public claiming that she, Frank, E. Howard Hunt, and others had driven to Dallas to shoot JFK. Marita claims she left before the shooting but did meet someone named "Ozzie" who was part of the conspiracy. The story could never be proven. Even Weberman concedes that Marita was lying. Frank, of course, issued a statement denying her charges. What happened next resulted in one of the more bizarre episodes in Frank's life. At the end of October 1977, Marita called Frank and asked him to come to New York to meet with her before she testified before the Congressional committee. Frank taped the call, and it definitely shows that Marita was the one who invited him. She even paid for his airplane ticket. She then contacted the NYPD and lied to them, claiming that Frank was coming to New York to kill her and prevent her from testifying. She told the same story to her teenage daughter, who got a gun and planned to shoot Frank. When Frank arrived at Marita's apartment at 11:00 P.M. on November 2, two NYPD detectives were waiting with their guns drawn to arrest him on charges of threatening her. He was taken to Riker's Island and processed for arraignment. His bond was set at $25,000. Frank retained his former Watergate lawyer Henry Rothblatt, who was able to have the bond lowered to $10,000, a sum Frank could afford. He was finally released on November 3. Two days later, Frank and Rothblatt appeared before criminal court judge Edwin Torres and heard assistant DA Alan Broomer tell the court that after an examination, the various tape recordings Lorenz had given them were found "to contain no threat."[16] Broomer said, "The lack of substantiation of her claims impairs her credibility." As a result, all charges were dismissed. But, there was yet another bizarre turn to the story. As Frank and Rothblatt were leaving the courthouse, they were met by Aron Kay, aka, the Pieman, who is a good friend of A. J. Weberman's. Kay was a "Yippie" (member of the Youth International Party, a radical political group) who got his nickname by throwing pies at various political and public figures. Frank, ever agile, saw the Pieman approaching and "took a quick sidestep, leaving most of the pie on the ground and on Kay's shirt." The photo that appeared with the news article shows Frank using his finger to sample a taste of what was left of the banana cream pie, the flavor chosen by Kay because of Frank's involvement with Banana Republics. Frank later filed a civil suit for false arrest against New York City and Lorenz. It was eventually settled in 1981 for the sum of $2,500 and the payment of attorney's fees. Frank said the $2,500 represented $1,250 per day for the two days he spent in jail.

If Frank had truly been a part of a conspiracy to kill President Kennedy and, as contended by Weberman and others, was the one who fired a shot from in front of the president, why would he wait until the morning of November 22, 1963, to fly to Dallas and carry out the mission? Logic dictates that he would have gone there at least the day before, and I know for a fact that he was in Miami that Friday morning of the assassination. There is no question that Frank was capable of pulling off assassinations, either personally or with the help of others. He was involved in a number of such plots to eliminate Castro and also had played a part in the assassination of Dominican dictator Rafael Trujillo. He admitted to the Rockefeller Commission that he had once been asked by CIA agent Macho Barker if he would be willing to participate in domestic assassinations. He told Barker he would do so, but only if the order came from someone much higher up the chain of command than Barker was. At the same time, Frank steadfastly denied having anything to do with the president's killing. The evidence is overwhelming that Frank did not fire the shot that killed the president in Dallas on November 22, 1963. He was not there.

Turning to the second question—Was he part of a conspiracy?—there is some evidence of his involvement. The answer to this question turns in large part on Frank's relationship with E. Howard Hunt and, possibly, Lee Harvey Oswald. During their lifetimes, Frank and Hunt steadfastly maintained and testified under oath that they did not actually meet until 1971 or '72, in connection with Watergate. Hunt acknowledged that he had heard of Frank Fiorini and the Havana leaflet missions when he was living in Miami in the early 1960s and heading up the Bay of Pigs project but said he never actually met him. Frank said that at that time he had heard of "Eduardo," Hunt's code name, but, likewise, had never met him. I agree with Gaeton Fonzi's conclusion that "there's a lot of circumstantial evidence that contradicts that contention."[17] As prominently as Frank figured in the affairs of the Cuban exiles in Miami during the early 1960s, it seems likely that he would have had contact with someone like Hunt. Frank participated in the Bay of Pigs planning at a high level. He was very close to Manuel Artime, the anti-Castro Cuban exile picked by Hunt to head up the government in exile, and considered him a good friend. I was present on numerous occasions when Frank went to see Artime. Hunt was also a good friend of Artime's. When Hunt was serving his Watergate sentence in 1973 and '74, two of his children lived with Artime's family in Miami. In addition to Artime, Hunt and Frank had close mutual friends in Macho

Barker and Pedro Diaz Lanz, both of whom met "Eduardo" at that time. In light of these relationships, it is certainly possible that Frank and Hunt knew and met each other years before they were willing to admit.

During his testimony to the Rockefeller Commission on April 4, 1975, Frank made a statement that, at the least, suggests that he knew Hunt before Watergate. He was being asked what evidence he had that the CIA was involved in his anti-Castro activities leading up to the Bay of Pigs in the early 1960s. Frank gave the following reply:

> *Well, number one, the activity that was going on in the Miami area, not only my activity, but everyone in the same position that I had, the comings and goings of people in and out of Cuba. Mrs. Geraldine Shamma, whom I recruited as an agent for the embassy, was traveling from Havana to Miami. And she had a home on Brickell Avenue, which was a safe house for the CIA. The Cubans who came from Havana would come to the safe house which she maintained herself with her own money, not CIA money, her own money. Bernard Barker would call her up, and she would tell him who was there, and he would come over to pick up these Cuban exiles to be sent over to be interrogated and debriefed. This is what Bernard Barker would do. And E. Howard Hunt, I believe, may have come over there. I don't think he did, but anyway, she met him traveling back and forth from Havana, where she met him, I don't know off hand. You would have to ask her. (emphasis added).*[18]

If Frank truly did not meet Hunt before 1971 or 1972, why would he have any knowledge of whether Hunt was ever at Shamma's safe house? After making that statement he tries to back pedal, saying they "would have to ask [Shamma]" how she met Hunt. Robert Olsen, the commission's attorney, then asked Frank, "You mean you subsequently heard or learned that she did possibly have some contact with Hunt?" and Frank replied, "*Oh, I knew for years, because, remember, I was in Brickell Avenue in Miami too*" (italics mine). Is Frank acknowledging here that, indeed, he did meet Hunt before Watergate? Unfortunately, Olsen never followed up on this point.

When examining any public statement made by Frank and Hunt, it must be remembered that both were spies and masters of the "limited, modified hang-out technique," where a grain of truth is offered but then a lot of non-truths are added to deflect suspicion from the spy making the statement. Frank's testimony to the Rockefeller Commission about mob involvement in the assassination may be one of the times he did not use this technique. If, in fact, Frank and Hunt knew each other in the early 1960s, why would they consistently deny such contact? Is there some dark secret that they shared? Following Hunt's death in January 2007, his son Saint John said that just before he died, Hunt wrote an account claiming that Vice President Lyndon Johnson had originated the JFK assassination plot. Hunt further claimed that in 1963 when he met with Frank at a Miami hotel, Frank asked him if he was willing to join the effort to "kill JFK."[19] As far as I know, this is the one and only time that Hunt stated that he knew Frank before Watergate. Hunt's claim that Johnson ordered the killing is pretty absurd and was probably offered as a limited, modified hang-out. On the other hand, was there some truth behind the claim that Frank was involved? I think it is highly unlikely that Frank would be soliciting Hunt to participate in the plot, but the reverse might be true. Hunt's CIA career suffered greatly as a result of the failure of the Bay of Pigs. Hunt was a very vain, egotistical man whose self-image did not match the reality of his reputation as a second-rate spy. At the same time, he was rash and had a demonstrated capacity for doing very risky things, including, possibly, participating in the assassination of a president. He had a personal ax to grind with JFK, who had hurt his career and his livelihood. If Hunt were involved in such a plot, it makes sense that one of the people he would turn to for help would be Frank, who had actually planned and participated in other assassination attempts. Frank had ties to the Cuban and American mobs and the Cuban exiles and would be in a position to coordinate contacts between those groups, each of which had its own motive for wanting to do away with JFK. To the extent that there was CIA involvement, Hunt, of course, had those contacts. There is no question that Frank was very patriotic and devoted to this country, but he also had an overriding agenda to get rid of Castro. What better way than to participate in a plot that would lead back to Castro and, hopefully, stir up enough sentiment to cause the United States to take action against him? I have no direct proof that Frank participated in the plot to kill the president. He consistently denied it. He even took a polygraph examination in November 1977 in which it was determined that he was telling the truth about not being involved.[20] However, there is a good reason that polygraph results have never been admitted into evidence by any court—the alleged scientific basis for the accuracy of the test has never been proven.

If Frank was involved in the plot, did he ever meet or know Lee Harvey Oswald? Right after Ruby shot Oswald, Frank said it was obvious that Oswald was a patsy or a fall guy. Sometime later that year he told me he believed that the Oswald who defected to the Soviet Union was probably not the same Oswald who later returned to the United States. He said the Russian KGB "planted Oswald as a mole" to carry out their mission to assassinate JFK. Frank publicly denied knowing or having any contact with Oswald before the assassination, but shortly after the assassination there was an article in the *Pompano Sun-Sentinel* purporting to quote Frank saying that Oswald had been in Miami a year before the killing to contact Miami-based supporters of Castro. The article also mentioned that Oswald had supposedly gotten into a fight with anti-Castro supporters at a rally in Bayfront Park. However, the FBI later investigated these claims and found them to be false.[21] They interviewed Frank, who denied ever making such statements. On the other hand, the author of the article, James Buchanan, and his brother Jerry were both officers in Frank's International Anti-Communist Brigade and knew Frank very well. Is this another modified, limited hang-out on Frank's part? Was Oswald in Miami, but for a different purpose? Additionally, in 1977, Senator Frank Church's committee on assassinations examined Oswald's diary and found a handwritten notation that appears to spell "Fiorini," the surname Frank was born with. It is also the name by which he was known in the anti-Castro community of the early 1960s, when Oswald's diary was being kept. Frank acknowledged that the diary entry might spell his name but suggested that it was there because Oswald planned to assassinate him because of Frank's ardent opposition to Castro.[22] Although it is true that prior to 1963 Castro had made several attempts to kill Frank, it is doubtful that Oswald was on such a mission for Castro. Frank was certainly well known in the Miami Cuban community, but there were other people such as Manuel Artime, former Cuban president Carlos Prío, and Pedro Diaz Lanz who probably had more notoriety than did Frank and would have been more likely targets for Oswald.

On the other hand, Frank's name may appear in Oswald's diary for a different reason—maybe as a contact person for Oswald in carrying out the plot and not as a target for assassination himself. Again, I have no direct evidence, except for the diary entry, that proves Frank knew Oswald. But, if Frank was involved on this basis, whom did Oswald think he was working for—the CIA, the anti-Castro Cubans, the Mafia? Frank had ties to all of them. If there was a conspiracy or a plot, the other question is, was it always planned for Dallas, or were there other contingencies? When President Kennedy scheduled his appearance in Miami for November 18, 1963, the original plan was to use a motorcade to get from the airport to the Americana Hotel in Miami Beach. However, this was later changed to using a helicopter because of threats coming primarily from the anti-Castro Cubans still upset about the Bay of Pigs. Did this thwart a plan to kill the president in Miami? If there was such a plan that included Frank, it is doubtful that he would have done the actual shooting since he would be easily recognized, but he could have had a hand in the planning or in coordinating things. In sum, there is a good chance that Frank was involved at some level in the plot.

Even if he wasn't, it is very likely that he knew much more about the assassination than he ever admitted. One of Frank's areas of expertise was intelligence and counterintelligence. When Frank first teamed up with Macho Barker in the early 1960s Barker told his superiors in the CIA that Frank had a network of 180 people inside and outside of Cuba that were loyal to him and who provided him with information. Frank also knew various mob figures, and it is likely that he did know E. Howard Hunt in those days. If the idea to assassinate JFK originated with one or more of these groups, Frank probably would have heard something about it before the actual act took place. If Frank did have specific information, he may have kept it to himself out of concern for his safety and that of his family. The Mafia, in particular, is known for exacting revenge on both stool pigeons and their families. As far as whether Frank worked with Hunt, one of the things that is interesting about Frank's Watergate experience is that he never blamed Hunt for what happened, even though it was Hunt's ineptness, in part, that led to their being caught. Frank never said anything derogatory, publicly or privately, about Hunt. Like Macho Barker, Frank remained loyal to Hunt to the end. Was this loyalty due to some secret that they shared?

The assassination of President Kennedy and the resignation of President Nixon are two of the most important and controversial political and social events of the twentieth century, and there is Frank, right in the middle of it all. One need not be a conspiracy theorist to believe, as Frank did, that there is a connection between these historical events. Frank thought that both grew out of a power struggle between an influential group of extremely affluent private citizens on one side and those in positions of leadership in the federal government on the other. Frank pointed out that it was the conservative Republican president Dwight D. Eisenhower who first identified what he called "the military-industrial complex" during his farewell address in 1961. Before becoming president, Eisenhower was the five-star general who led the Allies to victory in Europe during World War II. In the speech, he noted, "Our military organization today bears little relation to that known by any of my predecessors," pointing out the huge amount of money and resources being spent to maintain military power during the Cold War. He went on to issue the following warning,

The conjunction of an immense military establishment and a large arms industry is new in the American experience. The total influence—economic, political, even spiritual—is felt in every city, every State house, every office of the Federal government. We recognize the imperative need for this development. Yet we must not fail to comprehend its grave implications. Our toil, our resources and livelihood are all involved; so is the very structure of our society.[23]

The only thing missing from President Eisenhower's analysis is the role of an organization like the CIA in relation to the military-industrial complex. The avowed mission of the CIA is to provide for the security of our country, and it does so in conjunction with the military and the private businesses that have a vested interest in supplying the military forces. Frank believed that President Eisenhower was raising the question of just where the power in our country lies. Certainly, federal, state, and local governments appear to exercise political and economic power, but is there a force or a group that holds sway over them? Do the voters really control the process, or is our democracy just an illusion?

The CIA as a bureaucratic institution has a vested interest in maintaining its existence and protecting its image and reputation. For example, as part of the congressional investigation into Watergate, Senator Mike Mansfield wrote a letter to CIA director Richard Helms requesting that he preserve all files and information relating to Watergate. Helms blatantly ignored this request and destroyed audiotapes of CIA meetings about Watergate. More recently, in 2007, the CIA destroyed videotapes pertaining to the interrogation of suspected terrorists being held at Guantánamo during a pending congressional investigation. By the very nature of its activities, many of which are illegal—assassinations, engineering coups d'état, spying on American citizens—there seems to be little or no moral underpinnings driving the policies and the actions of the CIA. Ultimately, the CIA does what is good for the CIA. It played off of Frank's sense of patriotism and utilized his skills to fight Castro, and then cut him loose during

Watergate. Frank remained very patriotic about his country, but he was totally disillusioned with the CIA. He felt that he had been betrayed and misled during Watergate. He had absolutely no respect for the CIA and thought it did a "piss poor job" of providing security and intelligence.

At some point, individuals in the CIA destroyed incriminating information concerning its involvement in the assassination of President Kennedy. As discussed in the previous chapter, this information and documentation had been kept by the CIA in what was called the "Bay of Pigs file." Nixon's top aide, Bob Haldeman, has stated publicly that when Nixon spoke about the Bay of Pigs file they all understood him to be referring to the assassination documents as well. Why the CIA would associate these two events in the same file is unknown. Whether there were rogue agents secretly working as moles for Castro, who was the mastermind behind the assassination, or whether the connection was through someone like E. Howard Hunt, who was still employed by the CIA in November 1963, working with the anti-Castro exiles and/or the Cuban and American Mafias, there was CIA involvement. If the plot originated with the Mafia or with Castro and the Russians, and if the CIA was doing its job, one would expect, at the least, that there was some intelligence information being collected about it. The FBI has acknowledged that it had a file on Oswald before the assassination. Why wouldn't the CIA also have one, especially in light of Oswald's public connections to the Soviet Union? Rather than being the "lone gun nut" who killed the president, Oswald, given his background, including his alleged defection to Russia and his return to the United States after publicly renouncing his American citizenship, is likely to have been an intelligence agent or mole.

In 2007 former prosecutor and author Vincent Bugliosi published a 1648-page book, *Reclaiming History: The Assassination of President John F. Kennedy,* in which he concludes that Oswald was, indeed, acting on his own. If this is true, then the unanswered question is, just exactly who was Jack Ruby? Was he some zealot patriot who loved President Kennedy so much that he would kill the suspected assassin?

I think not. Ruby owned strip clubs in Dallas and had documented ties to the mob. Frank claims Ruby dealt guns and drugs for Castro. He shot Oswald and lost his own freedom to cover the trail that might have unraveled if Oswald had lived. This is the kind of tactic that a group such as the Mafia or the CIA might use. At the very least, the actions of Ruby provide evidence of some kind of conspiracy.

In 1971 President Nixon tried to obtain various classified documents from the CIA that might reflect badly on the Kennedy family, including the Bay of Pigs file. Frank believed that individuals in the CIA in conjunction with this shadow government of influential people engineered the bust at Watergate to force Nixon out of office and prevent him from getting these documents. As Frank said, "Nixon's goddamn lucky he got out without being shot like Kennedy was." Frank then had a warning of his own—"The people in this country don't realize how close we are to a fascist form of government, and as far as I'm concerned, the fascists are just as bad as the communists." These comments give rise to two ironies. First, Frank was truly patriotic, a real war hero, a man of action who firmly believed in the personal freedoms that exist in a democratic government. Frank's main problem with Castro and the communists was the totalitarianism and absolute lack of freedom of expression forced on Cubans by Castro's regime. Frank could have tolerated a socialist Cuba provided it was built on true democracy. And yet, this champion of personal freedom and democracy ended up being used, abused, and manipulated by the CIA and whatever other groups were behind the assassination of JFK and the forced resignation of Nixon. No wonder he was bitter about Watergate.

The other irony arises from the public perception that the whole Watergate experience, including Nixon's resignation, demonstrated the triumph of laws over men and that our system of justice worked properly. Frank's fellow burglar Rolando Martinez and Watergate lawyer Dan Schultz told us that this was the lesson of Watergate. However, if Frank is correct—that the CIA and the military-industrial complex engineered it—what we really have is outright manipulation of the system by people acting beyond the control of those of us who vote. Watergate and the assassination continue to raise the question posed by President Eisenhower—who is really in control of our country?

In conclusion, although Bob thinks that Frank may have been in Dallas that fateful day (Frank had the means, motive, and opportunity, and his alibi about being home all day has some holes in it), and I do not think he was anywhere near Dallas (based on when I recall seeing Frank, it would have been physically impossible for him to have been there), we both conclude that Frank probably knew the conspirators and had knowledge of the plan or plans that led to the assassination. We both agree that Frank was not a shooter but probably knew who the shooter or shooters were.

Most people have formed opinions of what happened in Dallas that day. We think Frank knew and, like the loyal soldier he was, took the secret to his unmarked grave. Like Gaeton Fonzi surmises, the plot "was designed to take us around in circles . . . and we are all still spinning."

11

Angola

It seems to be that my destiny will be in Africa.

—Frank's diary entry July 10, 1977

WITHIN A YEAR OF HIS RELEASE FROM PRISON IN 1974 FRANK BE-
came military and intelligence director for Wilfredo Navarro and his
anti-Castro group, United Cubans. Navarro was a Cuban refugee living in Miami who had publicly claimed his group was the legitimate
Cuban government in exile. Over the next fifteen years Frank and
Fredo would team up on a number of anti-Castro missions. In 1977,
one of those took Frank to Angola on behalf of the Afro-Cuban Committee, an outgrowth of United Cubans. The purpose was to provide
aid and training for the two rebel groups that were fighting the
communist-dominated government that was backed with money,
men, and arms by Castro.

Angola is located in southwest Africa, south of the mouth of the
Congo River. It had been a Portuguese colony for five hundred years.

Like many colonized lands, it desired independence, and on November 11, 1975, it declared just that by a proclamation of the People's Movement for the Liberation of Angola (MPLA). A fourteen-year armed revolution had been waged against colonial rule by several factions led by the stronger and better organized MPLA that had been founded in 1956. The MPLA's success grew out of its broad-based group of rebels from all sections and social classes of the country. Its appeal was based on its position against the divisive phenomena of tribalism and racism. Similar revolutionary movements have often failed because of their inability to unite warring factions, be they different tribes, religions, races, et cetera. In December 1977 the MPLA declared itself a Marxist party, which made it a target of certain interests who had soldiers like Frank. The MPLA guerrilla force that had fought the Portuguese was expanded to meet the threat posed by two rebel leaders, Holden Roberto, head of the FNLA party, and Jonas Savimbi, leader of UNITA. Training and structure of the MPLA forces was carried out with help from Castro. Frank's old boss . . . Frank's old job. But communism had put him on the other side, and now he helped Savimbi and Roberto train recruits. Castro was attempting to export his Russian communist revolution to Angola. In May 1977 Frank flew to England and met with those interested in overthrowing the pro-Castro government of Angola. Frank's longtime partner in espionage, Marita Lorenz, told the CIA, "Frank wanted me to fly to Angola in 1977 and take part in anti-Castro activity there."[1]

Through most of his adventures, including those involving Cuba, Frank kept a diary of his activities. Unfortunately, these diaries were in a storage locker destroyed by Hurricane Andrew. However, portions of a diary that Frank kept beginning in May 1977 survived. This diary detailed the events that led eventually to Frank's meeting rebel leaders Holden Roberto and Jonas Savimbi in the Angolan bush. Publicly, Frank's mission was to provide medical and humanitarian aid to the rebels. Privately, Frank agreed to train the rebels in guerrilla warfare and provide military advice to Roberto and Savimbi along with arms and ammunition. In exchange for this support, United

Cubans asked Roberto to recognize it as the legitimate Cuban government in exile. As a result of his efforts, in September 1977 Frank signed an agreement in Geneva pledging $150,000 to aid the fight against the Angolan communists and their ruling party, the MPLA. Adding to the intrigue is the fact that the Angolan who signed the agreement in consultation with FNLA head Holden Roberto, and who will be referred to as "Mr. V" in the following excerpt from Frank's diary, was a high-ranking member of the MPLA itself. He was obviously no communist. Pseudonyms and omissions have been employed by the authors.

London, England. 5/28/77. *I left NY airport at 8:00 P.M.—arrived Heathrow airport, London, England at approximately 7:40 A.M. I checked at the airport tourist counter for a hotel reservation—the hotels were packed because of the Queen's Silver Jubilee. I was fortunate to get a room at the Viceroy Hotel—Lancaster Gate, Hyde Park.*

While I was in NY I called Steve Dunleavy of the National Star *and told him about my trip to London and Brussels and that he needed to contact the representatives of the FNLA forces in London. Through him I made contact with Robert Warren—news editor of the* World News-*paper—in a pub two blocks away from his office. I spent several hours there with some of his chaps . . . He sent his oldest boy to get some newspaper clippings of some Englishmen involved with the FNLA in London—a Mr. C and a Mr. S.*

Mr. S called me at my hotel at 5:15 P.M. and a meeting was arranged. I had to do some talking to him. He agreed to meet me Sunday at the Park Hotel which is next door to my hotel. I was exhausted with no sleep in the last 48 hours. I was very careful looking behind my back for CIA and British Intell. So far, so good.

5/29/77. The weather was good and after a good night's sleep I went for a walk along the park for one and a half hours. I had breakfast at the Park Hotel next door, I bought some souvenirs for my wife. . . . I came back to the hotel to meet with Mr. S—military supply chief for

President Holden Roberto of the FNLA forces. . . . We sat down in a corner table—ordered a drink—and we talked. We went out to get Chinese food and talked—had dinner at 10:00 P.M. and talked—I went to a pub with Mr. S and talked. I got back to the hotel at 2:00 A.M. the following morning.

5/30/77. Mr. S came to my hotel, we went out. He brought me to see some friends. I knew he checked me out good. I gave him and President Roberto a deal they could not refuse—for an anti-communist Cuban government in exile. I offered them everything. He accepted in President Roberto's name. He said he would arrange a meeting with President Roberto for me and Mr. L. If we had to go to Angola to meet with President Roberto we would. Mr. S drove me to the airport and we talked more. . . . He was to keep in close contact with me in the USA.

6/1/77. The first week of June I received calls from Mr. S. He is trying to contact President Roberto who is in the bush. I asked for a cable and a document signed by President Roberto noting that he proclaimed on Angolan soil a government in exile.

6/14,15 & 16/77. I took my wife Jan to NY at the Holiday Inn. The day I arrived I made $1,000.00 with Malcomb Abrams of the Midnight *newspaper. Signed a contract to lecture—had an offer for a movie, book and an article for* Penthouse *magazine. Good, huh? I had a call from London, Mr. S—we talked.*

6/20/77. Miami. I spoke with Mr. S and Les Aspin this morning. They want me to go to Frankfurt, Germany to speak with President Roberto. Arrangements are being made for Mr. L to leave Caracas and go to West Germany to talk with President Roberto. We had a meeting with Nino Diaz, Marcos Diaz Lanz and —— on the 18th of June. I recommended that Nino Diaz be chief of the army. He accepted. Marcos Diaz Lanz as chief of the airforce—he accepted and Mr. R as chief of the navy—he accepted. I am to be the chief of Intell and security. In one day, Mr. L and I formed the military staff under us. We will control the military and exile government.

7/1/77. *Received July 1, 1977 at 8:35 P.M. a special delivery letter from Mr. S with a letter and two photostatic copies on FNLA paper from the Prime Minister of the FNLA.*

Lisbon, Portugal. 7/7/77. I arrived at the airport with no problems—I expected some. I picked my bag up and outside the airport terminal I flagged a cab. One came and before we left, the cab driver I had got into a fist fight with another cab driver. I rooted him to victory—we won— and he drove me to the Ritz Hotel—big and beautiful—something like the Fontainebleau. I checked into Room 138. I like Lisbon. I'm catching on to the language. I called Mr. G at the Rex Hotel—he came over in about one hour—when Mr. G arrived we talked for some time and we agreed on many things. He called a person by the name of Mr. V who was a commandant with the MPLA. Mr. V was a pleasant fellow and we spoke for some time. He had with him a beautiful young lady who spoke English. She is living with a man and Mr. V would like her to join him in his endeavor. Mr. G wants me to talk with officials of South Africa. I agreed to.

We went out last night to get dinner at the restaurant called "Faia," a communist hang out. The owner is a famous woman who was a fas- cist before she and her husband became communists. Her son is a won- derful singer and very involved in the PCP (Partide Communista Portugal). I noticed many famous painted communist PCP slogans on walls and buildings on my way to the hotel. This is a hot bed of com- munist intrigue.

7/8/77. *I woke up at 11:30 A.M. I went to the dining room and had a light lunch of shrimp salad. It was very good. I called Mr. G who was not in. Mr. V called me at 2:00 P.M. . . . Got a call from Mr. G, he is on his way to my hotel. He speaks of a few disasters—hope things turn out all right. So far, Mr. V is late. Mr. G came over and we talked about new developments. Mr. V is with some people and cannot come over as yet.*

He has agreed with Mr. G and wants us to join a coalition force backed up by South Africa which Mr. G represents. We expect to leave Portugal soon. He wants me to talk to the government of South Africa. He plans to be back at 8:15 P.M. He is getting me some maps of Angola. He is working hard to put me with their important people in the government and the tribal chiefs.

I called my home at 7:30 and spoke with Jan my wife. It is 2:00 P.M. afternoon in Miami. Tonight I have more work to do with Mr. G. He told me last night that Portugal Intell was tailing us—it has started.

7/9/77. Mr. V called at 12:20 A.M. I was asleep for a half hour and he came up to speak with me till 4:00 A.M. He is convinced we all should be together. He seems to be an Intell person. . . . I was awakened at 7:30 A.M. after two and a half hours sleep by Mr. D, a member of the FNLA. They were frantic trying to contact me. I said to sit tight. Mr. V told me that during the May coup in Luanda, Angola, 1977, the Cuban garrison surrounded the Russian Embassy for several days and it remains a mystery why. The Bulgarian Embassy—to a man—left prior to the coup attempt. The Cubans have increased their military strength to 20,000 troops, not counting the 600 Russian military personnel in Angola. The Cubans have 25 fighters and 10 bombers, 350 tanks and other military equipment. Their morale is low—one reason for the increase in troop strength. Reports are that Castro intends to increase his military force to 30,000 men by the end of 1977.—Mr. G came to see me at lunch. He was late because he had a strange call from a Paul —— who spoke English. At first, he would not identify himself but because he wanted to meet Mr. G in the lobby of the hotel Sheridan a few blocks from me, he gave a description of himself and said it was of utmost importance. Mr. G went and waited and Paul did not show up. It was strange. We had a talk and I wanted to take some pictures for my wife. We came back to his hotel and he arranged for Mr. V, myself and him to leave tomorrow for Switzerland and maybe Paris for a meeting. His government is interested knowing about my mission.

7/10/77. I was up late with Mr. G and Mr. V. I got back to the hotel at 3:40 A.M. I fell asleep at 5:00 A.M. and at 7:30 A.M. I received a call from London. David —— from the FNLA office in London was trying to contact me. He had a hard time trying to find me, but succeeded. I told him to tell the others to sit tight that I was here on company business and not to talk over the phone because I was under Portuguese Intell surveillance and possibly the other side. This place is like being in Russia—a hot bed of communist conspiracies. I told David I will contact him in a few days. They were concerned about my safety here in Lisbon. Mr. G called and will pick me up in a cab. We will go to —— (this address is to be kept secret). We arrived and walked up a flight of stairs to the third floor and waiting for us was Mr. V, his younger brother, his fiancée, her mother, her aunt and uncle (who are Angolans). Also a high ranking FNLA officer named ——. Mr. V, Mr. G and I talked alone—concerning the military situation that is coming—the talks with the other factions and in sending a demand in Luanda—the coming talk about our joining together in a united front against the enemy. We three will leave Monday, July 11 to Switzerland at 3:30 P.M. and maybe go to Paris later. Things look better and better as each day goes by. Mr. V wants me in the coalition that is being negotiated here in Lisbon between several revolutionary forces. The South African government wants this to happen and with Mr. G behind me I will succeed. Mr. G will contact the South African government to relay what is occurring between us—the next few days will tell the story. It is 5:15 A.M. and I cannot sleep. I have had twelve hours sleep in five days. It seems to be that my destiny will be in Africa—I will either succeed or fail—but I am sure my mission is on a correct course. As each day goes by I am more in the confidence of Mr. V and Mr. G. I suspect Mr. G is a high ranking Intell officer for South Africa. They are aware of me and through Mr. G will guide my course of action. I am thrilled at this great opportunity that came about—when I was in Miami—my wife felt what I felt and if she did not convince me to come to Lisbon—I may have missed this moment. We shall see.

7/11/77. I asked Mr. G how much he trusts Mr. V. He told me—not much at this point but he has to work him—if he sees there is a betrayal then his orders are to eliminate him. He has to call South Africa to make his report before we leave today. Mr. G called and I went to his hotel. South Africa sent two tickets—Mr. S was there—Mr. G introduced him to me. He said we need him so he will go to Geneva with us. We took a cab and went to my hotel to get my bag and then went to pick up Mr. V. He lives on a hill so when we had all our luggage aboard we were OK till we turned the corner—on these narrow streets—we then had to go up-hill. It was funny because Mr. G and I had to get out being the biggest of the four and with all the baggage we helped push the cab up the damn hill. Mr. G with his bad back. We made it to the airport and we began to have problems with the secret police—a woman and another official. Mr. S finally did straighten out the problem. In the meantime, after we boarded the plane to Geneva, a DC 9—real nice—beautiful trip one and a half hours. On the flight Mr. V told me that —— was a traitor. Mr. V and I get along real fine. He agrees with much of my plans (military) about Angola. He is on my side.

Geneva. 7/11/77. Mr. V and I spoke quite a bit on the plane. . . . I find Mr. V quite an intelligent man and he wants to give me his help for the things I want. We arrived at the airport—no problems—we got a cab . . . and went to the Hotel Royal . . . Geneva is very beautiful. I will open an account tomorrow at the bank. We four had a good talk till 9:00 P.M. We will rest till 11:00 P.M., get some food and go to sleep.

7/12/77. We walked and talked last night along the river till 3:00 A.M. . . . Mr. G told me that Mr. V has two and a half million in a numbered account and we spoke to Mr. S who is to return to Angola to make contact and get his mother and father out. He does not know all the plans we spoke about. We are sending Mr. S to the airport at 2:30 to return to Lisbon and Angola. We may leave after Mr. V withdraws the money and I open my account. We have to arrange a secret meeting for the signing of a pact we agreed upon. Mr. G is a lot of fun. We took loads of pictures.

Mr. V, Mr. G, Mr. S and I went to the Swiss bank. Mr. S got money from Mr. V then got into a cab for Lisbon. We are to meet him in Paris with a member of his group. Mr. G went back to the hotel and we went to buy some tape and bugging equipment. Mr. G spent $900.00 American. I bought two watches. On the way back to the hotel we were stopped by men from Angola. One was the minister of health in the transition government, later defeated and now with the FNLA and would you believe he knew who I was? He wants to talk so we agreed for 7:00 P.M. We talked and this man told me that it was urgent that I speak with rebel leader Holden Roberto. He would leave at once for Frankfurt, Germany. He is getting two passports for Mr. G and three visas for Zaire, Mr. V, Mr. G and myself. A lot of intrigue is going on. Someone told the minister of health that he thought that I was a Castro agent.

7/13/77. Woke up at 8:00 A.M., had breakfast with Mr. V while Mr. G spoke with Samuel —— for two hours. I showed him how to bug his conversation. Mr. V and I walked over to the train station and bought a plane ticket for B —— who is in Kinshasa, Zaire to Paris, Lisbon back to Zaire on Zaire airline. We will see him Friday in Paris (secret) it costs over $900.00. We also bought three one way tickets to Paris for us, it costs less than $300.00 and would take 45 minutes to fly to Paris from Geneva. We went back to the hotel Royal and made phone calls to Lisbon, Paris, Zaire. A lot of intrigue. Mr. G and I felt we were made in Geneva again. Some stranger said hello to him. Geneva was a beautiful place but expensive. We left at 8:15 P.M. and arrived in Paris about 9:00 P.M. The drive to the hotel was good and what I saw at night was pretty. We are staying at a middle class hotel so we don't get made in Paris. It is now 11:40 P.M. and I am really tired and hopefully I will sleep this night. Hope no one will find us.

Paris. 7/14/77. We made calls today. We went to the South African Bank of Paris. It was beautiful but cool. We had lunch at a nice restaurant, breakfast in the room. B will come tonight with documents and news of Savimbi breaking away from Roberto. Things are moving in Zaire and

Angola. Poor Lionel is stuck in Venezuela for at least two more weeks. I miss my wife. This place is very expensive. We spent $1500.00 today. I checked into the hotel, a very bourgeois hotel, I put a $100,000.00 belonging to Mr. V in my safe deposit box. He has two and a half million dollars. I think South Africa is backing him.

7/15/77. I went by cab to Le Grand Hotel. It's beautiful. Mr. V was waiting for me. We got to the safe deposit box. Mr. V asked me if he should change $4,000.00 American dollars instead of $2,000.00 American dollars. I said yes. Mr. V thought it would be best for me to get a room in the Le Grand Hotel near him. So we now have three hotels. Mr. V missed a call from the Zaire Prime Minister. We will talk to B on Sunday at a preliminary briefing and may have to go back with him to Portugal for final briefing. London will have to wait. Paris gets dark at approximately 10:00 P.M.

7/16/77. I got at least five hours of sleep. Called for breakfast in the room. I woke Mr. V and called Mr. G. We had to wait for a call from Lisbon and Kinshasa. Everything is OK. We may have to return to Lisbon. Mr. V wants me to go with him instead of going to London. Mr. V made calls to Lisbon and now wants to return tonight. I feel like a fucking gypsy. We went to the bar, he drank scotch and water and I drank Coke. We talked military stuff and plans. We got two tickets for Lisbon tomorrow. . . . I have a television, black and white, six channels—all the same program. Well, we will see what happens tonight. Mr. V may want to challenge me again at the rifle range. I beat him badly yesterday but last night I purposely made him win. If we go tonight, I'll beat his ass again.

Paris. 7/17/77. 2:20 A.M. Mr. V did it to me again. We went to the shooting gallery. I held back tonight and he shot good. We went back to hotel to my room. He wanted to read some of my clippings. He saw Marita Lorenz and asked me to call her in New York. I did, it was 1:05 A.M. in Paris. Marita said it was approximately 7:00 P.M. She spoke with Mr. V. He wants her to come over to meet him. He is very interested because she was the mistress of Fidel and Perez Hermenez of Venezuela. Mr. V spoke to me about Carlos the Terrorist. [Note: the Carlos discussed here is the infamous Venezuelan assassin used as a model for the book and movie The Jackal. *Carlos is now serving a life sentence in a French prison.] He met Carlos three times. He is not a good communist but his father is a political man in Venezuela and a communist. Carlos wants Mr. V to sell 300 bars of uranium to the West at $4,000,000.00 per bar. Carlos wants to retire at 33 years old before he dies. Mr. V will get me the specs and photos of the uranium. Carlos arranged the kidnapping of the OPEC ministers with the backing of Russian Intell. He was the planner of the Munich, Germany operation. Carlos is afraid of the Russian Intell service and wants to retire. Carlos received training in Cuba and Russia on terrorist activities and they were involved behind the scenes on these missions. I told Mr. V I would try to sell the uranium to the US government. Mr. V saw Carlos and a picture of the uranium bars in Madrid, Spain. Carlos plans another operation before the year is out. Mr. G came to the hotel and briefed us. Mr. V and I will go back to Lisbon and wait for B to bring documents and get briefed on when we will all get together on signing the documents. We were talking about Marita Lorenz and Mr. V wants me to send for her. Mr. G thought it was a good idea. I spoke to Marita and she will fly over tomorrow. We arrived in Lisbon at 2:20 A.M. On the plane I asked Mr. V if a CIA agent had debriefed him. He said Frank —— at the American Embassy did for a few hours.*

Lisbon. 7/18/77. I had breakfast in my room. Showered and shaved and checked on Marita's flight to Lisbon. Mr. G called me from Paris . . . R will be in today and will contact me. Mr. V is to give him $1,000.00 American. I believe or suspect that R is also an agent for South Africa. As each day goes by, I am taken into their confidence more and more. Agents of foreign governments seem to act and work alike. We are getting close to the ballpark. I called Mr. V's code name and left a message for him and said it was important. Mr. V called me at 7:30 P.M. and asked me to rent two autos. I got a Mercedes-Benz and another car for tomorrow. It looks *like we will travel. I reminded Mr. V of the pictures and specs of the uranium from Carlos. I am calling Mr. G in Paris to brief him on today. I had a very good dinner and hope to get a good night's sleep. I should call my wife. I really miss her. Can't wait to get home.*

7/24/77. I went with R to the airport for him to catch his plane to South Africa. I returned to my hotel and I am trying to call my wife. In the park below my hotel balcony, I could hear a loud speaker with a woman's voice. I understand some words which are political and understood her defending the Angolan President (communists). This place has a large communist party and supports the communist government of Angola. There are over one million Angolan exiles here and plenty of agents.

Lisbon. *7/20/77. R came in yesterday. He is quite a guy—and an explosives expert. Well connected. I was told to brief him, which I did. He is in agreement with my plans. If things go OK I asked him to be my aide and he agreed. I need someone like him to put me straight on African affairs. He's a very valuable man.*

9/21/77. I drove the small car part of the way from Lisbon to our hotel in the south of Portugal. A five to six hour drive. It was the first time I drove a small car and on a bad road in Portugal. It was dangerous and exciting. Mr. V drove, R drove and I went last. Since I came here I have seen a lot of confusion. I wish this would get over with. I need a rest and miss my wife. I called her three or four times and could not get a connection to Lisbon and to the USA. I'll call her when I get to Lisbon. The way it looks the time is near, it won't be long.

After the agreement was signed in Geneva in September 1977, Frank did travel to Angola by way of Kinshasa and met with Holden Roberto. In December 1981, Frank again went to Portugal and met with Mr. V and Chip in furtherance of their efforts to rid Angola of communist rule. We have been able to locate two diary entries that Frank made from that trip.

Portugal. Saturday/Sunday 1981. *I have been up almost all night with Mr. V talking about the coup d'etat that will occur in February, 1982. He has been calling Luanda, Angola for two days trying to reach two of his underground men who are ministers in the communist government. He received word last night that one of the ministers will arrive Saturday night at 11:00 P.M. Mr. V is one of twelve or fourteen men on the revolutionary council and in the last few days in Angola things are upsetting him because some of the ministers and vice-ministers have been replaced in the government and his fear was that his people were part of the purge. Later, good news arrived by phone in my room from Luanda that his people have survived and have been put in as head minister of security and other vice ministries. Mr. V left me at 10:30 to meet the arriving minister at the airport. I will make arrangements to take Mr. V to Washington D.C. I had lunch with Mr. V and the ex-Prime Minister at my hotel.*

Monday, December, 1981. *I met Mr. V and Chip at my hotel for lunch and we had a long discussion. I was forceful with Chip. I told him he must be forceful and aggressive. Mr. V wanted me to be tough with him. I told him he had to work with Mr. V because he has the ear of Washington D.C. In front of Chip, I made a call to Washington D.C. Chip told me he would work with Mr. V and wanted to go to Washington D.C. At 4:00 P.M. Lisbon time a call came through and I spoke with Howard Liebengood (former aide to Tennessee Howard Baker and Sgt. of Arms for the US Senate) who said hello to Mr. V and will see all of us in Washington D.C. this weekend. He was interested about Colonel Khadafi being in Angola for three days in the beginning of December 1981, and speaking with a Cuban secret agent official about President Reagan's assassination. Everyone is excited that they're going to Washington D.C. because Savimbi is there these last few days. Mr. V is going with me to meet the President of Chile (Pinochet) and the President of Columbia.*

Following the trip to Portugal in December 1981 and his return to the United States, Frank set up two meetings to plan his next

Angolan mission. The first was in April 1982 in London. An internal State Department memo from August 1982 reads as follows:

THE AUGUST 7 ISSUE OF PORTUGAL'S LEADING WEEKLY NEWSPAPER "EX-PRESSO" CARRIES A FRONT-PAGE EXPOSE ALLEGING A SOUTH AFRICAN PLOT TO ORGANIZE A COUP D'ETAT IN ANGOLA. ACCORDING TO "EX-PRESSO" THE COUP WOULD BE COORDINATED WITH MILITARY OFFEN-SIVES AGAINST LUANDA CARRIED OUT BY HIRED MERCENARIES AND ANGOLAN DISSIDENT GROUPS SUPPORTED BY SOUTH AFRICAN REGU-LAR FORCES. REPORTEDLY THE SAG IS ACTIVELY SEEKING MERCENARIES (TO INCLUDE ANTI-CASTRO CUBANS IN THE U.S.), WITH LISBON A PRIN-CIPAL RECRUITING AND PLANNING CENTER FOR THE OPERATION CODE-NAMED "OPERATION KUBANGO"... THE OPERATION WAS DECIDED UPON AT A SECRET MEETING LAST APRIL IN LONDON BETWEEN REPRE-SENTATIVES OF UNITA, FNLA, SOUTH AFRICAN INTELLIGENCE AND (DIS-SIDENT) MEMBERS OF THE ANGOLAN GOVERNMENT. ALSO PRESENT WAS FRANK STURGIS, DESCRIBED AS ONE OF THE WATERGATE "PLUMBERS," NOW AFFILIATED WITH AN ANTI-CASTRO ORGANIZATION HEADQUAR-TERED IN WASHINGTON.

UNDER THE PLAN, A COUP BY DISSIDENT MPLA ELEMENTS IN LUANDA WOULD BE COORDINATED WITH A MILITARY INVASION OF ANGOLA BY TWO COLUMNS AIMED AT LUANDA: ONE IN THE NORTH JUMPING OFF FROM ZAIRE, THE OTHER IN THE SOUTH LAUNCHED FROM NAMIBIA.

THE NORTHERN COLUMN WOULD CONSIST OF 500 MERCENARIES, TRANSPORTED TO ZAIRE VIA GABON, AND JOINED BY FNLA ELEMENTS. THE SOUTHERN COLUMN, CONSISTING OF MERCENARIES AND UNITA ELEMENTS, WOULD BE ASSISTED IN ITS ADVANCE BY A MAJOR ATTACK LAUNCHED BY SOUTH AFRICAN REGULAR FORCES, OSTENSIBLY DI-RECTED AT SWAPO BASES.

THE ULTIMATE OBJECTIVE IS THE INSTALLATION OF A MODERATE, PRO-WESTERN REGIME IN LUANDA, WHICH WOULD END OR DRASTI-CALLY REDUCE GOA SUPPORT FOR SWAPO; ACCEPT CONTACT GROUP PROPOSALS FOR NAMIBIA; NEGOTIATE THE EXIT OF CUBAN TROOPS

FROM ANGOLA; "POSSIBLY" ACCEPT POWER SHARING WITH UNITA AND
FNLA; AND ESTABLISH DIPLOMATIC RELATIONS WITH THE SAG.

SOUTH AFRICA IS FINANCING THE RECRUITMENT OF 2000 MERCE-
NARIES AND THE ACQUISITION OF EQUIPMENT FOR THE OPERATIONS,
WITH AN INITIAL INVESTMENT OF 5 MILLION DOLLARS. PRINCIPAL RE-
CRUITING GROUNDS ARE SOUTH AFRICA AND PORTUGAL, WITH EM-
PHASIS HERE ON EX-MEMBERS OF THE PORTUGUESE ARMY SPECIAL
FORCES. CONTACTS HAVE ALSO BEEN ESTABLISHED FOR RECRUITMENT.

Frank then went to Portugal for a follow-up to the London meeting (there would be a third in Miami) and to recruit special forces
guerrillas who had fought for the Portuguese army.

Another internal Department of Defense communiqué from the
U.S. embassy in Lisbon dated later in August 1982 states the following:

THE PRESTIGIOUS PORTUGUESE WEEKLY EXPRESSO PUBLISHED A
FOLLOW-UP AUGUST 14 TO ITS STORY OF LAST WEEK (REFTEL) REGARD-
ING AN ALLEGED SOUTH AFRICAN (SAG)/ANGOLAN DISSIDENT/MPLA-
INSIDER PLOT ("OPERATION KUBANGO") TO OVERTHROW THE CURRENT
REGIME IN LUANDA. THE LATEST PIECE, THOUGH LARGELY A RETREAD
OF THE EARLIER EXPOSE, ADDS TO THE CAST OF CONSPIRATORS BY
POINTING TO INVOLVEMENT BY ZAIRE AND POSSIBLY THE CIA. AT THE
SAME TIME, HOWEVER, THE NEWSPAPER ACKNOWLEDGES THAT THE
DOCUMENTATION UPON WHICH ITS STORY WAS LARGELY BASED MAY
NOT BE AUTHENTIC.

THE LATEST ARTICLE LISTS THE PARTICIPANTS AT THE LONDON MEET-
ING WHICH ALLEDGEDLY GAVE OVERALL APPROVAL TO OPERATION KU-
BANGO AS PEDRO FERNANDES AND PAULO TUBE (FNLA), ANTONIO DA
COSTA FERNANDES (UNITA), SOUTH AFRICANS GARY VAN DYKE AND
JACK ROLLINS (THE LATTER ALLEGEDLY AN ALIAS FOR THE DIRECTOR
OF THE SAG DEPARTMENT OF NATIONAL SECURITY), AND THREE ANGO-
LAN GOVERNMENT OFFICIALS LINKED TO HIGH-LEVEL GOA MEMBERS
UP TO THE LEVEL OF MINISTER. (COMMENT: AN EMBASSY SOURCE CLOSE

TO EXPRESSO TELLS US NEWSPAPER OFFICIALS HAVE ASSERTED TO HIM THAT THE THREE GOA OFFICIALS PRESENT WERE MEMBERS OF THE GOA SECURITY SERVICES. END COMMENT.)

ALSO ALLEGEDLY PRESENT WAS FRANK STURGIS, REPRESENTING A US-BASED ANTI-CASTRO CUBAN GROUP. THE ARTICLE NOTES STURGIS ALLEGED PAST TIES TO THE CIA AND SUGGESTS THAT HE MIGHT HAVE ATTENDED THE MEETING AS A CIA EMISSARY.

ACCORDING TO THE ARTICLE, THE LONDON GATHERING CULMI-NATED A SERIES OF MEETINGS, ONE OF THEM IN MIAMI AT THE END OF MARCH/BEGINNING OF APRIL. THIS INCLUDED STURGIS, VAN DYKE, ANGOLAN DISSIDENTS FERNANDO SIMOES AND VICTOR FERNANDES, HENDRIK VAAL NETO (FNLA), AND WILFREDO NAVARRO AND YANNU MONTEZ—THE LAST TWO DESCRIBED AS MEMBERS OF THE ANTI-CASTRO MOVEMENT, RESIDENT IN MIAMI.

THE STORY IN SEVERAL PLACES HINTS AT OR ASSERTS ZAIRIAN CON-NIVANCE IN THE PLOT, MOST NOTABLY IN ITS DESCRIPTION OF AN AL-LEGED DOCUMENT OUTLINING THE OPERATION AND DESCRIBING MILITARY EQUIPMENT NEEDS. THE DOCUMENT INDICATES 500 MEN WOULD PROCEED FROM GABON TO ZAIRE TO JOIN THE FNLA THERE IN PREPARING 3 BATTALIONS FOR A NORTHERN THRUST INTO ANGOLA. IT ALLEGES THAT THE FNLA HAS ALREADY OBTAINED PRESIDENT MOBU-TU'S PERMISSION FOR THIS. THE ARTICLE ASSERTS THAT RECRUITMENT OF MERCERNARIES HAS BEEN CARRIED OUT IN PORTUGAL BY A SOUTH AFRICAN FIRM, CAMREX INTERNATIONAL, DESCRIBED AS A LONG-TIME FRONT FOR THE SOUTH AFRICAN SECURITY SERVICES IN SPONSORING SUCH ACTIVITY. A PORTUGUESE FIRM OWNED BY AN ENTREPRENEUR FORMERLY BASED IN ANGOLA IS ALSO DESCRIBED AS A SOURCE OF FUNDS FOR THE OPERATION.

After England and Portugal Frank traveled to Belgium, which was known at the time by those who watch such things as a clearinghouse for spies and soldiers of fortune. By way of Belgium and Zaire he entered the Angola bush, where he trained Roberto's soldiers. He also went to military garrisons in two towns—Ninda and Lobito—in territory controlled by Savimbi in southern Angola.

Like Castro, Savimbi initially became a "celebrity" rebel leader in resource-rich Angola, and he made trips to the United States, where he was well received. He was another underdog on the world's stage of political struggle. But all that changed, and in the 1990s he became a belligerent revolutionary who continued the war long after treaties were signed and elections held. In September 1992 the Angolans democratically elected a president and a national assembly. Savimbi lost but refused to accept the results. He became an anachronistic leader of a long-suffering rebel group and he refused to stand down long after he should have. Savimbi was shot and killed by the Angolan army, under President José Eduardo, in February, 2006. Now the media calls him "Angola's greatest tragedy," who unfortunately kept the oil-and diamond-rich nation from succeeding. Roberto ran for president in 1991 but received only 2.1 percent of the vote. At his death in 2007, he was remembered as a "pioneer for national freedom from Portugal."

The Angola diary pages offer a glimpse into the secret activities of spy missions. The travel, the meetings, the worry of being found out, transferring funds into and out of secret Swiss accounts, planning coups, trying to figure out who can be trusted and how to liquidate those who cannot. And woven into the fabric of the intrigue are the very human aspects of calling home, picking up souvenirs, enjoying a good restaurant, and missing your wife and family. Angola was yet another chapter in Frank's forever fight against Castro's communist Cuba.

As a postscript, the communist Angolan ruling party, the MPLA that Frank had fought against, renounced communism in 1991.

12

It Was Always About Cuba

I am not a soldier of fortune. I do things because I believe in them. . . . Everybody else [from Watergate] is retired, but I'm still fighting my ass off against the Communists. I certainly don't want to die in bed. I want to go out in a blaze of glory, and take about 100 of my enemies with me.

—Frank quoted in the Miami Herald, *June 17, 1982*

SHORTLY AFTER FRANK RETURNED FROM ANGOLA, HE HEADED back to the more familiar territory of Central America. This time he would ply his trade in El Salvador, Costa Rica, Nicaragua, and Honduras.

Honduras is bordered on two sides by ocean—the Pacific on the south, the Caribbean on the north. It is east of Guatemala, northeast of El Salvador, and northwest of Nicaragua. Frank had set up an anti-Castro training camp in Nicaragua in 1975. Before Frank got there in the early 1980s, Christopher Columbus had hit the coast in 1502 and claimed the land for Spain, which ruled for the next three hundred years, until the country declared independence in 1821. Also before Frank's visit, the "Football War" had been fought with El Salvador in 1969. In the 1969 World Cup soccer competition, the two countries met in an elimination match. Built-up hostilities erupted, and on July 14 the El Salvadoran army attacked. A cease-fire was instituted a week later but the battle had been met.

Frank's stay in Honduras had more to do with the Sandinistas. The Sandinistas took their name from Augusto Sandino, who led a rebellion against the U.S. occupation of Nicaragua during the 1920s and '30s. Sandino was assassinated in 1934 by the Nicaraguan National Guard, who were trained and outfitted by the U.S. military, which was there to cement Somoza's hold on the country and keep it safe for U.S. investment. The Somoza family ruled Nicaragua from 1936 to 1979, when they were overthrown by the Sandinistas. Like most revolutionary groups, the Sandinistas were initially a group of student activists, this time at the University of Nicaragua in Managua. The Cuban communists were also knee-deep in this revolution when Frank got there in 1981. By the spring of 1979 no less than five guerrilla groups were operating throughout the country under the command of the FSLN (Sandinista National Liberation Front). Guerrillas and National Guardsmen were fighting on an almost continual basis. With the exception of William Walker, a whack job who declared himself president of Nicaragua in 1856, making English the national language and supporting the slave system, the United States' interest in Nicaragua was its viability as a candidate for what later became the Panama Canal. In creating the Nicaraguan National Guard and bolstering the reign of Luis Somoza, once again the United States had backed a powerful anti-communist who would turn tyrant and spark a revolution.

The Nicaraguan revolution had been aided by Cuba from at least 1967. The two countries had the same commitment to revolutionary guerrilla warfare. So when Frank arrived on the scene, he was training troops to go up against the same kind of revolutionaries he had trained in the mountains of Cuba twenty-four years earlier. Once again the wheel was coming full circle. By the early 1980s there were conflicts between the Sandinistas and other factions of the ruling junta. These factions, often in conflict with one another, became known as "contra-revolutionaries" or Contras for short. So to sum up the Nicaraguan political landscape, the Somoza family, with U.S. backing, ruled from 1936 to 1979, when the Sandinista communists staged a successful revolution and ruled until the U.S.-backed Contras, operating out of Sturgis-assisted camps in Honduras and Costa Rica, got into the act and President Reagan imposed a trade embargo on Nicaragua. Methods employed by the Contras were called into question, and in 1983 Congress prohibited federal funding of the Contras. This led to the "Iran Contra Affair," the practice of selling arms to Iran (to free American hostages held in Tehran) and funneling the proceeds from the arm sales to the Contras. At one point in the hostage negotiations, Frank and fifty Cubans offered to exchange places with the hostages in Iran. Having been tortured as a prisoner of Batista in the early days of the Cuban revolution, Frank felt that he and the other Cubans might be able to tolerate the situation better than the embassy hostages being held.

An article in the *Miami Herald* dated February 6, 1980, reported that United Cubans leader Wilfredo Navarro and "military advisor" Frank Sturgis met with Kamaran Movasaghi, the Iranian embassy's economic counselor in Washington, to check on the response to their offer to provide fifty Cuban exiles willing to trade places with the hostages. Frank emerged from the meeting stating that there was a very good possibility the hostages would be released by March 21. Movasaghi, however, told a reporter that he was only guessing that March 21 would be the date. He noted America's willingness to support a U.N. tribunal to look into Iran's grievances once the hostages were free and also the fact that March 21 would start the Iranian New Year. As it turned out, the hostages were released on January 20, 1981, minutes after Reagan was sworn in as president.

Frank and Wilfredo also asked the Iranians to allow them to set up a Cuban government in exile in Iran. In return, they volunteered to raise a Cuban-exile army to guard Iran's Afghanistan border.

During the 1980s the United States established a significant military base in Honduras to use as a jumping-off point for military operations in Nicaragua and El Salvador. Frank was there to train the

Contras fighting the Nicaraguan government and also to train the El Salvador military against the FSLN leftist guerrillas. Frank also assisted at the U.S. air base near Comayagua that serviced the huge C-5A cargo flights, and if all that wasn't enough, he helped train the Honduran army as it waged a small below-the-radar war against some communists of their own. But his main assignment was to help with the training of the Contras and the El Salvadoran army. This initiative included assassinations by government-sponsored death squads. In 1981, elections were held and Suazo Córdova's election changed Honduras from a military regime to a democracy.

In 2006, the Contras' enemy, Sandinista leader Daniel Ortega, was elected president of Nicaragua. When national elections had been held after the cease-fire in 1987, Ortega's Cuban/Soviet backed government had lost. An Associated Press article published February 10, 2008, described the force that Frank helped train:

> Today's Contras are a shadow of the movement the CIA built around a core of former soldiers who had served the dictatorship toppled by the Sandinistas in 1979. With U.S. arms and funds smuggled into Nicaragua from clandestine bases in neighboring Honduras, it grew into one of Central America's largest guerilla armies.

Although the former Contra soldiers watched the current situation closely, as former Contra commander Noel Valdez said, "But we're now in a context that is very different from the past."

ON APRIL 22, 1975, THE ASSOCIATED PRESS RELEASED A STORY UNder the headline, "Sturgis Claims Ballerina in Plot to Invade Panama." This story was from Paul Meskil's series in the New York *Daily News* in the spring of 1975. In this story, Frank relates a plot to invade Panama that was allegedly hatched by William Morgan, an Ohio-born adventurer who became a friend of Frank's when he was also an officer in Castro's army. Evidently the overly ambitious conspirators planned to overthrow the Panamanian government by blocking the canal with a sunken ship and taking control of the canal for "propaganda and extortion reasons." What gave the story legs was the list of those supposedly involved. It read like a Hollywood A-list. Ballerina Dame Margot Fonteyn de Arias and her husband, the son of Arnulfo Arias, a former president of Panama, were involved. Their job was to bury arms and ammunition at a designated location so they would be available to the invaders. The mission headed south, however, when Dame Margot and her ballet slippers were sent back to England and her husband took sanctuary in the Brazilian embassy in Panama. A letter reportedly signed by actor John Wagner showed that he had given $525,000 to Arias from 1957 to 1959. When asked about the letter, the actor said he was partners with Arias in a shrimp exporting business. Errol Flynn's name was bandied about, but Flynn said the only connection he had with Arias was that Arias had wanted to rent Flynn's yacht for a trip to Panama. Flynn claimed he had declined the rental.

In 1977, Arnulfo Arias was living in exile in Miami. Arias had been president of Panama three different times (1940–41, 1949–51, and in 1968 for two weeks). It was typical banana republic politics. He never served a full term in office, as he was deposed by a military coup on each occasion. In Miami he teamed with a group of anti-Castro Cubans, including Frank, and planned to assassinate General Omar Torrijos, the leading power in the military junta. Evidently a Cuban assassin was offered a million dollars to liquidate Torrijos, and Frank was to help the Cuban enter Panama through Costa Rica and exfiltrate him upon the mission's completion. This mission was never completed but, at least in Panama there was a deep water canal, running aground, as they did off the coast of Honduras, would have been more difficult to achieve. When the United States pressured General Torrijos to loosen his grip somewhat, Arias returned to Panama the next year. Six years later, in 1984, he once again ran for president and once again, in banana republic style, when the voting returns revealed Arias building a sizable lead, Manuel Noriega, who was in charge of the election, stopped the count and changed the results so that Arias lost to Nicolás Barletta by 1,700 votes. As a result of these election irregularities, Barletta was nicknamed "Fraudito," or "little fraud." (Makes you wonder what you have to do down there to be in the *grande* category.)

IN SEPTEMBER 1981, FRANK AND FREDO NAVARRO WERE INVOLVED in an ill-fated invasion of the American naval base in Guantánamo, Cuba. The mission was to send several boatloads of unarmed men under an American flag into a canal adjacent to the base. The goal was to stay long enough so that sympathetic nations would recognize them as the legitimate Cuban government in exile. However, Frank and his crew ran aground in the Turks and Caicos Islands. The Guantánamo "invasion" continued to be doomed when the U.S. Coast Guard intercepted and turned back one of the boats because there weren't enough life jackets on board. Another boat had fuel problems, and Frank and his crew of fifty-seven men had to be evacuated to a small island, Providenciales, in the Turks and Caicos. The only member of the "invading force" who ever reached Guantánamo was Geraldo Fuentes, who was taken there by the Navy for emergency treatment of acute appendicitis. Despite these setbacks, an article in the *Miami Herald* reported that Frank, ever fast on his feet, had proclaimed the mission to be a success because the real aim was to create a diversion so that a group of anti-Castro guerrillas could be infiltrated safely into eastern Cuba.[1]

In the meantime, the police commissioner of Providenciales, Stanley Williams, was not having much success with Frank and the other invaders. He said that most of them had been sleeping outside the police station and had not really caused any trouble, "so far." He then added, "They weren't supposed to have any money, but they must have some because they've been doing a lot of drinking."[2] However, he pointed out that the entire police force of the island consisted of himself and two other officers, so he had real concerns about crowd control. To make sure the invaders would all leave sooner rather than later, Commissioner Williams said he would not let Frank leave the island unless he took the other fifty-seven men with him. Despite this, Frank left the next morning in a small powerboat for a larger island, where he hired a sixty-five-foot boat, the *Captain Jack,* to go to Providenciales and pick up the crew and transport them back to the States. Frank then flew back to Miami. Two days later he found out that sixteen of the anti-Castroites had hijacked the *Captain Jack* and were on their way to "invade" Guantánamo. Again, luck was not on their side. The U.S. Coast Guard found them adrift after the engine and steering failed. They were arrested for operating a shrimp boat without a master and were towed to Miami. The remaining "invaders" were flown to Miami on a DC-3 chartered by Fredo Navarro, whose group, United Cubans, had sponsored the mission. Upon arriving in Miami, both "invader" groups faced scrutiny and interrogation by the Immigration and Naturalization Service. Seventeen of them had no passport or other "documents permitting them" to leave the United States and then reenter because they originally came to the States as part of the Marielita boat lift.[3] They were shipped to the federal prison in Homestead, where they faced deportation proceedings. An INS spokesperson commented, "We haven't had much success deporting Cubans over the past 20 years . . . but we'll put them through the proceedings anyway, if only to show them they can't just bounce in and out of the United States and then every time return to walk the streets at will."[4] This is a good example of the persistence of the official U.S. policy of hostility toward Cuban freedom fighters that was adopted as part of the deal to resolve the Cuban Missile Crisis in 1962.

DURING THE 1980S FRANK WAS INVOLVED IN SEVERAL BUSINESSES, including a bookstore and a video store. He opened his King Video store in North Miami's Dixie Plaza on December 13, 1980. He told the *Miami Herald* that he would not stock movies with Jane Fonda or Vanessa Redgrave in them due to their "political behavior," including their open support of the North Vietnamese communists.[5] For the first few years, the store was a success. Then a national chain moved in and drove Frank out of business. He also was self-employed as a "consultant" on "military matters for governments, rebel leaders, anyone who is anti-communist." In describing his colorful life Frank said,

I am not a soldier of fortune. I do things because I believe in them. . . . Everybody else [from Watergate] is retired, but I'm still fighting my ass off against the Communists. I certainly don't want to die in bed. I want to go out in a blaze of glory, and take about 100 of my enemies with me.[6]

Indeed, during the 1980s and beyond, Frank continued to work his "ass off" in the fight against Castro and communism. Since his days in Cuba, Frank had amassed a great deal of intelligence regarding the drug trade in the Caribbean. He used this knowledge to help both the FBI and the DEA and at least one defendant accused of drug crimes. On that occasion, Frank was hired by a member of the notorious Black Tuna gang, which controlled the distribution of marijuana and cocaine from Venezuela to the United States. Frank was able to obtain the details of a large drug shipment by a rival gang that could, in turn, be given to the DEA in exchange for a lighter sentence for the Black Tuna member. The district attorney was ready to make the deal. However, the Black Tuna guy apparently wanted to hedge his bet because he was caught trying to take out a hit on the judge and the prosecutor in his case. He ended up getting eighty-five years.

One of the more bizarre events that came from Frank's undercover work was his arrest by Dade County detectives on June 18, 1986, on charges of receiving stolen property. He faced up to fifteen years in prison. They claimed to have caught Frank in a sting operation where he promised to help free a prisoner in exchange for money. The deal was set up by a cop posing as a drug dealer who came to Frank for help with his alleged friend in prison. As a down payment, the cop gave Frank four Rolex watches valued at $4,000. He was then arrested. Frank's case went to trial on November 5, 1982, in Dade County with Frank's old friend Ellis Rubin conducting the defense. A key witness on Frank's behalf was John McCutcheon, group supervisor for the United States Customs Service in central Florida. He testified that

Frank had provided valuable information to Customs in "20 or 30 drug operations" and he believed that this was what Frank was doing during his encounter with the Dade County undercover officer. Ellis Rubin told the jury that Frank was gathering information for Customs and was only pretending to help the policeman posing as a drug dealer. As he put it, "It was a case of Frank conning the cop and the cop conning Frank. It would be humorous if Frank were not on trial."[7] After deliberating for three and a half hours, the jury returned a not guilty verdict. For once in his life Frank publicly displayed his emotions. With tears in his eyes, he personally thanked the jury as they left the courtroom. They told him they believed he was working for Customs when this happened.

IN DECEMBER 1989 A FRIEND OF FRANK'S, ABDUL NADER, ARRANGED for the two of them to fly to Tunis to meet PLO leader Yassir Arafat. This was one mission that probably had nothing directly to do with Cuba. In 1982, when Israel invaded Lebanon, the U.S. Marines escorted Arafat out of Palestine and into exile in Tunisia. Prior to leaving, Frank did not tell his wife, Janet, the purpose of the conference with Arafat.

On his return, Frank told his brother-in-law, James Hunt Sr., that Arafat wanted to hire Frank to upgrade his image. It has to be a cover story. Who would hire a Watergate burglar to upgrade his image? Frank had also lost his citizenship, been arrested, and sampled the wares of more than a few foreign and domestic penal institutions. Not exactly the kind of image one would choose to build for oneself. Surely there were others more qualified for that job. Jobs for which Frank was qualified may have been a more logical reason for the visit. According to Frank, pictures of the two and other more sensitive items were in a bag lost by the airline that was never found, or at least never returned. But a gift from Arafat to Frank was shipped separately and survived. It's a Christmas present, a delicate crèche fashioned from ivory. An unusual gift from an unusual host in an unusual location. During his meeting with Arafat, Frank was given a detailed outline of a proposed peace plan with Israel. Frank passed the document to an agent of the CIA who debriefed him. Three years later Arafat was officially recognized by the United States and was allowed to return to the Middle East.

UNFORTUNATELY, ON JUNE 16, 1989, FRANK'S GOOD FRIEND FREDO Navarro died after the car he was driving in Fort Lauderdale struck a concrete wall. A short time later, Fredo's group, United Cubans, became inactive. In 1990, Frank was asked to become the director of intelligence and counterintelligence and a guerrilla warfare instructor for the Cuban exile group PUND. (National Democratic Unity Party). It was definitely an "action group," still conducting missions into and out of Cuba. But it also served another purpose—to provide engineers and other people with the expertise to continue to operate Cuba's power grid, water supply, and other infrastructure in the event of an armed revolt to oust Castro. The group received a great deal of financial support from Daniel Rodriguez, a wealthy Cuban exile living in Coral Gables. He had made a fortune running tobacco plantations in Cuba and Nicaragua before Castro's revolution. PUND maintained an office in Miami's Little Havana that featured military maps of Cuba on the walls and a male mannequin dressed in camouflage. Missions conducted by PUND ranged from the somewhat bizarre to the very serious. For instance, on July 30, 1991, Frank held a press conference for the exile group that featured a "cloaked conspirator" who called himself Leandro. Speaking "through an air hole cut in the cloth," Leandro claimed to be a high-ranking official in Castro's government who was ready to lead a military uprising against Castro.[8] A spokesperson for the Castro government said, "The news conference was a farce fit only for a third-class burlesque theater and not the work of serious conspirators."

Admittedly, Frank was always adept at generating publicity for his cause—witness the 1958 kidnapping of Juan Fangio, the Argentinean Formula One racing champion, that Frank pulled off for Fidel. And he did have a good sense of humor. On the more serious side, in July 1991 two members of PUND, Gustavo Rodriguez Sousa and Tomás Ramos Rodriguez, were tried in a Cuban court on charges that they infiltrated Cuba from an inflatable raft landing twenty-five miles east of Havana for the purpose of assassinating Fidel and other members of his government. The prosecutor claimed the CIA had backed the mission. The pair was captured and confessed to being from the Cuba Freedom Army, the action wing of PUND. They said that Frank had recruited them and offered them $500,000 to carry out the mission.[9] They also said that he had provided the twenty-two-foot launch and dinghy that took them from the Bahamas to Cuban waters. They were convicted and sentenced to twenty years in prison.

STILL CONCENTRATING ON LATIN AMERICA, FRANK TOOK A TRIP to Argentina in January 1991. A Freedom of Information Act request produced the extract below, a translation from the Spanish language of an informational communiqué from the Embassy of the United States of Buenos Aires, Argentina, to the Secretary of State in Washington, D.C.—date of communiqué, January 1991.

Ex Nationalist leader Guillermo Patricio Kelly, who in his youth directed the Alianza Liberadora Nationalista (ALN) or Nationalist Liberator Alliance, a group with NAZI tendencies, presented in his program a North-American citizen, whom he identified as "The Colonel of United States Intelligence, Frank Sturgis" indicating that he (Sturgis) was responsible for the covert spying operation at Democratic Party headquarters in Washington D.C., that begat the Watergate scandal. Sturgis, who speaks an incomprehensible Spanish, admitted that he served a 14 month prison term for Watergate and then began to describe in terms reminiscent of a scene from a novel, his life as a guerilla with Fidel Castro, his experiences in World War II, and most recently Angola. The spectator (unsure as to whether this is a reference to an Argentine media source or the person relating the story from the Embassy) had the sensation that Sturgis developed his conspiracy theories to ultimately arrive at a point of suggesting that the same could happen to Menem (Argentina's president in 1991). Sturgis stated that he had advised President Reagan that he (Reagan) was going to be the subject of an assassination attempt organized by Khadafi and by the Cubans, and later, together with Kelly, the two spoke of the "conspiracy" concerning Nixon and the "conspiracy" that determined who assassinated President John F. Kennedy, whom Kelly tied to Marilyn Monroe. He then placed on the table the books, *Silent Coup* and *Kissinger,* . . . regarding Kissinger he also tied both Sturgis and Kissinger to espionage and Watergate.

The main course of the show arrived when Frank Sturgis referred in passing to the journalist Carl Bernstein, who is actually in Argentina, whom he accused of being a communist, a member of a family of communists and who had received support from the "international communist party and Fidel Castro." Sturgis said that Bernstein, owing to ideological problems, had brought about the fall of the Nixon presidency, and how he had the same designs with the Menem presidency. Kelly interrupted him to predict that this "conspiracy" would occur next March.

It's interesting to note that thirty-two years after Frank joined Castro in the mountains of Cuba, his Spanish still needed work, although to be fair, Cuban Spanish sometimes is difficult for people from other Spanish-speaking countries to understand. It is clear that his Watergate burglar status and his adjunct CIA activity had gained him some notoriety throughout the Americas. His activity in Angola is also mentioned.

On the humorous side, Carl Bernstein, not on Frank's holiday card list, happened to be in Argentina at the time, and Frank couldn't resist taking a shot at one member of the liberal media with whom he had crossed paths, if not swords.

After some of his visits to Latin America and the Caribbean, Frank talked about taking over an island of his own from which to launch attacks against Castro's Cuba. This way, he said, he would not have to worry about losing his citizenship as he had upon returning to the

United States from his December 1959 trip to visit President Ydígoras of Guatemala. Nor would he have to concern himself with the politics of any power-hungry heads of state.

As his wife, Janet, remembers, Frank had actually checked out several small islands. In the 1960s corporations and some very wealthy individuals were buying their own small islands in the Caribbean. Frank talked about setting up a Swiss account and doing just that. One he visited was "about half the size of Manhattan"; he said, "Give me fifteen good men and some real estate for the boats and planes . . . that's all I need."

IN ADDITION TO BEING IN CHARGE OF INTELLIGENCE AND COUN-terintelligence for PUND, Frank was commander of a training camp operated on land leased from their benefactor Rodriguez. It was located in the Everglades, adjacent to Fakahatchee Strand Preserve State Park, about 120 miles west of Miami. In February 1993, PUND member Iván Rojas was arrested along with four other Cuban exiles by the U.S. Coast Guard. The group was caught in a fishing boat sixty miles off the Cuban coast. The boat was loaded with "machine guns, assault rifles, and ten thousand rounds of ammunition."[10] To follow up on the story, news reporters looking into PUND found that the training camp in the Everglades had actually been leased by a nonprofit organization called The Society to Save the Wetlands, which Frank had incorporated under Florida law in November 1992 when the camp became operational. Frank told the media that the purpose of the group was to protect the ecology. Unpersuaded by this claim, federal ATF agents raided the camp on March 9, 1993, and seized "the bulk of their weapons, including Chinese-made AK-47s," but no one was arrested.[11] Frank denied that the two hundred to three hundred trainees were involved in commando activities. With his typical sense of humor, he said, "We are just a bunch of Boy Scouts learning about ecology." In response, the United States Customs Service delivered a letter to PUND warning that any further paramilitary activity would be considered to be a violation of the Neutrality Act. Undaunted,

Frank and Justo Regalado, vice secretary of PUND, held a news conference and announced that the weapons seizure would not prevent the group from continuing its aggression toward Castro's government. To emphasize the point, Frank displayed an AK-47 and demonstrated that it was a legal semi-automatic weapon. Despite his claim about being "boy scouts," Frank acknowledged that the camp in the Everglades was, in fact, a military base and that the group was "a 'belligerent' organization preparing war against Fidel Castro."[12]

When Frank spoke at the PUND press conference in March 1993, he was sixty-eight years old, and his war was not over. Since his break with Fidel in June 1959 Frank had spent thirty-four years actively trying to rid Cuba of his former friend and ally. Throughout his life Frank was steadfastly guided and motivated by his two major passions—anticommunism and anti-Castroism. He never wavered from these goals. He was training PUND guerrillas in the Everglades two weeks before his death.

Frank was often mistakenly identified in the press as a Cuban. Even the *New York Times* described Frank as a Cuban-American in his obituary. In fact, he was an American whose parents were Italian-Americans. However, he had devoted more than thirty years of his life to the Cuban exiles and their quest to overthrow Castro and rid their homeland of communism. So, it was fitting that following his death on December 4, 1993, the funeral took place at Rivero Funeral Home on Calle Ocho (Southwest Eighth Street) in the heart of Miami's Cuban community. A large number of people came to offer their condolences, including many Cubans and Cuban-Americans. Honor guards from PUND were posted at the head and foot of Frank's open coffin. Local and national media covered the funeral.

The Marine Corps paid tribute to Frank at his funeral with a twenty-one-gun salute and "Taps." Because he was a war veteran, the VA was supposed to provide money to purchase a headstone for the grave site. Despite numerous attempts by his wife, Janet, the VA never provided this benefit. Frank is buried in an unmarked grave in a cemetery south of Miami.

13

Uncle Frank

My God! That looks like my uncle Frank.

—*Jim Hunt to his wife, Laura, and dinner guests,*
while watching the **CBS Evening News**

SUNDAY, JUNE 18, 1972, WAS FATHER'S DAY. OUR GOOD FRIENDS MIC and Bernetia Akin had joined my wife, Laura, and me for dinner. The CBS Evening News was on, and out of the corner of my eye I saw photos of four men and heard the anchor say something about some Cubans and a burglary at an office building in Washington, D.C. I looked again and said, "My God! That looks like my uncle Frank." Another of the four looked like a man I knew as Bernard "Macho" Barker. I had met him in the early 1960s while spending summers in Miami with my uncle Frank and aunt Janet. I did not recognize the other two men, who were identified as Virgilio González and Eugenio Martinez.

Aunt Janet had introduced me to Frank in 1959 just before they were married. Frank was a handsome Italian/Latin-looking man with wavy dark hair, brown eyes, and a tan. He stood about six feet and was noticeably muscular with a stocky, solid build. He was smoking a filtered cigarette as he shook my hand. He had a firm grip and was in excellent physical shape. He looked me straight in the eye. Right away, I liked him.

So what was Frank doing in a national TV news story about a burglary by four Cubans in Washington, D.C.? I switched channels and was able to get more details. The burglars had been caught inside the offices of the Democratic National Committee, which was located in an office/apartment complex called the Watergate. This puzzled me even more. When I first knew Frank, he, like my aunt, was a Democrat and a supporter of President Kennedy. Frank met and spoke with Kennedy in 1960 during a presidential visit to Miami. The meeting was at the Fontainebleau Hotel, then the fanciest place on Miami Beach. Frank had introduced the former president of Cuba, Carlos Prío, to President Kennedy. I still remember my aunt proudly telling me to "shake the hand of the man who shook the hand of the president."

All that changed after the Bay of Pigs fiasco. Frank was part of the planned air attack that had been canceled by President Kennedy and was lucky to have escaped without being captured or killed by Castro. From that point forward he had no love for the Kennedys or the Democratic Party. Had this somehow led to his being involved in this burglary?

The other thing that struck me that Sunday in 1972 was the presence of Bernard "Macho" Barker. I had first met him when I was in high school spending part of the summers with Frank and Janet in Miami. Most days I accompanied Frank as he drove his Cadillac Coupe de Ville to various locations in Miami. We would often end up in the southwest section, where most of the Cubans fleeing Castro were settling. As we walked the streets, there were always a number of Cubans who recognized Frank and called out his name. Sometimes Frank would tell me in general what he was doing and about the people who were involved. That is how I learned that Macho Barker was what Frank called a "field director" for CIA operations in the Caribbean. Barker ran two realty companies as legitimate fronts to conceal his true work. Frank made frequent visits to see Barker, and I was always delighted to go along because of the chance to swim in his pool and catch a glimpse of Maria Elena. Barker was Cuban-American and his wife, Clara, was Cuban. Maria Elena was their very beautiful daughter, who was about my age. I had several dates with her, during which I was exposed to the *dueña* system used in many Latin countries. This required that an older female (often a relative) accompany the dating couple. I have to admit, I did not give this system high marks. On the other hand, it was in keeping with a girl whose father spent a lot of his time dealing with spies for the CIA.

As I saw the news that Father's Day, I wondered what a CIA field director was doing with Frank at the Watergate Democratic Party offices. I had last seen Frank before Watergate in February 1971 at the funeral of my aunt Laura in Miami. Although it was a sad occasion, we relaxed that evening by playing one of Frank's favorite board games, Risk. As usual, Frank won.

Frank was particularly bitter about the Bay of Pigs disaster. Some twenty years after it happened I flew to Miami on business and stayed with Frank and Janet over the weekend. On Saturday, Frank asked me to go with him while he made a few stops in "Little Havana." Frank talked about José Marti, one of the leaders of Cuba's fight for independence from Spain at the end of the nineteenth century. More than a military leader, Marti was a renowned poet and writer who was the founder of the Latin Literary Modernism Movement. He wrote the song that is still considered Cuba's unofficial national anthem, "Guantanamera." Frank spoke about him with the same kind of reverence that he felt for George Washington, which was fitting since each was considered to be the father of their respective countries.

We stopped at an office on Southwest Eighth Street and Frank dropped off some documents, and then we went to a diner and ordered Cuban sandwiches to go. "We'll eat them at a park down the street that I want to show you," Frank said. We parked on Thirteenth Avenue, which was also called Cuban Memorial Boulevard. As we entered the park area, Frank explained that there were three monuments in the park: one honoring José Marti and Spanish-American War hero Antonio Maceo that displayed their busts; the Island of Cuba Memorial, featuring a life-size sculpture of a Cuban peasant, or *guajiro,* brandishing a machete; and one dedicated to the 2506 Brigade and those who were killed or captured at the Bay of Pigs. When we got to that part of the park, I saw a simple obelisk engraved with the inscription "To the martyrs of the assault brigade, April 17, 1961." There was also a shield bearing the emblem of the 2506 Brigade, a cross superimposed over the Cuban flag. At the top of the obelisk a perpetual flame burned. Frank said they chose the flame not only because of the obvious symbolism that the fight for Cuban freedom would never be extinguished, but also because "if the son of a bitch that sent them to their deaths has a perpetual flame at his grave in Arlington, then they deserve no less."

Frank explained that the hundreds of candles and notes that were placed around a large ceiba tree near the Bay of Pigs monument were memorials left by Cuban exiles in Miami in remembrance of those killed and those who were and are being held as political prisoners by Castro. He told me, "You can look at them, but don't touch or you'll have *salao,* bad luck." It was obvious to me that the years had not erased the bitterness and betrayal Frank felt, particularly concerning President Kennedy.

When I asked my aunt Janet to describe Frank in a few words, she called him "idealistic" and a passionate dreamer. "He was a handsome version of Cyrano de Bergerac," she said. He was also a fearless fighter who passionately pursued his goal of overthrowing Fidel Castro from 1959 until his death in 1993. Even though he did not succeed, I do not see Frank as some kind of tragic figure. On the contrary, he followed his dreams and met every challenge head-on. In my opinion, his Watergate experience actually energized him to continue the fight against Castro. I measure Frank's success in life from the standpoint of how he lived it, not whether he achieved his ultimate goal. On that score, there is no question that he succeeded. To paraphrase a song by one of Frank's favorite singers, Frank Sinatra (the other was

Mario Lanza), Frank did it his way. As my aunt said, "Frank was definitely not a nine-to-five guy."

The first time Janet heard about Frank was in 1959 when she was having dinner with my aunt Laura and their friend Robin. They were dining at Capra's on Biscayne Boulevard in Miami, which was owned by Santo Trafficante, the Tampa-based Mafioso who lost a fortune when Fidel closed down the casinos in Havana. Laura told Janet that she'd recently seen Frank Fiorini, whom she had first met several years earlier in Norfolk, where Frank ran two nightclubs. Laura described him as a good-looking "adventurer" who had taken part in the Cuban revolution but who was now fighting against Castro. About a week later Janet met Frank when he stopped by to see Laura and Robin at the Admiral V, an extended-stay hotel in North Miami. It was late in the evening, and Janet, who was spending the night, was wearing a robe over her pajamas. She said that the first time she saw him it was like lightning had struck her and she felt like she had found her soul mate. As she joked later, "I first met Frank in a hotel room in my underwear." Within a year they were married.

Physically, Frank was a very strong man and had a lot of stamina, owing in part to his Marine Raider training. He routinely beat me at arm wrestling, making it look easy while reading the paper or smoking a cigarette with his other hand. I once challenged him to an athletic event I thought I could win—a fifty-yard dash. Frank said he would accept the challenge if I would accept his—my aunt would drop each of us in separate locations in the Everglades armed only with a pocketknife and we would see who would last the longest. I, of course declined, owing to the fact that I could never beat a guy like Frank, who could survive in the wild on such things as bugs, raw fish, roots, berries, and waterfowl that tasted like mud. No thanks.

One thing I remember about Frank was his sense of humor. He enjoyed a good joke, but he absolutely could not tell one. Once in October 1963, Frank, my aunt Janet, and I drove to Macho Barker's house. On the drive my aunt told a joke she had heard from her hairdresser—"What is six inches long and has two nuts?" The answer? "An

Almond Joy candy bar." We all laughed and Frank said he was going to tell the joke to Macho. True to his word, after we arrived, Frank told Macho the joke as follows—"Hey, Macho. What's six inches long and has two *cojones*?" I think I laughed harder at Frank's attempt than I had when my aunt told the joke. On one occasion, Frank used his sense of humor, albeit in a somewhat macabre vein, on the FBI, which maintained a perpetual tap on his home telephone. Most nights before going to bed he would pick up the receiver and say, "okay, guys, I'm going to sleep now. You can turn off the recorder." While his phone was being tapped, Frank got a call from his friend Larry De Joseph, who told him that Greta was dead and he didn't know what to do with her body. Frank told him that he would be right over and they could dispose of the body at a secluded location he knew of in the Everglades. Frank got to Larry's house and they loaded Greta's body into the trunk of Frank's Cadillac and headed out on the Tamiami Trail. They were still in Miami when they were pulled over by two Metro-Dade police officers, who said they were investigating a "possible homicide." The officers asked to search the trunk, and Frank opened it up to reveal the lifeless body of Larry's faithful dog, Greta, a dachshund, who at age fifteen had died of natural causes. They were taking her for burial in the Everglades. There was no "homicide."

In July 1962 I visited Frank and Janet at their home in Miami, down the street from the country club where Al Capone used to stay. Under the twin beds in the room I used I noticed several wooden crates. I asked my aunt what was in them and she said, "It's some of your uncle's anti-Castro stuff. You'll have to ask him what it is." When Frank got home later that day I did ask him about the crates. He said, "Oh, those are my anti-tank guns." I wasn't surprised. A year earlier when I visited he had two machine guns in crates sitting on the front porch. He took me to the backyard and opened the door to an outside storage unit containing an unmarked cardboard box that held six one-gallon metal paint cans. There were no identifying labels or marks on the cans. He pried one open to reveal a clear gel that smelled like alcohol or gasoline. He put a wooden stick in the can, and when he pulled it out, a hunk of the gel stuck to it. Frank then put his lighter to it and the gel almost instantly burned an intense white flame. While it was burning, Frank wiped some on the side of a metal garbage can, and again it stuck to the can while it continued to burn. Frank said, "What you are looking at is napalm." I had heard of napalm bombs and wondered why Frank possessed one of the main ingredients. Frank said that he planned to fire-bomb sugarcane fields in Cuba to disrupt the economy. I asked him how and where you went about buying napalm. Frank said, matter-of-factly, that he'd located a supplier in St. Louis and drove his Cadillac there to pick up a load, then drove it back to Miami. Just a couple of days' work for a guerrilla soldier.

A character trait of Frank's that I admired was his tolerance of other races and religions. It bothered him that some Miami Beach hotels discriminated against Jewish guests. Frank said that one of the things he admired about the Cuban people and their social structure was that there was little or no racial prejudice like there was in the United States. Castro's rebel soldiers came in a variety of colors.

One day Frank invited me to go with him as he made his rounds. We rode in his Cadillac to the southwest section of Miami and stopped at a small café that served Cuban coffee. Frank never drank American coffee (though he always made coffee for my aunt in the morning), but he loved the Cuban kind, made very strong and dripped through a long cone-shaped filter (the Cubans joke that if you don't have a filter, use your sock), then served in small cups with loads of sugar. I liked it too. We waited with our coffee while Frank went into a back room to "meet with some guys." He came out about fifteen minutes later and said, "Come on, we're going for a ride." As we drove west on SW Eighth Street, Frank pointed out all of the store signs in Spanish and said that most of the Cuban exiles were settling here in what was being called "Little Havana."

After a short ride we pulled up in front of a house that had a large outbuilding in the backyard. We exited the car and I followed Frank to the backyard and saw that the outbuilding housed a car-repair business. One of the two bay doors was open, and we entered to see a group of three Latin-looking men whom Frank introduced simply as "some Cuban friends of mine." They were loading metal canisters with paper leaflets, approximately three-by-five inches in size, that they removed from cardboard boxes stacked throughout the garage bay. There must have been thousands of leaflets. Frank grabbed a handful and gave them to me. They were similar to the ones I had seen at Frank's Coral Gables house when I first met him. He said, "You can keep these as souvenirs. We'll be dropping them over Cuba later this month." The main message on the leaflets was *"Fidel fracaso"*—"Fidel failed." On the reverse side were instructions for making bombs out of such things as gasoline and cleaning fluid.

In addition to the boxes of leaflets, I noticed a number of other boxes that looked very similar to the one that held the napalm cans that Frank had shown me the day before at his house. These were stacked near a door that led to another part of the garage. I didn't ask Frank about them, but about a week later I found out exactly why those boxes were there.

Later that week, he took me to a marina south of downtown Miami and showed me his PT boat and one of his cabin cruisers that he used for clandestine incursions into Cuba. This is where I first met Pedro Diaz Lanz, the former chief of Castro's air force (who, like my uncle, was fighting to overthrow Castro), and Pedro's brother, Marcos, who also had been a Cuban air force officer.

On the day before I was to leave for Cincinnati, Frank took me to a lunch meeting he had with two Cuban men at Los Basquos, a Basque restaurant located on SW Eighth Street in Little Havana. He was always very generous with me when it came to food and entertainment. We then drove to the same garage we had previously visited, followed by the two Cubans who'd had lunch with us. This time, both bay doors were closed and we entered through a small side door. There we saw the same three Cubans from the week before. One of them locked the door behind us and pulled down a shade to cover the window. We then entered the back room through the door near where I had earlier seen what looked like cardboard boxes of napalm. The room was made out of concrete block, and there were no windows. There were three separate piles of one-gallon cans stacked on the cement floor along the walls. There was a mound of sand next to one of them. In the center of the room there were empty bomb casings with fins at the rear similar to ones I had seen in Army/Navy surplus stores. Frank explained that one pile of cans contained napalm, and another pile contained explosive material. The third group of cans was going to be filled with sand for ballast. Each of the bomb casings would be cut open at the front end, and, as Frank demonstrated on one that had already been opened, three of the cans fit perfectly into the hollow core. To make the bombs, one first put in the explosive, then the napalm, and then the ballast. Once the cans were filled, two of the Cubans would reattach the front of the casing with metal strips and screws holding a detonator. Frank said it was important to fill the bombs in the order indicated and not place the napalm or explosives at the front so that the screws wouldn't inadvertently puncture them. This sounded like excellent advice to me. Armed with these instructions, I spent the next several hours helping to make bombs, which were to be used on the sugarcane fields of Cuba in an effort to overthrow Castro's communist government. My charter membership in Frank's International Anti-Communist Brigade was finally being put to use.

Everyone was being very slow, careful, and deliberate in handling the explosives and the napalm, so the work was taking longer than expected. It was past dinnertime when Frank decided to stay and have one of the Cubans drive me to his house so I could pack and get ready to leave on the bus in the morning. It was 11:30 P.M. before I went to bed that night, and Frank was still not home. In fact, he still wasn't there the next morning before Janet took me to the bus station. She seemed a little worried but not ready to push the panic button. When I got home I called to let her know that I'd arrived safely and also to check on my uncle. She said he was there and I should ask him what had happened. He told me that a few hours after I left, the garage was raided by FBI and ATF agents. They evacuated a four-block area around the garage because of all the explosives and the napalm. He said the good news was that he had not been arrested and probably wouldn't be due to his CIA connections, but the bad news was that they had confiscated his beloved Cadillac as evidence. Unfortunately, he never saw that car again.

During another summer visit I had the chance to watch Frank put together a mission that involved a surreptitious incursion into Cuba. Two anti-Castro Cubans had asked for his help in getting a fast boat. We picked them up in Little Havana and then drove to a marina located on the Seventy-ninth Street Causeway. There we met "Captain Andy," who looked a lot like movie and TV star Troy Donahue. His secretary looked like Sandra Dee, but with a more developed and surgically enhanced upper body. Sometimes when hanging out with my uncle I felt like I was in a movie or on a TV show. Frank told Captain Andy that he wanted to rent a racing hull. These boats were built by the Bertram Yacht Company in Fort Lauderdale. They had a distinctive V-shaped hull, in twenty-five- to thirty-one-foot-long configurations that allowed the boat to cut through the waves at forty mph or more with power from twin engines. Racing hulls by Bertram consistently won the annual Miami to Nassau powerboat race. Captain Andy showed us his racing hull, which had an open upper deck with no cabin. The wheel and power controls were located on a stalk in the stern. He offered to give us a test drive, so Frank and I and the two Cubans hopped on board. I took a position near the bow and, like the rest who stood in the front, I held onto the hull railing. Captain Andy maneuvered the boat out into Biscayne Bay and then "opened her up." As promised, the boat was extremely fast, especially in light of its length of thirty-one feet. The waves in the Bay were calm, so it was smooth sailing even at the fast speed. All that changed when Captain Andy took the cut from the Bay to the open sea, where the waves were very choppy. He firewalled the engines again, and we hit a wave that threw the bow of the boat and me along with it up into the air. Fortunately, I landed on the deck when I came down. From there, I crawled to the rear of the boat, where I sat on the deck for the rest of the trip back to the marina.

As we tied up at the dock, Frank told Captain Andy that he wanted to rent the boat and would be back to take care of the paperwork and payment after dropping off the two Cubans back in Miami. When we took them back to Little Havana, one of them gave my uncle an envelope full of cash. Frank and I then returned to the marina, where Frank signed the rental agreement using the alias Frank Hamilton and gave Captain Andy the cash. Frank said they would pick up the boat in the morning. On the way home, Frank told me that the mission was to drop one of the Cubans in Cuba and bring another Cuban back to Florida. Frank said they were all members of an anti-Castro underground organization operating inside Cuba. The money for this mission had been provided by wealthy anti-Castro, anti-communist individuals from Latin and South America. He said that even though the CIA was not directly involved, one of the Cubans had told him that they had a "green light" from the Agency. I asked him about the alias he used, Frank Hamilton, and he showed me a Florida driver's license and social security card issued in that name. He told me that Frank Hamilton was just one of many aliases he had used. When I asked him where he'd gotten the phony ID, he said, "It's easy. You just have to know the right people. In a pinch, I can make my own. I have a whole drawer full of these at home." He said that over the years he had used thirty-three different false identities. As far as the mission was concerned, sometime later, Frank told me that the boat was intercepted by the Coast Guard near Islamorada, just south of Miami, and the mission had to be aborted. "So much for the green light. You just can't trust the CIA," he said. But he was so impressed with the speed and performance of the Bertram racing hull that he bought two of them to use in his war against Castro.

During the time I spent with Frank he introduced me to some interesting people. I met Carlos Prío, former president of Cuba; Geraldine Shamma, the wife of a wealthy Cuban who operated a "safe house" for the CIA; Manuel Artime; Macho Barker; the Diaz Lanz brothers; and, on one occasion, a lady named Dickey Chapelle. Frank told me that she was a photojournalist who did work for *National Geo-*

graphic magazine. She began her career during World War II, during which she jumped with paratroopers behind enemy lines. Frank first met her in the Sierra Maestra mountains when he was a captain in Castro's rebel army. He said she was the "toughest woman" he had ever known, "braver than most men," adding, "and, she cusses like one." Frank did not like women who used the "f" word, but in her case he made an exception. We met her for lunch and she was actually circumspect about her language, owing to the fact that my ten-year-old cousin Gale was with us. Dickey told us that she had done work all over the world, and, like Frank, she was an ardent anti-communist. She proudly wore the wings that had been awarded to her in World War II signifying that she was a paratrooper. She said she was planning to do a story about Frank, so after lunch, we went to a state park, where she took a number of pictures. She also took some shots that included me, my aunt Janet, and my cousin Gale. I remember Frank showing me proofs and prints of these photos a few weeks later. I have never seen them since and my aunt believes they were part of the papers and documents that were lost during Hurricane Andrew. Several years later I asked Frank about Dickey Chapelle and the planned article and he said that she had recently been killed by a land mine while on patrol with a squad of Marines fighting in the Vietnam War. She was the first journalist to be killed in that war and the first female war correspondent casualty ever. As far as I know, she never finished or published the piece about Frank. The U.S. Marine Corps honors her with an annual award given in her name to the top female Marine.

Frank was a good-looking man. He was also gregarious and hospitable and could be very charming, all the things we associate with charisma. It is not surprising that women, in particular, were drawn to Frank, though I have no doubt that he was faithful to my aunt. I was with him one time sitting at the bar of a lounge in one of the hotels on Miami Beach. We were waiting for Frank's friend Hymie Levine to meet us there. The bartender was an incredibly beautiful young woman with what she said was naturally blond hair. I ordered a draft beer and Frank got his usual, a Coca-Cola. After serving us she began to talk, complaining about how bad her married life was. It seemed her husband wasn't paying enough attention to her "sexual needs." She described in detail the sexy things she did to try to get him interested, but nothing worked. She asked Frank what he thought she should do. He refused to take the bait and said, "Honey, you'll just have to keep on trying." He then looked at me and said, "Remember this, kid, women are the ruination of mankind . . . God love 'em."

Frank once provided some other advice about the opposite sex. Without going into the details, I managed to lose my virginity to a married older woman at a birthday party Frank and I attended. On the drive home, I began to worry about what had just happened. What if her husband found out about it? Had someone taken pictures of me while all this was going on? Would I be blackmailed? To a fifteen-year-old who had just lost his virginity, these were important issues. I therefore decided to confide in Frank and told him the whole story, including my belief that something had been put in my drink. He told me not to worry about it. He said that when he was sixteen he lost his virginity when one of his uncles took him to a whorehouse in Philadelphia and paid a prostitute. He laughed and said, "At least you didn't have to pay for it." I said, "But what about her husband and any pictures?" Frank said, "He won't cause any trouble. When I was in Havana, before I married your aunt, I used to bang her, as did a bunch of other guys. Believe me, her husband is not mad. In fact, he was probably hiding in the closet and watching the whole thing. He won't bother you." I took his advice to heart and stopped worrying about it. When Frank told you not to worry, you didn't worry.

Frank sometimes took me along when he conducted his anti-Castro business and meetings at various Miami Beach hotels and restaurants. One of my favorite places to go was an Italian pizzeria and restaurant on Miami Beach called Sonny's. The atmosphere was casual and the pizza was delicious—New York–style with fresh dough that was tossed in the air by the cooks. Besides the food, the unique attraction was Tony, the singing waiter. He was a big, barrel-chested Italian who sang opera like Mario Lanza, one of Frank's favorite singers. He had a beautiful voice and sang a capella with perfect pitch. I had no idea why he wasn't singing on a stage somewhere.

Frank and I went to Sonny's one night to meet my aunt Janet and my aunt Laura, who had gone to a Tupperware party. We were the first to arrive, and as we walked to an empty table I noticed two men dressed in dark suits sitting at the back of the restaurant. One of them waved at Frank and motioned us to come over. They both stood up, and Frank introduced me as his nephew, "the college student," to "Mr. Trafficante" and "Mr. Mannarino." They were both cordial as we made small talk. They encouraged me to stick with college. "Or you might end up like your uncle," Mr. Trafficante said. We all laughed, and Frank and I went back to our table. Once there, I asked Frank who these guys were. He said, "They're both Mafiosos. Santo Trafficante is head of the Tampa mob. Sammy Mannarino is head of the Pittsburgh mob. I met them when I was Fidel's gambling czar in Havana. They owned the Sans Souci casino and hotel as well as other gambling interests. They lost a fortune when Fidel took over. They're not very happy about it, either."

At the time I had no idea just how connected and high up these mobsters were. They were both top-level dons. According to Scott M. Deitche, author of *Cigar City Mafia*, Trafficante was a frequent visitor to Sonny's. The owner of the restaurant, Joseph "Chicky" Chierico, was "a well-rounded criminal with arrests for gambling and assault." He was also a member of Trafficante's crime family. I do not believe that my uncle was ever a "made man." As my aunt jokes, "If Frank was a made man we would have had a lot more money than we did." But, there is no question that Frank knew these people and others like them.

The other real-life gangster that I met through Frank was Hymie Levine, whom I saw quite a few times, especially when I was a college freshman living with Frank and Janet. Frank told me that Hymie was a former partner of mobster Dutch Schultz's. Frank was an expert on the history of the mob in the United States. He said Schultz's real name was Arthur Flegenheimer and his parents were orthodox Jews. He was known for using brutal means to kill and torture people.

Schultz was thirty-two years old when he was assassinated in 1935 by rivals in the New York mob. Before that, Schultz and Hymie were partners and controlled the slot-machine business in Upstate New York. I remember Hymie as a short Jewish man with a potbelly who loved to smoke cigars. Even though he had been Dutch Schultz's partner, I did not see Hymie as someone who could brutally torture or kill someone. But, who knows? After all, Hymie was a made man. He lived in a small hotel/apartment in South Miami Beach, where Frank and I visited him often.

Hymie was also a guest at Frank and Janet's house on many occasions. He loved cigars, and most times Frank brought a few to give to him. I never talked to Hymie about his gangster life, but in doing research for this book I discovered that he was fairly high up in the mob. According to a 1955 report from the Senate Special Committee to Investigate Organized Crime headed by Senator Estes Kefauver, in 1944 Hymie was part owner of The Dome, a "notorious gambling establishment located in Irving Park, just outside Chicago." He also was identified as a major player in the slot-machine rackets. Frank said he met Hymie in Havana while enforcing and collecting for the tax stamp that Fidel required on each gambling device. It was Hymie who introduced Frank to such mobsters as Santo Trafficante and Sammy Mannarino. The gambling tax hit Hymie particularly hard because of the large number of slots that he controlled.

When I knew Hymie, it was my impression he was not working and had retired from whatever he had previously done. He did not live lavishly—his hotel suite was modest but clean. He ate well. Sometimes we would meet him for lunch at Wolfie's, the New York–style deli on Miami Beach. Huge corned beef sandwiches and "mile-high banana pie" were the specialties of the house. I recently asked Janet if she knew how Hymie supported himself and she laughed and said, "Maybe like all the other gangsters, he lived off of Social Security." However, there may be another explanation. Just before Dutch Schultz was killed, he supposedly buried a waterproof safe containing $7 million that nobody has been able to find. Maybe Hymie had a similar 401(k) plan of his own. Unfortunately, while I was living in Miami, Hymie suffered a stroke that left him partially paralyzed. Frank, ever the loyal friend, helped Hymie through this difficult period, visiting him at least twice a week. Frank was always ready to go to the aid of a friend in need.

Although Frank was not a member of any crime family, he was definitely a family man in the best sense of the word. Through all of his adventures and schemes, Frank maintained a strong family life with my aunt and her daughter, Gale, and, later, with Autumn, Janet's granddaughter, whom they adopted. I remember well when Frank called me to tell me about the adoption. He was so excited. He told me it was the best thing that ever happened to him. At the time, Autumn was three years old and she went with them to the probate court for the hearing. My aunt said that when the judge asked them to raise their right hands to swear them in, Autumn raised her hand too. She then asked Janet, "Where's Judge Wapner?" Autumn thought they were going to be on the TV show *The People's Court.* Frank was totally devoted to Autumn. He made up fantastic adventure stories to tell her at bedtime, as his grandfather Vona had done with him. Janet told me that sometimes his tall tales would put him to sleep before Autumn. Frank's favorite place to vacation was Disney World in Orlando, an interesting choice for a person who had been all over the world. He first took Autumn when she was just six months old and made many repeat trips thereafter. Her bedroom was filled with practically every doll or figure manufactured by Disney. Frank was a huge part of Autumn's life, and his death in 1993 hit her hard. Frank was a good father.

Frank was a good husband, too. From my personal observations, it is apparent that Frank and Janet deeply loved each other. Watergate attorney Dan Schultz told us the same thing—"Frank sure loved his wife." The letters Frank and Janet wrote during his Watergate incarceration speak to this. Frank did his best to keep his family life separate from his lives of adventure. To protect my aunt, he rarely shared the details of his exploits with her. In fact, over the years, I think Frank told me more about these things than he told her. For instance, all of the plans to assassinate Castro that Frank described to the Rockefeller Commission had been told to me in private years earlier.

Janet, who knows about astrology, prepared Frank's chart and found that he was a "double Sagittarius," meaning that both his birth sign and his ascending sign were in this constellation. She said people with this configuration often become priests and are generally very intelligent. Both of these features fit Frank. He gave serious thought to becoming a priest before joining the Marines in World War II. Frank's intelligence is documented in the psychological testing and evaluation that was done as part of the multiple pre-sentence investigation reports (PSIs) ordered by Judge Sirica during Watergate. The other thing about Sagittarius that fits Frank is the separate, dual manifestations, half man and half horse, a balance of strength and intelligence. For whatever reason, Frank was able to compartmentalize and separate his role as a soldier of fortune/spy from his role as father and husband. What I find remarkable is that he was able to do this and still maintain his mental balance and stability, especially after the horrors he saw and experienced as a Marine Raider. As reported in his PSI, the psychological evaluation and testing found Frank to be well-adjusted, gregarious, and confident. Frank was also a typical Sagittarius in a very literal sense—he was an excellent archer. The farsightedness that had made him a precision sharpshooter and sniper gave him a distinct advantage with a bow and arrow too. Frank told me that when he trained Fidel's rebel army in guerrilla warfare he showed them how to make a bow and arrow out of plants and materials at hand that could kill someone, a skill he learned as a Marine Raider.

Frank is the only uncle I ever had with two last names. When I first met him I knew him only as Frank Fiorini; Sturgis was not used until around the time of Watergate. As recounted earlier, on September 23, 1952, he successfully changed his name from "Frank Angelo

Fiorino" to "Frank Anthony Sturgis," shortly after being introduced to the espionage business by an Israeli spy working for the underground, Haganah. When my aunt Laura first met Frank in the mid-1950s in Norfolk, where he owned and managed several nightclubs, he used the Fiorini name. That is the name he used in Cuba and when I met him in 1959 and when he married Janet.

A. J. Weberman believes that there is some nefarious significance in the fact that Frank's name was "Fiorini" while the petition he filed is in the name of "Fiorino."

I disagree with him. In Italian, the word *fiorini* is a plural noun meaning "little flowers." The singular form of the word is *fiorino*. It is common for Italians with such last names to use the plural and singular forms interchangeably. For example, in researching information about the mobster Sammy Mannarino, I found that his last name was sometimes spelled "Mannarini." There is another meaning for the words *fiorini* or *fiorino*—they refer to gold coins that were minted by the Republic of Florence when it was an independent city-state. The coins first appeared in 1252 and were issued and circulated until 1505. In English they are referred to as gold florins. The Italian word for soldier—*soldato*—derives from the coins that were paid to Roman legionnaires, distinguishing them as paid, professional fighters as opposed to slaves and others who had been conscripted into the army.

In December 1993 I flew to Miami for Frank's funeral. I am proud to say that I was asked to stand as an honor guard by his coffin. Also posting with me was Frank's good, loyal friend and fellow Watergate burglar Rolando Martinez. Two weeks before, when Frank was training anti-Castro commandos at his beloved camp in the Everglades, he complained about what looked like an insect bite on his back. It itched and swelled and then went away after a few days. At the time Frank recalled that in July of that year he had suffered a similar "bug bite" while standing outside the PUND office in Little Havana. It produced symptoms exactly like the subsequent one he received in the Everglades. There are a number of mysteries surrounding Frank's life—Was he involved in the JFK assassination? Did Frank and E. Howard Hunt know each other before they met during the Watergate debacle? Did Frank drop bombs on a sugar plantation in Haiti as a warning to dictator François "Papa Doc" Duvalier? Did he supply the gun to Arthur Bremer that was used in the attempted assassination of Governor George Wallace? Did he know the truth behind the death of J. Edgar Hoover? Therefore, it is no surprise that there is mystery surrounding Frank's death. There are those who claim that Frank was actually assassinated by Castro's agents. They point out that Frank died suddenly within days of being hospitalized and diagnosed with stomach cancer. They claim that during the Cold War the Soviet Union's KGB developed a blowgun weapon to deliver a cancer-causing toxin that would likely be taken to be a bug bite. They believe that this weaponry was given to Castro's G-2 secret police and intelligence agents. Frank certainly made no secret of his hatred of Fidel and his "belligerent" efforts to oust him. Just two years earlier, in 1991, these efforts included a plan to assassinate Castro and high-ranking Cuban government officials. Why wouldn't Fidel try to kill Frank? He had tried before in 1959 after Frank left Cuba for Miami. Frank had tried to kill Fidel. Castro's agents certainly knew where the PUND office and the camp in the Everglades were. They probably had Frank's home address. Finding Frank in a location where some sort of blowgun could deliver a small needle or dart would be easy enough. Whether this is what actually caused Frank's death will never be known for sure. An autopsy was not performed. What is known is that for thirty-four years Frank lived his life as an ardent anti-Castro anti-communist. As he once told the Rockefeller Commission, "It was about Cuba . . . it was always about Cuba."

As mentioned in the introduction, this book began as a song. Frank's death and the remarkable things he did furnished the necessary animus. I wanted to not only relate the varied adventures he had but also to capture what motivated him to do the extraordinary things he did. The answer to that was easy—Cuba and the attempt to overthrow his old friend and fellow guerrilla Fidel Castro. Frank was truly enchanted with Cuba. Of all the places he had been in the world, he said Cuba was the most beautiful. He admired the Cuban people and their culture. He felt "at home" in Cuba and among Cubans. So I called the song "Cuba on My Mind." I wrote six verses that covered some of the highlights of Frank's life: Angola, the Trujillo and Kennedy assassinations, and, of course, Watergate.

I then thought about Frank and the personal relationship he had with Fidel. What would Fidel's reaction be to news of Frank's death? At one time they were very close friends who trusted each other. They lived together in mountain camps and shared meals together. They fought against a common enemy. Frank's guerrilla expertise and the guns and ammunition he delivered contributed significantly to the success of Castro's revolution. Frank and many others believed that Fidel was going to establish a democratic government. Fidel betrayed that trust when he opted for totalitarian communism instead. For his part, Fidel also felt betrayed because Frank spied on him, calling him "the most dangerous CIA agent ever." After all the years, could these mortal enemies ever find common ground? In a more general sense, after a half century of Castro, could there ever be reconciliation between Cuba and the United States?

The obituary that appeared in the *New York Times* erroneously identified Frank as a "Cuban-American," a mistake other newspapers had made during Frank's lifetime. Frank always said he didn't mind the error because he was proud of his association with Cubans over the years and his devotion to their struggle to rid Cuba of Castro and communism. But, what would Fidel's reaction be to this misidentification? Could he ever accept Frank as a Cuban or, at the least, an honorary Cuban, even though they ended as mortal enemies? On the other side of the coin, could Frank, the ardent anti-communist, ever accept his onetime friend, Fidel? I therefore added a chorus to the song, written in Spanish, in which Frank addresses these questions to Fidel from the grave. In closing, I offer the following song:

CUBA ON MY MIND

I woke up with Cuba on my mind,
Camping out in the Angola bush, 'bout a thousand dreams
*   behind.*
I woke up with Cuba on my mind.

I woke up with Trujillo on my mind.
I was in the Dominican, with the CIA on the line.
I woke up with Cuba on my mind.

I woke up with Duvalier on my mind.
I was down in Port-au-Prince, makin' gangsters toe the line.
I woke up with Cuba on my mind.

¿Somos ambos Cubanos? (Are we both Cuban?)
Somos todos humanos (We are all human).
Soldados por fortuna (Soldiers of fortune).
Encantados a la Cuba (Enchanted by Cuba).

I woke up with JFK on my mind.
They say I shot him from the grassy knoll, but I never took the
*   time.*
I woke up with Cuba on my mind.

I woke up with Fidel on my mind.
Checking into the Watergate with Nixon and his kind.
I woke up with Cuba on my mind.

I woke up with freedom on my mind.
Wading through the Everglades, headin' southward one more
*   time.*
I woke up with freedom on my mind.

¿Somos ambos Cubanos? (Are we both Cuban?)
Somos todos humanos (We are all human).
Soldados ya olvidados (Soldiers now forgotten).
Si, somos ambos Cubanos. (Yes, we are both Cuban).

Adios, Paquito, vaya con Dios (Good-bye, Frankie, go with God).

Cast of Characters

Yassir Arafat (1929–2004) Leader of the Palestine Liberation Organization, whom Frank met with in Tunisia in 1989. Arafat conveyed his peace plan to Frank, who relayed it to the U.S. government.

Arnulfo Arias (1901–1988) President of Panama on three occasions (1940–1941, 1949–1951, and for two weeks in 1968).

Jacobo Árbenz (1913–1971) President of Guatemala from 1951 to 1954, when he was ousted by a coup organized by E. Howard Hunt and the CIA.

Manuel Artime (1932–1977) Leader of the Cuban government in exile in Miami. If the Bay of Pigs had been successful, he would have been the head of the new government. He was captured in the Bay of Pigs and ransomed out.

Joaquin Balaguer (1906–2002) President of the Dominican Republic from 1960 to 1962, from 1966 to 1978, and from 1986 to 1996. He was a protégé of Trujillo's.

Alfred Baldwin III (1936–) FBI agent who was a lookout for the Watergate burglary and who later turned state's evidence and testified against Frank and the others.

Bernard "Macho" Barker (1917–2009) Field director for CIA operations in Latin America and one of the Watergate burglars.

Fulgencia Batista (1901–1973) Dictator of Cuba from 1933 to 1940 and president of Cuba from 1940 to 1944. He led a successful coup against then-president Prío and became head of the ruling junta from 1952 to 1959, when he was ousted by Castro.

Autumn Benken Frank and Janet's adopted daughter. The apple of Frank's eye.

Carl Bernstein (1944–) One of the two *Washington Post* reporters who covered the Watergate story.

Lorenzo Berry A Dominican dissident involved in Trujillo's assassination. On behalf of the CIA, Frank shipped assassination weapons to Berry's Wimpy's Market in the Dominican Republic.

Rómulo Betancourt (1908–1981) President of Venezuela from 1945 to 1948 and again from 1959 to 1964. Survived an assassination attempt ordered by Raphael Trujillo. Widely known as the father of Venezuelan democracy.

Orlando Bosch (1926–) A physician who organized one of the first anti-Castro groups, MIRR (Revolutionary Insurrectional Recuperation Movement), and a close friend of Frank's.

Douglas Caddy (1938–) The lawyer who was first called after the Watergate arrests.

Michael Canfield (1948–) Co-author of *Coup d'État in America,* which claims that Frank and E. Howard Hunt were involved in JFK's assassination.

"Carlos the Jackal" (aka Ilich Ramirez Sánchez, 1949–) Venezuelan radical terrorist who crossed paths with Frank in 1981.

Carlos Castillo (1914–1957) President of Guatemala from 1954 until his assassination in 1957.

Ángel Castro (1875–1956) Spanish immigrant to Cuba who fathered Fidel and Raúl Castro out of wedlock.

Fidel Castro (1926–) Born Fidel Alejandro Ruz. He was imprisoned for opposing Batista, and on his release went to Mexico, where he met Che Guevara and raised an army. He returned to Cuba and overthrew Batista in 1959.

Dickey Chapelle (1919–1965) An award-winning female photojournalist embedded with U.S. troops during World War II, Korea, and Vietnam who first met Frank during Castro's revolution in the Sierra Maestra mountains.

Clio Chivano Brother-in-law of Fulgencia Batista and partner of mob figure Norman Rothman in the Havana casino business.

Camilo Cienfuegos (1932–1959) One of the commanders of the July 26th Brigade and a hero of the Cuban Revolution. He died in October 1959 when his Cessna disappeared on a flight from Camaguay to Havana. Frank believed Camilo was shot down by a Cuban air force pilot on orders from Raúl Castro because of his relationship with Frank.

Lucius Clay (1897–1978) Known as the "father of the Berlin airlift." Following the Allied victory in World War II, he was military governor of Germany. Frank was in his personal honor guard.

Suazo Córdova (1927–) President of Honduras from 1982 to 1986. He was democratically elected in 1982, ending eighteen years of military rule.

Robert Curtis One of Frank's recruits for Operation Sword, which had as its goal ransoming the USS *Pueblo* and her crew.

William "Wild Bill" Donovan (1883–1959) Soldier, lawyer, intelligence officer who headed up the World War II Office of Strategic Services (OSS), which eventually became the CIA. He helped organize Edson's Marine Raiders.

François "Papa Doc" Duvalier (1907–1971) President of Haiti from 1957 to 1964. His formal title was "President for Life, Maximum Chief of the Revolution, Apostle of National Unity, Benefactor of the Poor, Patron of Commerce and Industry and Electrifier of Souls."

Jean-Claude "Baby Doc" Duvalier (1951–) Ruled Haiti upon his father's death in 1971 until 1986, when he was overthrown by a popular uprising. He was exiled to Spain. His nickname was "Cesta Cabeza," or "basket head."

Allen Dulles (1893–1969) First civilian director of the CIA, from 1953 to 1961. Also a member of the Warren Commission. He was forced to resign as a result of the Bay of Pigs fiasco.

Merritt "Red Mike" Edson (1897–1955) Medal of Honor recipient and leader of the First Marine Raider Brigade during World War II.

Daniel Ellsberg (1931–) Member of the Rand Corporation think tank working for the Pentagon who leaked *The Pentagon Papers* on June 13, 1971. This led to creation of the White House Plumbers and eventually the Watergate break-in.

John Ehrlichman (1925–1999) Counsel and assistant for domestic affairs to Nixon during Watergate. He was fired by Nixon and served eighteen months in prison for the Watergate cover-up.

Juan Manuel Fangio (1911–1995) Argentinean Formula One world champion kidnapped by Frank and others to promote Castro's revolution.

W. Mark Felt (1913–2008) Deputy director of the FBI during Watergate who was later revealed as Woodward and Bernstein's "Deep Throat" confidential source.

Dr. Lewis Fielding Daniel Ellsberg's psychiatrist, whose office was burgled by Barker, Martinez, and de Diego.

Angelo Fiorini Frank's father.

Errol Flynn (1909–1959) Hollywood movie star who lived in Cuba and filmed the revolution with director Victor Pahlen.

Gaeton Fonzi Former federal investigator into the JFK assassination and author of *The Last Investigation* (1993).

Alfredo Gamonal One of Fidel's look-alike bodyguards, who was killed in an ambush at a memorial service for one of Castro's friends.

Sam Giancana (1908–1975) Chicago mob boss from 1957 to 1966. Frank was acquitted with "Sam the Cigar" in relation to assassination attempts on Castro. He said, "The CIA and the Mafia are different sides of the same coin."

Lina Ruz González (1903–1963) Fidel and Raúl Castro's mother, who was a cook in Ángel Castro's household.

Max Gonzalez Anti-Castro Cuban activist who assisted Frank on covert missions.

Virgilio González One of the Watergate burglars who, like Frank, was a CIA contract operative who took part in the Bay of Pigs.

L. Patrick Gray (1916–2005) Acting director of the FBI from 1972 to 1973. His nomination for director was withdrawn after he admitted destroying Watergate documents given to him by Nixon counsel John Dean.

Ernesto "Che" Guevara (1928–1967) An Argentinean who trained as a doctor and joined Castro's revolution after meeting him in Mexico in 1956. He met Frank in 1958 in the Cuban mountains while preparing for the revolution and they compared notes on guerrilla warfare. He was executed at the direction of the CIA.

H. R. "Bob" Haldeman (1926–1993) Chief aide to Nixon during the Watergate scandal. He was fired by Nixon and served nineteen months in prison for the Watergate cover-up.

J. Edgar Hoover (1895–1972) Director of the FBI for thirty-seven years.

Dorothy Hunt (1920–1972) Wife of E. Howard Hunt. A career CIA agent, she died in a mysterious plane crash in Chicago on December 8, 1972.

E. Howard Hunt (1918–2007) Career CIA agent who planned the Bay of Pigs invasion and the Watergate break-in.

Jim Hunt Sr. (1918–2001) Father of co-author Jim Hunt and Frank's brother-in-law. Not related to E. Howard Hunt.

Jim Hunt Co-author of this book and Frank's nephew.

Lyndon B. Johnson (1908–1973) Thirty-sixth president of the United States.

John F. Kennedy (1917–1963) Thirty-fifth president of the United States. He was assassinated in Dallas November 22, 1963.

Alan Kessler Attorney for Frank in his citizenship case.

Meyer Lansky (1902–1983) Born Major Suchowlinsky. Member of the crime syndicate heavily into gambling operations in Florida and Cuba. He was well known to Frank when Frank was Castro's gambling czar.

Marcos Diaz Lanz Brother of Pedro Diaz Lanz. He was also in Fidel's air force and also left to become important in the anti-Castro movement in Miami.

Pedro Diaz Lanz (1926–2008) Like Frank a daredevil bush pilot. He was the head of Castro's air force until he was co-opted by the communists. He then became an important member of the anti-Castro exile working for the CIA.

Hymie Levine A partner of Dutch Schultz's in the slot-machine business. During Batista's reign, he contracted the slot-machine business in Cuba. Frank looked after him.

G. Gordon Liddy (1930–) Former FBI agent and Treasury Department employee who, along with E. Howard Hunt, directed the Plumbers and the Watergate break-in, for which he served five years in prison.

Marita Lorenz (1939–) Fidel's mistress in 1959 who, along with Frank, helped smuggle intelligence to the CIA (including future missile sites) and helped plan plots to assassinate Fidel.

Gaspare Magaddino (1908–1970) U.S. mob figure out of Detroit who was reputed to be an assassin without equal.

Jeb Magruder (1934–) Deputy director of the Committee to Reelect the President (CREEP) who served time for a Watergate conviction and perjury.

Sammy Mannarino (1920–1993) With his brother Gabriel ran the Pittsburgh mob and was involved in the casino business with Santo Trafficante in Cuba.

Carlos Marcello (1910–1993) New Orleans crime boss introduced to Frank by Hymie Levine. He was deported by Robert Kennedy.

Eugenio Rolando Martinez Career CIA agent and one of the Watergate burglars. He was a close friend of Frank's who made more than two hundred incursions into Castro's Cuba.

Rolando Masferrar (1918–1975) A rival of Castro's who headed up *Los Tigres,* a guerrilla organization to protect and support Batista.

James McCord (1924–) A former FBI and CIA agent arrested with Frank, Rolando Martinez, Virgilio González, and Macho Barker at the Watergate break-in.

Paul Meskil (1923–2005) Reporter for New York *Daily News* who did a series of articles on Frank in 1975.

John Mitchell (1913–1988) Nixon's attorney general who became director of CREEP and who authorized the Watergate break-in.

Kamaran Movasaghi The Iranian embassy contact with whom Frank and Wilfred Navarro negotiated a proposed hostage exchange wherein anti-Castro Cuban hostages would be exchanged for the fifty-two Americans being held in Tehran.

Wilfredo Navarro Head of anti-Castro group United Cubans in Miami. Frank was the group's military advisor.

Colonel Nichols One of two embedded CIA agents at the U.S. embassy in Havana whom Frank reported to in 1959.

Richard Nixon (1913–1994) Thirty-seventh president of the United States. He was toppled by Watergate and resigned in 1974.

Pastorita Nuñez A female commander in Castro's rebel army. Castro appointed Frank to help her in her position as casino czar.

Larry O'Brien (1917–1990) Head of the Democratic National Party during the Watergate break-ins.

Lee Harvey Oswald (1939–1963) Alleged assassin of JFK.

Victor Pahlen Hollywood movie director who filmed *The Truth About Castro's Revolution* with Errol Flynn while the revolution was actually occurring.

Katherine Parsons Frank's mother's sister, with whom Frank and his mother lived in Philadelphia during Frank's school years.

Francisco Quesada An Argentinean anti-Castro military colonel invented by Frank to help raise anti-Castro funds and support and, on occasion, serve as a scapegoat.

Holden Roberto (1923–2007) Chief of the FNLA (National Liberation Front of Angola), one of two factions at war in Angola with the communist MPLA backed by Cuba. Frank trained Roberto's rebels and provided military and financial support.

Félix Rodríguez (1941–) CIA operative who tracked down Che Guevara, leading to Guevara's execution.

Henry Rothblatt (1916–1985) One of the lawyers who defended the Watergate burglars.

Norman Rothman (1914–1985) Ran the Sans Souci casino in Cuba. Frank's good friend, nicknamed "Roughhouse," he coordinated the smuggling of arms to Castro.

Alex Rorke (1926–1963) Frank's good friend and fellow anti-communist fighter. In September 1963, Alex and the airplane he was in disappeared while he was on an anti-Castro mission.

Ellis Rubin (1925–2006) Frank's longtime Miami attorney, who represented Frank in many matters.

"Stretch" Rubin A mobster who worked for Norman Rothman in the slot-machine business in Cuba. Frank saved his life by stopping Castro's rebel soldiers who were about to execute him.

Jack Ruby (1911–1967) Born Jack Rubenstein. Killer of Lee Harvey Oswald. Connected to the underworld.

Andrew St. George Embedded reporter who covered Castro's revolution and who featured Frank in much of his writing

Romeo Vasquez Sanchez A communist who assassinated Carlos Castillo, president of Guatemala.

Augusto Sandino (1895–1934) Led a rebellion against the U.S. occupation of Nicaragua during the 1920s and '30s. Assassinated in 1934.

Joaquim, Louis, and Sergio Sangenes Anti-Castro CIA agents. Joaquim, codename Sam Jennis, was Frank's primary CIA contact.

Jonas Savimbi (1934–2002) Chief of UNITA (National Union for the Total Independence of Angola), one of the two factions at war in Angola with the communist MPLA (Popular Movement for the Liberation of Angola) supported by the Russians and Castro.

Dan Schultz Defense counsel for the Watergate burglars.

Dutch Schultz (1902–1935) Real name Arthur Flegenheimer. He made a fortune bootlegging and was later in the slot-machine business with Hymie Levine.

Geraldine Shamma Anti-Castro underground figure who worked with Frank to overthrow Castro.

Earl Silbert Prosecuted the Watergate burglars.

John Sirica (1904–1992) "Maximum John"; the presiding judge in the Watergate trial, known as a hard-line jurist.

George Smathers (1913–2007) Democratic senator from Florida who helped Frank regain his citizenship after losing it for serving as an officer in Castro's rebel army.

Carlos Prío Soccarrás (1903–1977) President of Cuba from 1948 to 1952, replaced by a coup headed by Batista. He lived in exile in Miami until he died in 1977.

Anastasio Somoza (1896–1956) Ruled Nicaragua from 1936 to 1956. His son, also Anastasio (nicknamed "Tachito") ruled Nicaragua from 1967 to 1972 and from 1974 to 1979. He was replaced by the Sandanista Daniel Ortega.

Janet Sturgis Frank's wife from 1960 until his death in 1993 and aunt to co-author Jim Hunt.

Mary Sturgis Frank's mother, who died when Frank was in prison serving time for the Watergate break-in.

Ralph Sturgis Frank's stepfather. In 1952, Frank had his name legally changed to Sturgis. This created a second identity for Frank.

Mario Terán A Bolivian army sergeant who executed Che Guevara on October 9, 1967.

Nora Odell Thompson Frank's first wife and the mother of Ron Thompson.

Ron Thompson Frank's stepson, who for many years thought Frank was his real father.

Omar Torrijos (1929–1981) Anti-communist de facto leader of Panama from 1968 to 1981, when his airplane blew up.

Charlie "The Blade" Tourine (1906–1980). A member of the Genovese crime family. His nickname came from his proficient use of the knife when dealing with recalcitrant debtors and business rivals.

Santo Trafficante (1914–1987) Ran the Tampa mob and owned the Sans Souci casino in Havana. He was well known to Frank.

Rafael Trujillo (1891–1961) Dictator of the Dominican Republic from 1930 to 1961. Frank assisted the CIA in his assassination.

"Mr. V" High-ranking Angolan government official who worked secretly with Frank to overthrow the communist-controlled government.

Major van Horn CIA agent imbedded in U.S. embassy in Havana. Beginning in January 1959 Frank spied on Castro and reported to him.

Tony Varona (born Manuel Antonio de Varona y Loredo; 1908–1992). Loyal supporter of President Prío Soccarrás who plotted a counterrevolution against Fidel with the help of Frank and the CIA. He founded the MRR (Movement for the Recovery of the Revolution), which is still active in Miami today.

Angelo Vona Frank's maternal grandfather, with whom he and his mother lived in Philadelphia. Born in Italy and a father figure for Frank.

Alan J. Weberman (1944–) Yippie and co-author of *Coup d'État in America*, which claims Frank and E. Howard Hunt assassinated JFK.

Frank Wills (1948–2000) Watergate security guard who discovered the break-in.

Bob Woodward (1943–) One of the two *Washington Post* reporters who covered the Watergate story.

Clark Woolan CIA agent working out of the U.S. Consulate in Santiago. He was the first to recruit Frank to spy on Castro.

Miguel Ydígoras (1895–1982) President of Guatemala from 1958 to 1963. Frank negotiated with him to establish anticommunist guerrilla training camps.

Frank Sturgis Time Line

1924   Born Frank Fiorini in Norfolk, Virginia, to Mary Vona Fiorini and Angelo Fiorini, both of whom were born in Italy.

1926   Parents separate; sister dies; Frank moves to the home of his aunt Kathleen Parsons in Philadelphia, where he lives until 1942.

1942   At age 17, enlists in the Marines; trains at Parris Island, South Carolina. Selected for elite First Marine Raider Brigade (Edson's Raiders). On December 15, leaves for American Samoa.

1943   Leaves Samoa for New Caledonia, where he sees action. In May, leaves New Caledonia for Guadacanal, where he distinguishes himself in combat. Also sees action on New Georgia Island and in the British Solomons. Is wounded twice and jumps a hospital ship to rejoin his unit.

1945   Receives an honorable discharge from Marines on October 23 after thirty days of treatment at a psychiatric facility for "war neurosis."

1946   Spends six months as a Norfolk police officer. Quits after a confrontation with a sergeant at roll call over cops being paid off.

1947   Joins the U.S. Naval Reserve at Norfolk air station and serves from November 9, 1947, to August 30, 1948. While there becomes a skilled airplane pilot.

1948   Joins the U.S. Army on August 31; serves as General Clay's honor guard in Berlin during the airlift. Holds top secret clearance with the Army security agency in Germany. Has a relationship with a Hungarian actress who's with Israeli intelligence. Helps her in her espionage activity during the next two years in Europe.

1952   Moves back to Norfolk, where he owns/manages the Top Hat bar in Virginia Beach. On September 23, changes his name to Sturgis.

1956   Travels to Miami, meets former Cuban president Carlos Prío Socarrás. (Frank's uncle, Angelo Vona, had married a Cuban woman, who became the source of Frank's Cuban involvement.)

1957   Meets Fidel at a theater in Miami, beginning a lifelong involvement with Cuba. Travels to Cuba and begins running arms into Cuba for Fidel Castro. Becomes a captain in the Cuban Rebel Army in charge of training guerrilla soldiers and chief of security and intelligence for the Cuban air force. Befriends Che Guevara.

1958   Buys two planes (a B-25 bomber and a C-40 transport), guns, and four boats (a sixty-three-foot Coast Guard cutter, sixty-three-foot yacht, *Quesa*, and two sixty-footers that could do fifty knots). Kidnaps Juan Manuel Fangio, world-champion race car driver, to publicize the Cuban revolution. Starts working for the CIA. Is offered $1 million by the mob to kill Castro.

On July 24, Customs agents raid Frank's residence in Miami and seize "large quantities" of rifles, machine guns, ammunition, and dynamite.

On July 30, Frank returns from Cuba and is arrested for conspiracy to ship arms from the U.S.

1959   On January 1, the Cuban revolution ends. Castro assumes power and establishes a communist government. Castro puts Frank in charge of the Cuban casinos. Frank meets U.S. mob bosses. Breaks with Fidel and leaves Cuba on June 30 and works with anti-Castro Cuban underground and CIA in Miami.

        On October 21, makes leaflet drop over Havana, which leads to break off of diplomatic relations between the United States and Cuba. Draws up and practices plans to assassinate Castro. Airlifts agents with radio equipment into Cuba and also makes a bombing run. Arrested on return trip from Guatemala and charged with service in a foreign military. Loses his citizenship and regains it with help from Florida senator George Smathers and the CIA.

1960   Participates in failed assassination attempt on Castro with Marita Lorenz. Visits various Latin American countries and Caribbean Islands seeking help for invasion of Cuba.

1961   Helps plan and is part of Bay of Pigs invasion of Cuba. Marries Jim Hunt's aunt Janet.

1962   Is approached in Miami and asked to do a domestic assassination.

1963   The USS *Pueblo* is captured by North Korea. Frank goes to Mexico to capture a Russian espionage "trawler" to trade. Within a week of JFK's death, Frank is interrogated by the FBI about the assassination.

1972   On June 17, Frank, Macho Barker, Eugenio Martinez, Virgilio González, and James McCord break into the Democratic National Headquarters for the second time and are discovered and arrested.

1979   Travels to Angola to help rebels fighting communist government and teach guerrilla warfare.

1981   Goes to Honduras to train Contras, the El Salvadoran army, and the Honduran death squads. Makes a second trip to Angola. Trains rebels in the Angolan bush for Holden Roberto. Interacts with Venezuelan terrorist "Carlos"—later known as "the Jackal."

1989   Visits Yassir Arafat in Tunis. Arafat shares elements of his peace plan. Frank is debriefed by CIA on return trip.

1993   Dies in Miami under suspicious circumstances.

Notes

Chapter 1: From Priest to Patriot
1   A. J. Weberman, *Coup D'Etat in America* (New Rochelle, New York: Third Press Publishing), Nodule 6, 15.
2   Ibid., 15.
3   Rockefeller Commission on CIA Activities, Testimony of Frank Sturgis (April 4, 1975), 25.
4   Ibid., 25.
5   Roy Grinker, M.D. and John P. Spiegel, M.D., "Brief Psychotherapy in War Neuroses," *Psychoanalytic Quarterly* (Jan. 14, 1944), 274.
6   Diagnostic and Statistical Manual-IV-TR (American Psychiatric Association, 2000) 218.
7   Weberman, *Coup D'Etat in America,* 15.
8   Grinker and Spiegel, "Brief Psychotherapy in War Neuroses," 274.

Chapter 2: A Spy Is Born
1   Rockefeller Commission on CIA Activities, Testimony of Frank Sturgis, 32.
2   Frank Saunders letter to Judge John Sirica from The Papers of John Sirica, Library of Congress (Feb. 27, 1973), 6.

Chapter 3: The Cuban Revolution
1   Rockefeller Commission on CIA Activities, Testimony of Frank Sturgis, 89.
2   Ibid., 44.
3   Ibid., 38.
4   Ibid., 40.
5   Ibid., 40.

Chapter 4: Anti-Communist

1   Rockefeller Commission on CIA Activities, Testimony of Frank Sturgis, 52.
2   Ibid., 49.
3   Jan. 4, 2008, http://www.jfkmontreal.com/john/lennon.
4   Rockefeller Commission, Frank Sturgis Testimony, 48.
5   Paul Meskil, "Secrets of the CIA," *New York Daily News,* April 22, 1975.
6   Rockefeller Commission, Frank Sturgis Testimony, 33.
7   Rockefeller Commission, Frank Sturgis Testimony, 49.
8   United States, April 1, 1959, FBI memo, reprinted @ Cuban Information Archives, June 5, 2007, http://cuban-exile.com/doc_126-150/doc0147.html.
9   Ibid., 6.
10   "I Plotted Castro's Death, Sturgis Says," *Miami Herald,* 2 April 21, 1975, 15.
11   Ibid., 15.
12   Rockefeller Commission, Frank Sturgis Testimony, 88.

Chapter 5: Anti-Castro

1   A. J. Weberman, *Coup D'Etat in America,* Nodule 7, 12.
2   Paul Meskil, "Secrets of the CIA," *New York Daily News,* April 20, 1975.
3   Ibid.
4   Weberman, *Coup D'Etat in America,* Nodule 10, 53.
5   "Ex-Phila. Flier on Castro Raid," *Philadelphia Inquirer,* Oct. 31, 1959.
6   A. J. Weberman, *Coup D'Etat in America,* Nodule 7, 15.
7   Ibid., 15.
8   Ibid., 16.
9   Rockefeller Commission, Frank Sturgis Testimony, 92.
10   Paul Meskil, "Secrets of the CIA."

Chapter 6: The Bay of Pigs

1   United States, House of Representatives Hearings Before The Select Committee On Assassinations—Assassination of President John F. Kennedy, Deposition of E. Howard Hunt (Washington D.C., Nov. 3, 1978), 32.
2   "The Bay of Pigs—The Truth," Nov. 5, 2006, http://archive.newsmax.com.

Chapter 7: Missiles, Missions, and the Sword

1   A. J. Weberman, *Coup D'Etat in America,* Nodule 7, 63.
2   "Fiorini Swashbuckled with the Anti-Castro Crowd," *Sun Sentinel-Ft. Lauderdale News,* April 25, 1972.
3   Ibid.
4   A. J. Weberman, *Coup D'Etat in America,* Nodule 7, 105.
5   "Guerilla Landing in Cuba Reported," Associated Press, July 3, 1962.
6   F.B.I. Memo Summary, 6/8/67 reproduced @ www.maryferrellfoundation.org

7   Ibid.
8   Ibid.
9   Ibid.
10   Ibid.
11   Ibid.
12   Ibid.
13   Paul Meskil, "Secrets of the CIA," *New York Daily News,* April 20, 1975.
14   A. J. Weberman, *Coup D'Etat in America,* Nodule 13, 23.
15   Ibid., 59.
16   http://havanajournal.com/politicsentry/Sherry-Sullivan-tries-to-cash-in-on-1963 -CIA-mission-to-Cuba.
17   "Pentagon Finds U.S.—Cuba Flight Was a Hoax," UPI, June 4, 1964.
18   F.B.I.-139-4089-394; Weberman Nodule X-25, 36, 37.

Chapter 8: Watergate—The Burglary
1   *U.S. v. Keith,* 407 U.S. 297 (1972).
2   *U.S. v. Barker, II,* 546 F.2nd 940 (D.C. Cir. 1976).
3   Ibid.
4   *The New York Times,* Obituaries, Jan. 24, 2007.
5   *U.S. v. Barker, II,* 546.
6   Ibid.
7   Eugenio Martinez, "Mission Impossible," Nov 11, 2006, http://www.watergate.info/ burglary/martinez.shtml.
8   *U.S. v. Barker, II,* 546.
9   Eugenio Martinez, "Mission Impossible."
10   Frank Saunders letter to Judge John Sirica from The Papers of John Sirica, Library of Congress (Feb. 27, 1973), 2.
11   *U.S. v. Barker, II.*
12   United States, Nixon White House Tapes (Washington D.C., Sept. 15, 1972); Nixon. archives.gov/virtuallibrarytapeexcerps/index.php.
13   Frank Saunders letter to Judge John Sirica, 3.
14   G. Gordon Liddy, *Will: The Autobiography of G. Gordon Liddy* (New York: St. Martin's Press, 1980), 54.
15   Frank Saunders letter to Judge John Sirica, 5.
16   Ibid., 5.
17   *U.S. v. Barker, II.*
18   Nixon White House Tapes (Washington D.C., May 1, 1972).
19   Ibid.
20   Frank Saunders letter to Judge John Sirica, 4.
21   Ibid., 5.
22   Ibid., 3.
23   "Watergate Burglar Frank Sturgis Dies," *Miami Herald,* December 5, 1993.
24   Frank Saunders letter to Judge John Sirica, 5.

25   Deposition of G. Gordon Liddy, *Dean v. St. Martin's Press,* U.S. Dist. Ct. DC, No. 92-1807, Dec. 6, 1996, 85–86.

26   *Wells v. Liddy,* 186 F.3rd 505 (4th Cir. July 28, 1999).

27   Eugenio Martinez, "Mission Impossible," Nov 11, 2006, http://www.watergate.info/burglary/martinez.shtml.

28   John Sirica, *To Set the Record Straight* (New York: W.W. Norton & Co., 1979), 35.

29   Deposition of G. Gordon Liddy, 96.

30   Eugenio Martinez, "Mission Impossible."

31   Ibid.

32   Ibid.

33   Ibid.

34   Frank Saunders letter to Judge John Sirica, 2.

35   Ibid.

36   "Five Held In Plot To Bug Democrats' Office Here," *The Washington Post,* June 18, 1972.

37   Eugenio Martinez, "Mission Impossible."

38   Ibid.

39   "The Bugs at Watergate," *Time* magazine, July 3, 1972.

40   Deposition of G. Gordon Liddy, 104.

41   "A Chat with Elusive E. Howard Hunt," *Miami Herald,* June 19, 1997.

42   Eugenio Martinez, "Mission Impossible."

43   "Five Held in Plot to Bug Democrats' Office Here," *The Washington Post,* June 18, 1972.

44   Eugenio Martinez, "Mission Impossible."

45   Saunders letter to Sirica, 4.

46   Papers of Judge John Sirica, Library of Congress.

47   Deposition of G. Gordon Liddy, 107.

48   Ibid., 106

49   http://educationforum.ipbhost.com/index.php?showtopic=5670, March 13, 2007.

50   Deposition of G. Gordon Liddy, 119.

51   E. Howard Hunt, *Undercover: Memoirs of an American Secret Agent* (New York: Berkley, 1974).

52   Saunders letter to Sirica, 3.

53   E. Howard Hunt, *Undercover: Memoirs of an American Secret Agent.*

54   Deposition of G. Gordon Liddy, 108.

55   Saunders letter to Sirica.

56   Deposition of G. Gordon Liddy, 111.

57   Ibid., 116.

58   Eugenio Martinez, "Mission Impossible."

59   James McCord, *A Piece of Tape: The Watergate Story: Fact and Fiction* (Rockville MD: Washington Media Services, 1974).

60   Letter of Norman A. Carlson, Director U.S. Bureau of Prisons to John Sirica, July 13, 1973, from the Papers of John Sirica, Library of Congress.

61   "Five Held in Plot to Bug Democrats' Office Here," *The Washington Post,* June 18, 1972.

62   Saunders letter to Sirica, 3.

63   "Five Held in Plot to Bug Democrats' Office Here," *The Washington Post,* June 18, 1972.

64   Warren Hinckle and Bill Turner, *Deadly Secrets: The CIA-Mafia War Against Castro and the Assassination of JFK* (New York: Thunder Mouth's Press, 1981, 1992).

65   *The Washington Post,* June 18, 1972.

66   Ibid.

67   Ibid.

68   Ibid.

69   Ibid.

Chapter 9: Watergate—Law and Disorder

1   George W. Howard, Chief U.S. Probation Officer memo to Judge John Sirica, (Sept. 13, 1972) from the Papers of John Sirica, Library of Congress.

2   Ibid.

3   John Sirica, *To Set the Record Straight* (New York/London: WW Norton & Company, 1979) 37.

4   Ibid., 57.

5   Ibid., 52.

6   George Howard memo to Judge John Sirica.

7   John Sirica, *To Set the Record Straight,* 58.

8   Ibid., 58.

9   Ibid., 59.

10   Eugenio Martinez, "Mission Impossible."

11   Ibid.

12   Tony Ulasewicz, *The President's Private Eye: The Journey of Tony U. from NYPD to the Nixon White House* (New York: Macsam Pub. Co., 1990).

13   Nixon White House Tapes, June 21, 1972.

14   Rockefeller Commission Testimony of E. Howard Hunt (March 4, 1975), 83.

15   Maurice Stans Testimony, U.S. *v. Liddy et.al,* (U.S. Dist. Ct., DC, No. 1827–72, Jan. 23, 1973).

16   John Sirica, *To Set the Record Straight,* 67–70.

17   Ibid., 69.

18   Ibid., 70.

19   Frank Saunders letter to Judge John Sirica, 3, 10, 11.

20   Ibid., 5, 8, 11.

21   Ibid., 5.

22   *U.S. v. Barker, II,* 546 F.2nd 940 (D.C. Cir. 1976).

23   John Sirica, *To Set the Record Straight,* 89.

24   *U.S. v. Barker, II.*

25   *U.S. v. U.S.* District Court 407 U.S. 297 (1972).
26   John Sirica, *To Set the Record Straight*, 89.
27   Ibid., 90.
28   Ibid., 90.
29   Frank Saunders letter to Judge John Sirica, 6.
30   Ibid., 12.
31   John Sirica, *To Set the Record Straight*, 94.
32   John Sirica,"After the Dam Broke," *The New York Times*, April 24, 1979.
33   Sirica, *To Set the Record Straight*, 96.
34   Ibid., 97.
35   Ibid., 111.
36   http://www.edwardjayepstein.com/archived/watergate_print.htm
37   John Sirica, *To Set the Record Straight*, 118.
38   *U.S. v. Barker, II.*
39   Ibid.
40   Frank Saunders letter to Judge John Sirica, 6.
41   Report of George J. Steinfeld, M.D. (June 12, 1973), from the Papers of John Sirica, Library of Congress.
42   Ibid.
43   Ibid.
44   Ibid.
45   Norman Carlson letter to John Sirica (July 2, 1973) from the Papers of John Sirica, Library of Congress.
46   Ibid.
47   Ibid.
48   Jack Anderson, "Watergate Burglar Spins Yarn," *Springfield Daily News,* April 16, 1974.
49   Milt Sosin, "Nine More Months for Sturgis," *Miami Herald,* Jan. 9, 1974.
50   Samuel Dash letter to Judge John Sirica, Sept. 19, 1973, from the Papers of John Sirica, Library of Congress.
51   George Howard memo to Judge John Sirica.
52   Hunt testimony, Select Committee on Assassinations (3 Nov. 3, 1978), 29.
53   George Howard memo to Judge John Sirica.
54   Ibid.
55   Ibid.
56   Ibid.
57   Ibid.
58   *U.S. v. Barker, I.*
59   "Judge John Sirica," *Time* magazine (Jan 2, 1974).
60   Ibid.
61   Nixon White House Tapes (May 12, 1973).
62   Federal Rule of Appellate Procedure 35.
63   *U.S. v. Barker, I.*

64   Ibid.

65   Ibid.

66   Ibid.

67   Ibid.

68   *U.S. v. Barker and Martinez,* 546 F. 2nd 940 (U.S. Court of Appeals D.C. Circuit, 1976).

69   Ibid.

70   "Nine More Months for Sturgis," *Miami Herald.*

71   "Miamian Will Try to Clear Watergate Burglar," *Miami Herald,* March 17, 1986.

72   Gene Miller, "Watergate Split: $200,000 Four Ways," *Miami Herald,* Feb. 23, 1977.

73   Letter written by Richard Galiher, in possession of the authors.

74   "Watergate Burglar Says Break-in a Plot by CIA," *Miami Herald,* Sept. 4, 1978.

75   Rockefeller Commission Report, Ch. 14 "Involvement of the CIA in Improper Activities for the White House," 172.

76   Ibid, 206.

77   United States, Central Intelligence Agency, "Family Jewels" (Washington, D.C., 2007), 105.

78   Ibid., 420.

79   Ibid., 420.

80   Rockefeller Commission Report, Ch. 14, 181.

81   United States, Central Intelligence Agency, "Family Jewels," 457, 552, 554.

82   E. Howard Hunt obituary, *The New York Times,* Jan. 24, 2007.

83   Rockefeller Commission Report, Ch. 14, 183.

84   Ibid., 184.

85   Ibid., 185.

86   Ibid., 185.

87   Ibid., 185.

88   Ibid., 193.

89   Ibid., 107.

90   United States, Central Intelligence Agency, "Family Jewels," 353.

91   Ibid., 356.

92   Rockefeller Commission Report, Ch. 14, 194.

93   Ibid., 195.

94   *High Times,* Interview with Frank Sturgis, April 1977, 32.

95   Ibid.

96   Ibid.

97   Rockefeller Commission Report, Ch. 14, 205.

98   *High Times,* Interview with Frank Sturgis, 32.

99   United States, Central Intelligence Agency, "Family Jewels," 406.

100   Ibid., 392.

Chapter 10: The Assassination of a President

1 Rockefeller Commission, Frank Sturgis Testimony, 85–88.
2 Erik Hedegaard, "The Last Confessions of E. Howard Hunt," *Rolling Stone*, Jan. 23, 2007.
3 Gaeton Fonzi, email to authors, April 2007.
4 David Talbert, *Brothers: The Hidden History of the Kennedy Years,* (New York: Simon and Shuster, 2007).
5 Report dated December 30, 1963, to James J. Rowley, Chief, Secret Service, reproduced at http://www.cuban-exile.com/doc_051-075/doc0066.html.
6 Rockefeller Commission Documents, Memo from Pete Clapper to Robert Olsen, April 3, 1975.
7 Rockefeller Commission, Frank Sturgis Testimony, 22.
8 *High Times*, Interview with Frank Sturgis, April 1977.
9 Ibid., 28.
10 Gaeton Fonzi, *The Last Investigation,* 79.
11 Ibid., 81.
12 FBI Report 3/8/92 reproduced @ http://assassinat.iquebec.com/susp_124-10179 -10310.htm?1&weborama=-1.
13 Ibid., 6.
14 Rockefeller Commission Report, Ch.19, 5.
15 http://mcadams.posc.mu.edu/3tramps.html.
16 "Sturgis Dodges a Pie as Court Clears Him," *Miami Herald,* Nov. 5, 1977.
17 Gaeton Fonzi, *The Last Investigation,* 78.
18 Rockefeller Commission, Frank Sturgis Testimony, 103–4.
19 Erik Hedegaard, "The Last Confessions of E. Howard Hunt," *Rolling Stone,* Jan. 23, 2007
20 "Reds Are Framing Me as JFK'S Killer," *Midnight Globe,* Nov. 29, 1977, 7.
21 Gaeton Fonzi, *The Last Investigation,* 80.
22 "Reds Are Framing Me as JFK'S Killer," *Midnight Globe,* Nov. 29, 1977, 7.
23 Public Papers of the Presidents, Dwight D. Eisenhower, 1960, 1356.

Chapter 11: Angola

1 CIA memo 28990 22 July 22, 1977.

Chapter 12: It Was Always About Cuba

1 Jay Ducassi, "'Invade' Mission Was Only a 'Trick,' 'Sturgis Says'," *Miami Herald,* Sept. 10, 1981: 2a.
2 Barry Bearak, "Beset by Woes, They're Cubans Disunited," *Miami Herald,* Aug. 29, 1981: 15a.
3 Ibid., 15.
4 Jay Ducassi, "'Invade' Mission Was Only a 'Trick,' 'Sturgis Says'," *Miami Herald,* 4a.
5 "Watergate Burglar Opens Shop in N. Miami," *Miami Herald,* Dec. 13, 1980: 2b.
6 "Plumbers Live Quietly," *Miami Herald,* June 17, 1982: 1a.

7   "Sturgis Says He Was Working for Customs," *Miami Herald,* Nov. 5, 1986: 1a.

8   "Cloaked Conspirator Taunts Castro," *Miami Herald,* July 30, 1991: 2b.

9   "Miamians Accused of Plot on Castro," *Miami Herald,* July 10, 1991: 4a.

10 "Environmentalists Seek Castro's Ouster," *Miami Herald,* Feb. 10, 1993: 1b.

11 "Agents Seize Weapons," *Miami Herald,* March 10, 1993: 1a.

12 Ibid., 1a.

Index